Volume Seventeen

The Encyclopedia of

Photography

THE COMPLETE PHOTOGRAPHER:
The Comprehensive Guide and Reference for All Photographers

WILLARD D. MORGAN
General Editor

GREYSTONE PRESS/NEW YORK

Title Page Picture Credits:

Copal Company Limited

HANS BURST/*Zeiss Ikon Photo*

LOU BERNSTEIN

GEORGE L. HONEYCUTT/*Charlotte Observer and News*

Copyright © MCMLXIV BY THE GREYSTONE PRESS

100 AVENUE OF THE AMERICAS

NEW YORK 13, NEW YORK

Cover and Book Designed by Harold Franklin

MANUFACTURED IN THE UNITED STATES OF AMERICA

Table of Contents   # Volume Seventeen

PSYCHOLOGICAL PORTRAITURE

PHILIPPE HALSMAN
[Philippe Halsman's work includes studio, still-life and industrial location photography, but he is best known for his portraits, over 90 of which have been *Life* magazine covers. Here he tells how he gets some of the many varied effects for which his portraits are famous.] All photographs by Philippe Halsman.
• *Also see: Lighting in Portraiture; Portrait Photography; Portraiture Outdoors; Portraiture with the Speedlamp.*

AT LEAST 90 PERCENT OF ALL pictures taken have people in them, but of these only a very few are portraits. Even a picture showing nothing but a human face is not necessarily a portrait—it may be only a record of an expression, or a meaningless snapshot. A picture of John is a portrait only if it is an attempt to show what John is really like.

Showing what a person is like means characterizing him. And we realize that portraiture is truly nothing but characterization. Consequently, if we want to make a portrait and not just a snapshot, we must ask ourselves what kind of person our subject is and what we want to say about him.

SELECTION

The main problem of every art is selection. A writer setting out to tell a man's life story could find himself stuck interminably in describing the first day—every hour and every minute of it. A photographer who wants to make a portrait is faced with a similar variety of possibilities. He can photograph the person formally or informally, outdoors or indoors, in the studio or in the subject's home. He can photograph him in close-up,

A great portrait of a great lady. The camera position and the lighting helped give an intimate close-up of Mrs. Eleanor Roosevelt, who was directed skillfully by the photographer.

in a long shot, against an infinite variety of backgrounds, and with an infinite variety of lighting.

Many photographers are so overwhelmed by all these possibilities that they cannot make up their minds how to start. They expect advice and instruction from an experienced portraitist. But the expert cannot make the choice for you. Only you know your subject, and your portrait will tell not only what the subject is like but also what you see in him.

Before he picks up his camera, the photographer must know what he wants to say about his subject. If it is his girl, and he likes her exuberant smile, he might try to capture this with a fast shutter speed, outdoors where the light is bright or with flash or speedlight. If the subject is a man, and the photographer likes his straightforward, serious expression, he might want to work in a quiet room and try to capture just that.

The decision about what you want to try to capture is the most important element in producing a portrait, and the moment you have made it, everything else becomes easy and logical—you simply ask yourself what background will add force to the characterization, what lighting will emphasize its mood, and so forth.

Photographic portraiture has usually been taught on a very low and purely technical level. The photographer is warned of the danger of foreshortening; he is introduced into the mysteries of the 45-degree lighting, and of low and high key, which only adds to his embarrassment of choice.

What has been overlooked completely is that every technical step the photographer takes introduces new psychological values. Different lightings produce different moods; camera angles emphasize and de-emphasize characteristics. Even darkroom techniques modify the character of a picture and consequently the character of the subject. This is what the photographer must keep in mind and if he knows the characteristics he wants to show, each successive technical step must be taken in the same direction to

emphasize the point he wants to make.

Of course a human being is not like a mathematical formula, and the portraitist has to be warned of too much rigidity in his approach. He should not be hypnotized by the desire to capture the quality he considers most important. Any human being is complex and unpredictable, and preconceived ideas should not act as blinders that will prevent the photographer from capturing the accidents that happen in almost every sitting and are sometimes more revealing than anything the photographer can figure out beforehand.

In the fog of the innumerable possibilities that face the photographer, his guiding beacon must be the first analytical selection of what he will be seeking in the sitting.

It would be wrong to think that after making up his mind, the photographer has only to apply his technique. During the sitting itself, he must continue to be a psychologist. I would go so far as to say that many photographers who are absolute masters of technique fail as portraitists because they don't pay enough attention to the psychological part of a sitting.

THE PSYCHOLOGY OF THE SITTING

We must remember that a portrait sitting is an extremely artificial situation. The poor sitter feels constantly observed, put to a test, not only by the critical eye of the photographer but also by the pitiless lens of the camera. He feels awkward, self-conscious, intimidated, and absolutely unnatural. Very few people are able to lose their self-consciousness immediately and behave in front of the camera as though it were not there. In most cases the photographer has to help his subject. Savages who have never seen a camera, and children less than four years old, have no camera shyness, but the more intelligent, complicated, or insecure a person is, the greater will be his difficulty in losing self-consciousness.

Are there any tricks? Very often I am asked by young photographers, "What do you say to an actress when you photograph her?"—as if there were some magic sentences that always produce photogenic expressions, and which a beginner could learn by heart to use at a critical moment. My answer is: there are no magic formulas.

ENCOURAGING THE SITTER

The photographer must be more concerned about the feelings of his subject than about his camera and his lighting. He must realize that sometimes complete silence is the best climate for the subject; on the other hand, silence sometimes makes the sitting a frightening affair. Usually I speak all the time, trying to find a subject that interests the sitter, trying to make it seem that the topic of our conversation is more interesting to me than taking of the picture itself. If I make remarks that concern my subject they are always encouraging. If I see that there is some progress, I immediately mention it.

A professional portraitist once told me that his client complained that he looked stupid in all his portraits. "Why do you blame me?" answered the photographer, "Why don't you complain to your parents?"

This witty portraitist was wrong, because it was his duty to influence and stimulate the subject's expressions, and to capture them at moments of his own choice. Even a man with a constantly stupid expression can lose it in a careless moment and give the photographer a unique opportunity.

We thus come to the paradoxical conclusion that very often it is not the good photographer who makes the good portrait, but the good psychologist. In many sittings I have felt that what I said to the client was more important than what I did with my camera and my lights.

I have in my files two pictures of the Duke and Duchess of Windsor looking directly at the camera. In the first one they look tense, tired, and old. I took the picture, then said, "You shouldn't look at the camera with that expression. You are in our eyes the most romantic couple of this century—the man who gave up a throne for the woman he loved." My subjects re-

laxed, smiled, and suddenly—an amazing thing—they looked years younger. The picture made a *Life* cover.

It is remarkable how much the state of our mind controls our features. Our face not only reflects all our emotions but actually can look taut and young or sagging and old.

One day Gloria Swanson came to my studio overworked and enervated from the tensions of her career. She was crying, and when she stopped there was a tired woman in front of my lens. I took her for a walk in the park, talked with her, and finally got the idea of asking her to put on her black gloves. This attribute of feminine coquetry stimulated her into an entirely different mood. For twenty minutes there was an exuberant flirtation with the camera, and when finished I told her, "You know, Gloria, you look twenty years younger now." "I don't *look* it, Dr. Halsman," she answered, "I *am* twenty years younger now."

CANDID PHOTOGRAPHY IN PORTRAITURE

It seems that portraiture is going more and more in the direction of informality and of the candid approach. Candid photography has the advantage of sometimes making very striking and truthful statements, but it also has the disadvantage of often being only the reflection of an isolated and passing moment. We have the feeling that the person is really caught, but not caught in his entirety.

But as a method, it is a good and valid approach, not only for the reporter but also for the portrait photographer. Instead of asking a child to sit still in front of the camera, you can ask him to play in front of the background you have selected, or in the area where you have set up your lights. For adults, a good working method is to photograph your subjects in a favorite or characteristic position, doing the things they usually do. For example, you might ask a writer to write a few sentences, and then photograph him while he does so. By using this method the writer will be in his element and you will have helped

him to be himself.

REPRODUCING A MOOD

Sometimes it is impossible to reproduce an actual situation, but you can try to recreate the mood. I once had to photograph the French actress Cecile Aubry, who was not particularly beautiful but was a very interesting mixture of an innocent child and provocative woman. The first pictures of the sitting had little expression, and showed merely a moderately attractive girl with slightly protruding teeth. Then I remmbered the movie *Manon,* in which she had starred, and said, "Imagine that a man you have never seen before is standing in front of you, and that you slowly open your dress." Cecile put her hands to her neckline, her eyes grew dark and strange, and suddenly I had a portrait full of inexplicable tension and appeal.

Some subjects are so tense and self-conscious that nothing seems to help. In such cases a relaxing drink will often help. I made one of my most successful portraits of a woman writer lying on a couch and so "relaxed" that she didn't know what was happening to her.

I must confess that I have never used tranquilizers on my subjects, but I suspect that they might help in some particularly difficult cases.

The photographer must improvise in trying to help his subject. He must be sensitive to whatever is disturbing the subject. He must be prepared to discover that in many cases the cause of the trouble is his own behavior. There are many books that teach darkroom techniques and how to light for portraiture, but there are no books to teach the psychology of a sitting. Reading the works of the great psychologists will help because it will clarify our thinking about the subconscious forces that influence our actions and reactions.

But more important than that is experience and the cultivation of one's own sensitivity. A portraitist who isn't sensitive to what is going

This outdoor portrait of Audrey Hepburn was made against an olive-tree background in Italy.

Changes in mood or psychological state can make a subject look younger or older. These two unretouched discards of the same Gloria Swanson sitting show dramatic differences in expression. (See text)

on in the mind of his subject during a sitting will never become a good portrait photographer.

WHO IS PHOTOGENIC?

The portrait photographer will soon find out that some people are easy to photograph, that their portraits "flatter" them. Other people are different—photographs don't seem to "do justice" to them. The former are photogenic; the latter are not.

The quality of being photogenic is the strange gift of appearing in most photographs at least as attractive and usually more attractive than one is in reality.

Photogenic Features

What are photogenic features? The main attributes are high cheek-bones, hollow cheeks, a strongly drawn jaw line, and, if you want to be handsome, small features. If you are more interested in showing character, you can afford the luxury of having a big nose and a big mouth. The bone structure of all our great film beauties is the same: Garbo, Dietrich, Loretta Young, Elizabeth Taylor, Kim Novak—all have big eyes, small noses and mouths. They have high cheek-bones, hollow cheeks, and strongly defined jaws, which guarantee a marvelous distribution of highlights and shadows under any lighting condition.

It is strange to notice how photogeneity has affected our ideal of beauty. Since we select our most beautiful women for the purpose of

photographing them, high cheekbones are now considered an attribute of beauty. But Flaubert only 100 years ago described Madame Bovary as attractive *in spite* her high cheekbones. All the Madonnas and goddesses of the Renaissance have oval, flat, definitely non photogenic faces. The only exception is Botticelli, whose every angel, saint, or goddess has higher cheekbones than does Loretta Young.

A woman full of charm is rarely photogenic, a sculptural beauty almost always. It is easy to reproduce the features of the latter because a photograph, which is necessarily still, is a good likeness of a face which is usually in repose. Charm, however, consists of a fleeting change of expressions, constantly surprising and delighting us. It is photogenic in a movie, but in a still picture we always have the feeling that it is somehow not enough, that one picture cannot capture the changing quality we call charm.

MINIMIZING PHYSICAL DEFECTS

Defects in a human face, hardly noticeable to the human eye (because the face is usually mobile and the eye cannot concentrate on them) appear with surprising force in a still photograph. Protruding ears, asymmetrical features are frozen still in a picture, ready to be compared and measured. Therefore the photographer has to be careful not to expose them to such comparison. He will not photograph protruding ears straight-on. If one eye is bigger than the other he will try to turn the subject's face in such a way that the perspective shift will adjust the difference.

Most human faces are asymmetric, and therefore the photog-

Right: *Lighting imparts a mood to a picture and is consequently a means of characterization. Lighting can make a profile look like a drawing or sculpture. Using one light to left of camera (top) minimizes modeling and outlines profile against the white background. The same lighting plus a spot (bottom) adds modeling and creates a more dimensional effect.*

Left: *When Halsman was confronted by the volatile Aldous Huxley he decided to interpret him in this active characterization. A Rolleiflex and electronic-flash lighting was used.*

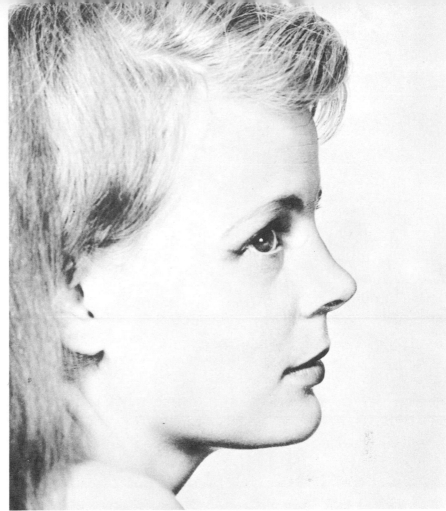

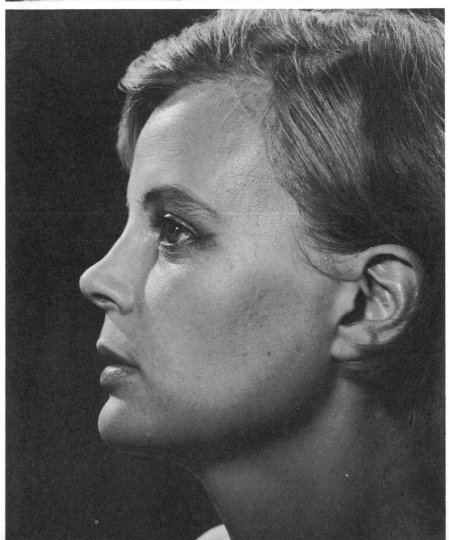

Above: *By simply tilting a face the emotional values are changed. The expression at the left is more expectant and receptive; at the right more reflective and scrutinizing.*

Right: *When Halsman told actress Anna Magnani that he did not do glamour portraits and that all her wrinkles would show, she said, "Don't hide them! I suffered too much to get them."*

rapher should start a sitting by comparing the sides of the face and determining which is the more attractive. It would be wrong to photograph a person from the least photogenic side; terrible fights occur when one of the actors in a scene is forced to sacrifice his photogenic side to the photogenic side of a colleague.

But it is not enough to have photogenic features to be photogenic in the full sense of the word. Many photographers think they have discovered a wonderful model when they see a girl with a perfectly photogenic face, only to be disappointed later when they have her in front of the camera. Besides being morphologically photogenic, a successful model has to be psychologically photogenic as well. She cannot be self-conscious and still in front of the camera; she has to be natural and completely unaffected. Great models have in addition an artistic gift for being creative and imaginative in front of the camera.

LIGHTING

Many photographers make the mistake of considering lighting only as a means of illuminating the subject. More than once I have seen a photographer take a meter reading, mumble that he didn't have enough light, and set up another light. This would indeed make the subject lighter, but would also introduce new shadows criss-crossing with the others, and disfigure the subject still further.

In a good portrait, lighting serves a different purpose. We must realize that a photograph is a flat two-dimensional piece of paper, while our subjects are three-dimensional. It is only with light that we can show this quality, and produce the illusion of depth. Lighting must sculpture a face. It can be employed also to beautify, to hide imperfections. Finally, lighting imparts a definite mood to a picture and is consequently a means of characterization.

Photography uses many kinds of lighting: photofloods, spots, flashbulbs, electronic flash, bouncelight, and the natural light it finds anywhere, outdoors or indoors—sun, diffused daylight, daylight indoors, artificial light indoors.

Start With One Floodlight

How do we learn lighting? I learned it by experience, and I earnestly recommend this method to others. I started by buying one floodlight, and by making all my portraits with that alone. I noticed that when I placed it near the camera and aimed it head-on at the subject, it flattened the face, produced few shadows, and consequently tended to remove the lines and wrinkles. When I raised my light, shadows appeared under the nose and chin and the face began to look three-dimensional. If I raised it still more, the eyes disappeared in the shadows of their sockets, the cheek hollows were accentuated, and the lighting imparted a gloomy, almost tragic mood. I noticed also that the shadows of the nose reached and crossed

the line of the mouth, disturbing its design.

If I held the light just above the level of the subject, and to one side of the camera, I obtained the 45-degree lighting so dear to most teachers of lighting. If I put my light lower than the face, the nose and other features threw shadows upward. The eyes caught a lot of light and the face looked unusual, often mysterious or forbidding. (This is the light abundantly used in mystery or horror movies—good to characterize a Frankenstein or Dracula, but it can also lend an air of unbearable mystery to a beautiful woman.)

By moving my light to the side I could light just one side of the face, leaving the other side black. And finally, by putting the light behind the subject I created a silhoutte. When I experimented with the profile I noticed that I could draw its outline when I had my subject against a black background and the light behind him. And I could draw a dark profile line when I had my subject against a light background and had my light source in front of him, coming from the direction of the back of his head.

I realized, however, that one light limited my photography. The shadows were often too strong and my pictures too dramatic and harsh. Nevertheless, I still use only one light in many of my portraits. It has unusual force, translating three-dimensional forms with an extraordinary plasticity.

Adding a Second Light

The next step in the beginning of my career as a portrait photographer was the acquisition of a second floodlamp. I used it first only to fill in the shadows produced by the first light. I noticed that besides lightening the shadows, my fill-in was also introducing a set of shadows of its own, which usually were displeasing and destroyed the plas-

Group portraits can be extremely difficult. Halsman arranged this group of five Eisenhower brothers in order of age at first, but found the picture to be too static. He asked Ike to tell a joke and shot at the moment of the punch line. A multiple-flash set-up using three flashlamps in reflectors.

Light position introduces psychological overtones. From top: overhead, high front, straight front, and floor level; expression remains the same, but the mood and characterization change. More detailed explanation in the text.

ticity of the one-lamp lighting. It was particularly unpleasant when the shadows partially overlapped, creating gray and black areas.

The only way to keep these secondary shadows at a minimum was to keep the fill-in light as close as possible to the lens. I noticed also that the smaller the reflector of the fill-in, the more pronounced were the edges of its shadows. Consequently the fill-in I now use is a diffused floodlight in a huge reflector which I keep as near as I can to the camera. My fill-in is usually half as strong as my main light, and by moving it closer to the subject I soften my lighting, remove wrinkles and lines, but also lessen the plasticity of my picture. By moving the fill-in farther away I achieve a contrary effect. The shadows become deeper, the lines stronger, and the whole picture grows more plastic and dramatic.

Using Two Lights

Once in a great while I use two lights as main sources of illumination. For instance I might place both at the sides of the subject for crosslighting, which sometimes creates interesting and dramatic effects.

The second light can be used not only as a fill-in but to light the background, or by pointing it at the subject from the rear to get backlighting or rimlighting.

Two lights can produce an infinite variety of lightings. One of the pictures that did the most for my career in America was made with two floodlights which cost less than $3 each. It was sold to Elizabeth Arden, won an Art Directors' award, and launched the career of its model, Constance Ford, who is now a well-known actress.

The more lights used, the more complicated it is to control them and to avoid the accidents that they produce, such as overlapping shadows and disturbing highlights. Many portrait photographers usually start a sitting with five lights. In front of the subject the have a main

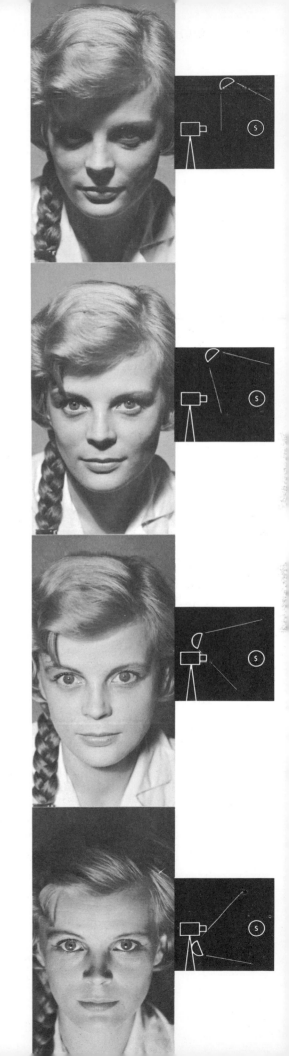

light, and near the camera a fill-in. Behind the subject they have the light which is used to control the illumination of the background.

At each side, to the rear of the subject, is a light which the portraitist can turn on if he wants edgelighting or if he wants to put a highlight on the hair. These two are, as a rule, spotlights with barn doors which keep the light confined to a narrow beam and prevent it from spilling over into the lens. Although the five lights are not always used together, they are usually sufficient for any lighting effect the photographer wants to produce.

INCANDESCENT LIGHT SOURCES

The artificial lights available to the photographer are these: floodlights with reflectors of various diameters, spotlights, and banks of lights. Most photographers are interested only in the power of these light sources, but we must also consider their character. A spotlight has the advantage of a narrow beam which can light a small area; with barn doors or a snoot, it can be concentrated at a very small point. The light rays of a spot are almost parallel, and they throw shadows with sharp outlines, giving to the objects they strike an added dimension of precision and plasticity. A floodlamp is softer; its rays are divergent, and consequently it is good for lighting large areas. The shadow outline is less precise and the entire aspect of the picture is softer.

Reflectors

Insufficient attention is paid by most photographers to the question of the reflector. A good reflector may add to the intensity of the light as much as 100 percent. Some reflectors achieve this not by an improved reflecting surface but simply by concentrating the light rays in a small area (a "hot spot")—a fault extremely common in flashbulb reflectors and even more common in speedlight units. It is in the interest of the electronic-flash manu-

Another famous group of five brothers shows skillful positioning of the Rockefellers for this portrait.

This serene character portrayal of Ricki Sonia Huston utilizes many of the important points presented in the text.

facturer to claim a high guide number for his product, and by measuring the light intensity in the center of the hot spot he can prove his exaggerated claim. Hot spots are, however, very dangerous for the photographer, producing an extremely uneven illumination, and they must be avoided.

Another important factor is the size of the reflector. The bigger it is, the softer will be the shadows and the softer the over-all effect. One must realize, however, that the bulb emits more light than the reflector, and that only by covering the reflector with spun glass or some similar substance (which usually weakens the light by 50 percent) does the whole reflector become a homogeneous light source. This, of course, is only desirable when the photographer is trying to avoid shadows. In this case the relative distance of the light source from the subject and the ratio of the size of the light source to the size of the subject enter into consideration. The closer the light, and the larger it is in relation to the subject, the softer and flatter will be the lighting. The farther the light source, and the smaller it is in relation to the subject, the more outlined will be the shadows. On the other hand if a light in a room is very far removed from the subject, it also illuminates the entire room, which

Drama critic Walter Kerr in front of a theatrical background. "A portraitist who isn't sensitive to what is going on in the mind of his subject during a sitting will never become a good portrait photographer," says Halsman.

acts as a kind of reflecting fill-in.

Sometimes it is in the photographer's interest to use a spot as a main light, in order to impart strength and precision to the subject. Sometimes it is better to use a flood as a main light, even a diffused one in a huge reflector, to produce a much softer effect.

FLASH AND SPEEDLIGHTS

For magazine assignments in France (before I came to this country) I used either available light or floods which I carried with me. When I came here, I found that most magazine photographers were using multiple flash for reportage. I had absolutely no difficulty in switching to this new method because there is no basic difference between light sources—flood, flash, or electronic flash. There were no modeling lights in my flash units, but I remembered so well the light-

A touch of candid quality is seen in this strong close-up of William Holden.

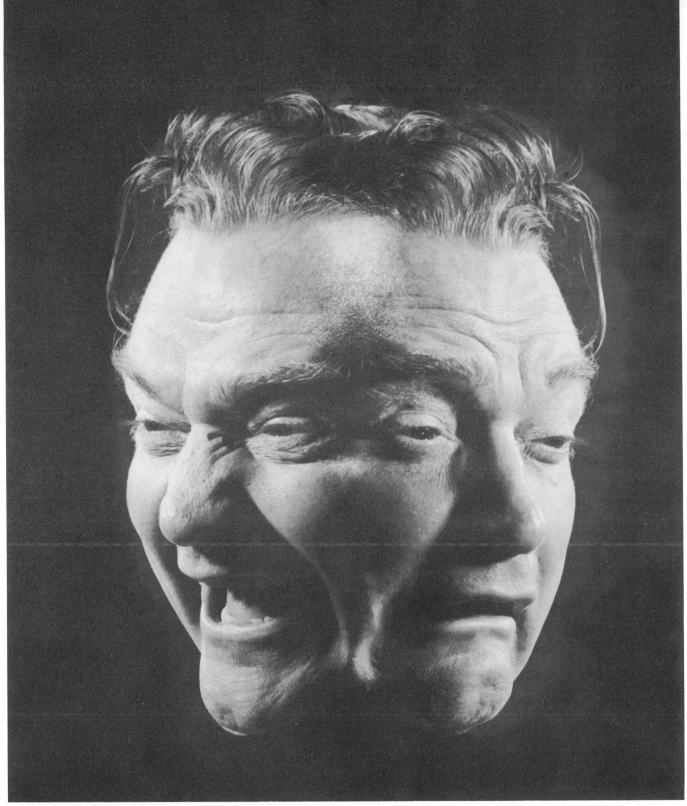

This portrait of Red Skelton gave the photographer a chance to have some fun. Two negatives were sandwiched together in the enlarger with this result.

ing effects I had produced with floods that I had only to place the flashbulbs in the same position to obtain the same results.

Many photographers think that flash produces a different quality of light than flood, and that speedlight has still other characteristics of its own. Most photographers overexpose when they are using flash, burning up the faces in the foreground, creating stark, chalky flesh tones against a relatively dark background. This has come to be considered typical of flashbulb lighting.

When electronic flash first appeared on the market, the manufacturers recommended increasing the developing time, which led to blocking-up of highlights. A colleague of mine complained that he could not get any flesh tones with speedlight, and bet me that I couldn't either. I put my two daughters in front of my camera, made a close-up portrait, developed

the film for the normal time, and won my bet.

COLOR VALUES OF LIGHTS

There is, however, something that differentiates the quality of light from the three basic sources. Photoflood is of lower color temperature, that is, it is higher in red as compared with its blue content. This makes the reds in the subject appear lighter than normal, and tends to wash out flesh tones, lips, and so on, unless exposure is carefully controlled. Flashlamps have a somewhat higher color temperature, and thus have a little more blue light, which brings up skin tones a bit better (the washed-out faces often produced by flash exposures, as I have pointed out, are always the result of overexposure, overdevelopment or both—they are *not* characteristics of the light source).

Electronic-flash illumination is much like daylight; if anything, it is a little colder, having a color temperature near 7000 K, as compared with about 6500 for average daylight. In black-and-white photography, this high blue content tends to affect the blue and green parts of the panchromatic sensitivity more than the red; it is equivalent to shooting through a pale blue-green filter. This darkens all the reds in the picture, and tends to emphasize skin blemishes, freckles, and so on. Some photographers claim that electronic flash " penetrates the skin deeper" but there is really no mystery about it; it is simply a matter of color balance.

Flash and electronic flash are usually used in small reflectors, which produce a harsher illumination than floodlights. In my studio I use speedlights in very big reflectors, and sometimes have difficulty later in distinguishing between the pictures I have made with speedlight and those made with floodlighting.

I recommend that the would-be portraitist proceed the same way I did—to learn portrait lighting with floods, to remember what the position of lights does to the subject,

A touch of informality, an unusual background, and Susannah York all add up to this successful outdoor portrait.

and to use the same arrangements with flash and electronic flash.

More and more speedlights now come with modeling lights in their reflectors. It is imperative that, when using several speedlights, their modeling lights lights be proportionate to the watt-second rating of the units, so as to permit judging the relative intensity of the light visually.

As I mentioned before, it is difficult to create rimlighting or hairlighting without using spots. Since there are no spots designed for flash or speedlight, I make black hoods which I put on my reflectors to keep light from spilling into areas where it is not wanted, confining the beam to the hair or the outline of the head.

BOUNCELIGHT

Flash and speedlight are being increasingly used indirectly. Instead of being turned on the subject, the light is directed against the ceiling or a wall. Many photographers think that when they use bouncelight it is scattered throughout the whole room, producing a soft effect which remains more or less the same whenever they use this technique.

This in an absolutely false conception. Bounceflash illuminates a limited area of the room, which thereupon becomes a source of light in itself. Consequently, if you bounce light against a ceiling, the ceiling becomes a sort of huge reflector shooting light down on the subject, lighting the top of the head, hiding the eyes in shadows, and producing an effect similar to that of the floodlights in the very high position, described earlier. Similarly, bouncing your flash- or speedlight from the wall facing the subject will create a flat head-on lighting. Although in bouncelighting the entire room becames more or less illuminated and fills in some of the shadows, we should not consider it to be a kind of soft, all-pervading lighting, but think of it in the old familiar terms of directional lighting.

If we want to use bouncelight, our first considerations should be: How will it mold the subject's face? What mood will it impart to the photographer? Bouncelight can give a gloomy mood if it comes from

the floor. We can make a crosslighting by bouncing light from two opposite walls; we can use bounce to produce a silhouette, and so on.

Very often we hear the recommendation to use bouncelight for color photography. Unfortunately, this is impossible in most rooms. Only in a perfectly white empty room will the bounced light keep its original color. If you bounce light in a white room with a lot of brown furniture, doors, and woodwork, the bounced light will have a distinctly brown tinge. It is even more dangerous to bounce light in a room with colored wallpaper. To shoot with bouncelight in such a place, you must bring your own reflecting surfaces—white paper or aluminum foil.

DAYLIGHT

In my discussion about artificial lighting I purposely put great emphasis on what the photographer can do with only one light, because everything on earth is actually lit by one light: the sun. Thus, everything I said about the effects produced by one artificial-light source applies also the effects one can achieve in direct sun. Of course the sun at any given moment is stationary, and it seems that we cannot adjust it. But we can turn and place our subject so that the sun's light strikes him head-on, sidewise, as a rimlight, or so that it silhouettes him. We can even make the sun shoot its rays from below, by putting a mirror on the ground. Finally, we can select the time of day, and shoot with the sun in the position we prefer.

I try to avoid shooting between 10 a.m. and 2 p.m. because of the overhead position of the sun. The early-morning and later-afternoon hours are usually the best. Many photographers use flash as fill-in, but its directional nature always produces a feeling of artificiality. I prefer to use as a reflector a white sheet or a piece of cardboard on which I have pasted aluminum foil. White-sand or light-concrete surfaces furnish marvelous natural fill-in. With the help of reflectors it is possible to shoot against the sun, using it as a secondary source for edgelighting or crosslighting. But very few people can keep their eyes open in bright sunlight. Even the reflector usually makes them squint, and consequently it is much easier to do portraiture when the sky is overcast, or in the shade.

Pictures taken in sunshine differ in mood from pictures taken in the shade or under overcast sky. The photographer should take care that the nature of the lighting does not weaken or even destroy the mood of the subject.

CAMERA POSITION

As important as lighting is the relative position of the camera to the subject. Even camera distance plays an important role; the closer the camera, the greater the distortion due to the effect of perspective. Everything that is close is exaggerated; everything that is distant is minimized. A hand that is closer to the lens than the face suddenly appears enormous. When close-up lenses are used at a distance of less than three feet, the face becomes distorted, the nose and mouth appear disproportionately big, the crown of the head becomes small, and the subject's features take on a particularly coarse look.

This is the reason why old-fashioned portrait photographers always used long-focal-length lenses and shot their clients from afar, keeping the hands and features pleasantly proportioned. On the other hand there are instances in which closeness can be used to advantage. When I photographed Durante, I used Proxars on my Rolleiflex in order to exaggerate his nose, knowing that Durante's nose was in the eyes of the American public as important as the man behind it.

Even though they are ugly and disproportionate, pictures taken at close distances evoke in the viewer the feeling of closeness and intimacy, and are more dynamic than pictures taken from a greater distance.

CAMERA ANGLE

The camera angle is even more important than the distance. A low position of the camera makes the subject appear tall and towering. A high position makes him appear small and less important. Strange as it may seem, the position of the camera influences our appraisal of the subject. When the camera looks down on the subject, we subconsciously also look down on him. When it looks up we are also looking up, and the subject appears to us large, domineering, forbidding.

Camera angle is one of our most important means of characterization. Our eyes are instinctively attracted by the actual center of the picture. It is as if they were following the axis of the light rays. We can subsequently crop the portrait and put the actual center in one of the corners of the print, and our eyes will still be attracted to it. Thus the picture axis becomes one of the most important means of calling attention to the part of the subject which is most significant to the photographer.

Almost every face is asymmetric, and since each side is different, the choice of one or the other already implies characterization on the part of the photographer. In some cases it is the most important choice the photographer can make. I remember the famous French writer André Malraux. From the left side his nose has an elegant hump and reminds one of the beak of an eagle; he looks handsome and romantic. From the right side his nose is turned up like the bill of a duck, altogether out of key with the man's romantic reputation.

EMPHASIZING FEATURES

I usually start a portrait sitting with my camera at eye level. I know that by raising the camera I will emphasize the forehead, and that by lowering it I will emphasize the chin and jaw. In our mind, the forehead is a symbol of intellectual capacity; the chin and jaw stand for energy and physical strength. Consequently it is in our interest to photograph a boxer from a low camera position to emphasize his brawn.

Conversely, when photographing a scientist we will raise the camera to put symbolic stress on his brain. When I photographed Dr. Robert Oppenheimer I naturally used a high camera position. Looking at the result, the words highbrow and egghead come automatically to mind. Here, however, a word of warning is necessary. If the expression of Dr. Oppenheimer had belied the strong (but only formal) camera-angle characterization, the photograph would not be a valid portrait. As it happens, the expression of intense intellectual concentration is interpreted and emphasized by the high camera position.

In the case of women, where one photographs more for beauty than for character, one should avoid a too pronounced distortion. We raise and lower the camera to a lesser degree, and our choice is not so much brow versus jaw as eyes versus mouth.

Poets have said that eyes mirror the soul and that the mouth is the ever-open door to sin. As a matter of fact most people associate eyes with intelligence ("bright-eyed"), or with honesty, innocence, and so on. The mouth is usually associated with sensuousness.

This knowledge can often be of great help. If a girl sends a picture with an application for a job that requires intelligence and efficiency, she should not choose one that emphasizes her mouth—unless her secret desire is to seduce her future boss. If it is, it would be wrong for her to send a picture emphasizing her eyes as the symbol of her intelligence and qualifications.

One day I had to photograph a very beautiful Polish writer. One picture was to be for her book jacket, another for her fiancé. In the first she looked at you with big and knowing eyes; you had the feeling the woman had a lot so say. In the picture for her fiancé, the camera was focusing on her mouth.

BACKGROUNDS

The problem of backgrounds is so complex that I can only scratch the surface of it.

A background can be neutral, an even surface of a single tone that will make the face or figure of the subject stand out.

In this intimate close-up Peter Freuchen is seen as a great patriarch, the master of the seven seas. Note the background map and positioning of his hand on the top of a globe.

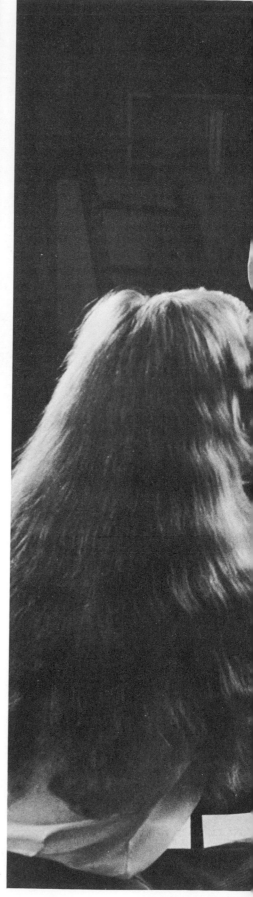

These two portraits were made at the same instant with two cameras in different positions. Halsman was demonstrating that change in camera position not only changes aspect of face but also alters the significance of an expression.

It can be purely formal, that is, it can add graphically to the portrait through its design or composition.

It can be storytelling or informative, in the way in which some photographers use it: they surround the subject with all kinds of objects which tell us about the interest or profession of the sitter. The great danger of this approach is that many forget that the main object of the portrait is the subject himself, and not the composition of the background.

It can be a characterizing background without telling a story. A background of books will characterize a person as an intellectual. Sometimes a background can be used as a contrast. When I photographed William Bendix against a very feminine, frilly curtain, the ruggedness of his features was accentuated doubly. A fashion photographer who had the unfortunate duty of photographing rich and prominent but unattractive elderly ladies solved his problem by creating very beautiful backgrounds and putting his aging subjects unobtrusively against them. Later, viewers would exclaim, "What a beautiful picture!" and add "What a beautiful picture of Lady X!"

It can be a symbolic background, in which there is an interrelation between the subject and the background which gives an added meaning to the whole, for instance, a picture I once made of a surrealist painter with a background of money.

It can be a symbolic background, chosen not for the sake of composition or to contribute information but to give a certain mood to the entire picture—a portrait of a young girl against a spring landscape, or of a shady-looking character in a dark street.

The photographer must be very careful in selecting a background to see that its mood does not weaken the mood of the subject.

A smiling face in a sunlit landscape will give us the feeling of

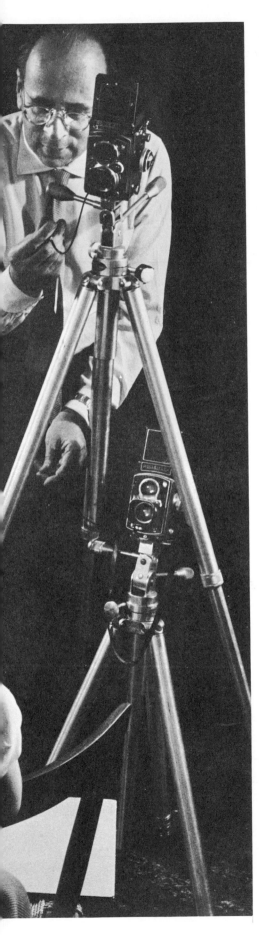

gaiety and cheer. A forbidding background of approaching storm would lessen the effect of gaiety but possibly introduce a new one; a smiling face against a threatening storm might mean defiance or unconcern.

COLOR

It is only natural that all the considerations discussed in the preceding pages should also be applicable to the color portrait, since the only thing that distinguishes it from the black-and-white one—and I apologize for the obvious truism—is color. But color is not just something that is there.

Color is a descriptive and emotional factor of great strength. Its emotional power can be illustrated by the way we use color words to describe moods or characteristics: to feel blue, to see red, to be yellow. The Russian movie director Sergei M. Eisenstein of *Potemkin* fame was probably the first to make an extensive study of the emotional associations produced by color and of their application in photography. There is a tremendous difference in characterization between a color portrait made in the cold light of a cloudy day and one made in the reddish glow of the setting sun.

Great thought should be given not only to the coloring of the light (once in a double portrait I tried to underline the character difference of two sisters by lighting one with warm and the other with cold light), but also to the color of the background. It was only natural that, in order to emphasize the ice-cold beauty of Grace Kelly, I photographed her for a *Life* cover against a cool gray-blue background. And when I photographed the fiery Mexican actress Maria Feliz, I used warm-colored lights and an orange-red backdrop.

I do not think it is necessary to belabor this point, however. The connection between color and emotion has been discussed by many writers at great length, and in the end, the photographer's taste, and what he wishes to express, are the governing factors. I would like, however, to warn the reader against trying to use too many colors in one portrait. It cheapens the over-all effect and destroys the power of characterization or the mood which

can be achieved by allowing one particular color to dominate.

IN THE DARKROOM

Many photographers assume that with the taking of the picture the creative process in finished. They are likely to give their film to a photofinisher and accept his prints as the final product of their effort. One of the most famous photojournalists, Cartier-Bresson, works this way with a photofinisher who knows his standards and goals. An equally famous photojournalist, W. Eugene Smith, feels that he has to make all his prints himself, and has been known to spend innumerable hours trying to make one perfect print.

As for myself, I make the greater part of my prints myself, because in my opinion the creative process continues with every step. It is my belief that one of the prime aims of photography is to reproduce three-dimensional reality on a two-dimensional surface. I want to show volume and texture, proximity and depth. As a rule I don't like completely black nontransparent shadows, but even more I dislike overexposed, washed-out areas which don't say anything, and which I call *anonymous*. Too soft photographs (which are often simply overexposed and not sufficiently developed prints) lack strength and often appear anemic or muddy. A good print should have punch and detail. Its tonal scale should start with pure white and gradually lead to a complete black.

But it is wrong to think that every negative can produce only one kind of perfect print. Printing a negative is interpreting a negative. If we use soft paper, we will produce softer and less dramatic pictures. If we use paper of high contrast, our prints will be more forceful, dramatic, even strident. And finally we can make either a light or a dark print, making it look gay, transparent and delicate, or gloomy, heavy and tragic. Therefore while printing a negative we should first ask ourselves what atmosphere we want to convey.

Even dodging can introduce or destroy emotional values. I remember a picture I made of a couple sitting by the fireplace. The room was dark. They were lit by the firelight and the picture had a mood of mystery and intimacy. I had no time to make the print myself and gave it to an experienced printer. The printer burned in the highlights, held back the shadows and presented me proudly with the finished print. It showed two people in a normally lit room. It was a technically perfect photograph but all its mood was destroyed.

We have talked only about printing, but the photograph depends entirely on the quality of the negative. If the negative is slightly overexposed and slightly underdeveloped, shadows show details and the highlights are not blocked-up. With the help of different grades of paper we can make any kind of print we desire. It's easy to make a print which has what so many photographers call good print quality.

The tendency of the present-day photographer who uses available light, however, is to underexpose and overdevelop. The result is a negative with underexposed transparent shadows and with highlights blocked up by overdevelopment. It gives an effect as if the picture were taken in a coal mine. Normal-looking faces appear gloomy and overdramatic. We realize suddenly that by underexposure and overdevelopment alone we are superimposing on our picture an extraneous mood which can either play in our favor or disfavor. If we photograph people in a slum area, underexposure and overdevelopment will intensify the mood of abject poverty and gloomy suffering. If we underexpose and overdevelop a gay birthday party, the coal-mine effect of the pictures will contradict the mood of enjoyment we are trying to capture.

CROPPING

Most photographers approach the problem of cropping from the point of view of pleasing composition. They establish rules like "the horizon line must divide the picture in a proportion of one to two," or they try to apply the Golden Section.

However, one can approach cropping also from the viewpoint of psychological values. We can establish the rule that if the subject touches the top edge of the photograph, he will appear tall, and if we leave a lot of air above him, the space will make him appear small. If a profile is cropped in such a way that it seems to be bending down, we have subconsciously the feeling of downbeat. The picture might appear, depending on its expression, thoughtful, scrutinizing, menacing, or pessimistic. If the same profile is cropped so that the face seems to be turned upward, the feeling of upbeat will make the profile look (again depending on expression) either proud, expectant, receptive, or optimistic.

The more background there is in the picture, the quieter and more diluted its essence. Closer cropping eliminates the parts of the picture which have little meaning, and makes it more forceful and dynamic.

It is good to put the psychological center of gravity close to the center of the print, since our eyes usually look into the center of a picture.

INTERRELATION OF TECHNIQUE AND EMOTION

Photographic technique has always been taught like any other craft. The fact that each technical step introduces new psychological values and modifies the emotional impact of the finished picture has never been adequately explained.

The essence of portraiture is characterization, and we understand now also that each technical step is an additional means of characterization. A portrait is a statement made by the photographer about his subject, and he must see to it that his technique reinforces the statement and does not dilute or obscure it. How wrong it would be, for instance, to try to make a somber and forceful portrait of a sad person by producing a flatly lit, delicate, and lightly printed photograph.

Not long ago a young photographer showed me his pictures and complained that none of them was ever published. "I am not interested in technique," he said, "I am only interested in capturing emotion. But the editors seem to be blind." I

The delicacy and dreamy quality of this quiet portrait gives it great power. Note how the backlighting is used to outline the figure. Frontlighting is subdued.

looked at his pictures. The young man was shooting in the city streets with his 35 mm camera, and sometimes had captured real emotion. However his pictures were so weak, so drab, the emotion so lost and diluted, that his work did not present any interest.

I said, "There are actors who feel their part deep within them, but when they read their lines, their face and voice remain expression-less. Their emotion does not move us. To transmit emotion you must know how to project it. Every real artist must know his technique."

CONCLUSION

It is the fate of every explainer to be misunderstood. I hope that no one has understood me to say that one can take any empty expression and through clever manipulation of each technical step, achieve great emotional impact. The best diamond cutter and polisher will not be able to transform a piece of glass into a valuable jewel. It will remain a worthless bauble.

What I have been attempting to show is that, in a portrait sitting, we have to try to capture the essence of a human being. When we think we have achieved it, we must be sure not to leave it diluted and lost in our picture. We have to show it with utmost clarity and force, and each technical step must contribute to this end. This is the meaning of the interrelation of technique and emotion. An uncut diamond has only a potential value. Only after it is cut and polished does it shine in the dark.

The Alcazar, a fairytale castle famous in Spanish history since 755 and now partially open to the public as a Museum of Arms, is a beautiful example of the kind of photograph sought by travel editors and tourist bureaus. (Photo: William Vandivert)

PUBLICITY PHOTOGRAPHY

LIDA LIVINGSTON
Vice President, Infoplan, New York

[Revolutionary changes have been taking place in the field of public relations. Here an author who is active in the field presents the very latest information from a practical viewpoint with information given about photography as a public-relations tool, including industry and business, entertainment and the arts, government, selling and purchasing. Photographers and publication editors will find a wealth of material in this complete presentation.]

• *Also see: Advertising Photography; Color Photography for Advertising; Picture-Story Production; Psychological Portraiture.*

THE GROWING FIELD OF PUBLIC relations increasingly recognizes still photography as an important communications tool. Every known photographic technique is used from reportage to portraits, from high key to low key, from micro to macro, from underwater to aerial, from realism to impressionism.

Public-relations photography is a demanding field. While the portraitist and advertising photographer must satisfy only one client and the photojournalist or news photographer only one editor, the public-relations photographer must satisfy both the client and editor. And since a public-relations photograph must contribute to a client objective, a perfect public-relations photograph must combine the storytelling requirement of the editorial picture with the "sell" of an advertising picture.

SIMILARITIES BETWEEN PUBLIC-RELATIONS AND NEWS PHOTOGRAPHY

It might seem that the public-relations and advertising photographers would use similar methods, since both take pictures to fill given client objectives. But in practice, the public-relations photographer more often exercises the same viewpoint as the photojournalist, since public

Above. *Aerial view of a new model village, built as part of Spain's land-reclamation program to bring agriculture to areas that have been empty and arid for centuries.*

Right: *Close-up of a modern Madrid apartment building was made for publication in newspapers and magazines to educate the American people, particularly the business and financial community, on the progress and achievements of modern Spain.*

relations, unlike advertising which occupies paid space, must earn its place in magazines, newspapers, or television.

Many news photographs are a record of events as they happen, while others are created—among these, Joe Rosenthal's magnificent Pulitzer Prize-winning "Flag Raising on Iwo Jima." In selecting the four Marines for this famous picture, Rosenthal was functioning in the manner of the best public-relations photographer: casting, framing, directing, and recording action to

achieve maximum viewer response to a given situation.

This goal of maximum viewer response should be the public-relations photographer's objective, whether his assignment is to photograph a presidential candidate or canned peas in a salad.

Except in client-controlled media, such as an annual report or house organ, the public-relation photograph must be an entity in itself: The objective is to achieve a photograph so persuasive that the editor is impelled to use the desired words. The mink must look so soft and luxurious, the diamonds so clear and dazzling, that the editor almost automatically writes "lovely, luxurious mink" or "exquisite diamonds."

TYPES OF PUBLIC-RELATIONS PHOTOS

Public relations photographs can be divided into four fairly distinct classifications:

Straight news. Here the photographer functions like a press photographer, covering any newsworthy aspect of an event.

Manufactured news. This is a created event which might reasonably have occurred.

Service feature. This is the most frequent type of public-relations photography. Products, services, facilities are presented in terms of reader service and interest.

Atmospheric feature. Here photographic excellence is the key to acceptance. In this category are most tourism photographs and some industrial photographs.

PUBLIC-RELATIONS PHOTOGRAPHY FOR BUSINESS AND INDUSTRY

Within the broad scope of public relations for business and industry, photography generally is of three types:

1) News and feature photos of company events, activities, and services.

2) Portraits.

3) Product publicity—from face creams to hats to household furnishings to buildings, from transistors to computers, from livestock to food to fashion.

Within the news and feature categories, the public-relations photographer may simply record scenes and situations, or he may direct the action, casting, and situation. Portraits can be simple head shots or can show the subject in relationship to his business or industrial environment, his hobbies, or other interests.

The greatest variety of techniques and specialized skills are required to make the broad category of product publicity interesting enough to publish.

MEDIA REQUIREMENTS

Business and industrial organizations use public-relations photographs in newspapers, trade publications, magazines, annual reports for shareholders, and internal or external company publications. Photographs may be made for one outlet, on an exclusive basis; or planned for utilization in a variety of media. The requirements of the primary outlet usually determine approach and technique. Photographic requirements vary according to the particular medium, its audience, policy, and viewpoint of the individual editor.

In furnishing photographic material the public-relations professional tries to adhere to the pictorial policies of the specific publication. Trade and technical publications want photos which provide reader service—a new product, a new package, a new technique, a new service, a successful sales-promotion display. Many are interested in photographs of new advertising campaigns, particularly successful ads,

A continuing public-relations objective is to find different mediums through which to tell a client story. This photo illustrated a story on the wide range of color of Emba mink, and was made to the specifications of a syndicated beauty editor, who provided it to her more than 100 subscriber newspapers.

"Distinctively U.S." is the criterion for photographs placed abroad to stimulate travel to the United States. This program, being carried forward under the slogan, "Travel a New World—see the U.S.A.," divides its photographs into two general categories: photographs of historic places such as this one of the Alamo, and photographs of modern developments such as the Pittsburgh skyline, Los Angeles traffic circles, and modern hydroelectric plants.

and new or successful sales-promotion devices. They are also receptive to portraits and informal photographs of industry and company leaders relating to a news or feature story. A variety of trade publications accept cheesecake as "brighteners."

Newspapers are using more and bigger photographs. Tabloid newspapers and the photo syndicates are often receptive to girl and gag photos. Cheesecake photos rarely appear in a conservative newspaper, but are acceptable in national news or men's magazines. There is demand for larger and more dramatic photos for women's pages, notably in food and fashion.

Front-page photographs must have a high news quotient or an extra measure of human interest. Pictures of lesser news value may appear on the front pages of early editions of afternoon papers as fillers. Some newspaper-picture editors insist on a pretty girl, or at least a human-interest picture "above the fold" on every edition. Consequently, particularly appealing or attractive public-relations photos may appear on front pages of newspapers even though they have little actual news value.

PHOTOS FOR SYNDICATES

Photographs placed with news, photo, and feature syndicates, such as Associated Press, United Press International, Wide World, King Features, North American Newspaper Alliance, NEA, Bell, Central Press, Metro, and smaller syndicates, must be exclusive. Different photos covering the same theme or event may be placed with competitive media. Frequently, in food, fashion, home furnishings, business, and science, photographs are made for a particular syndicate according to the specifications of the interested editor. In this circumstance, variations of the photograph are not

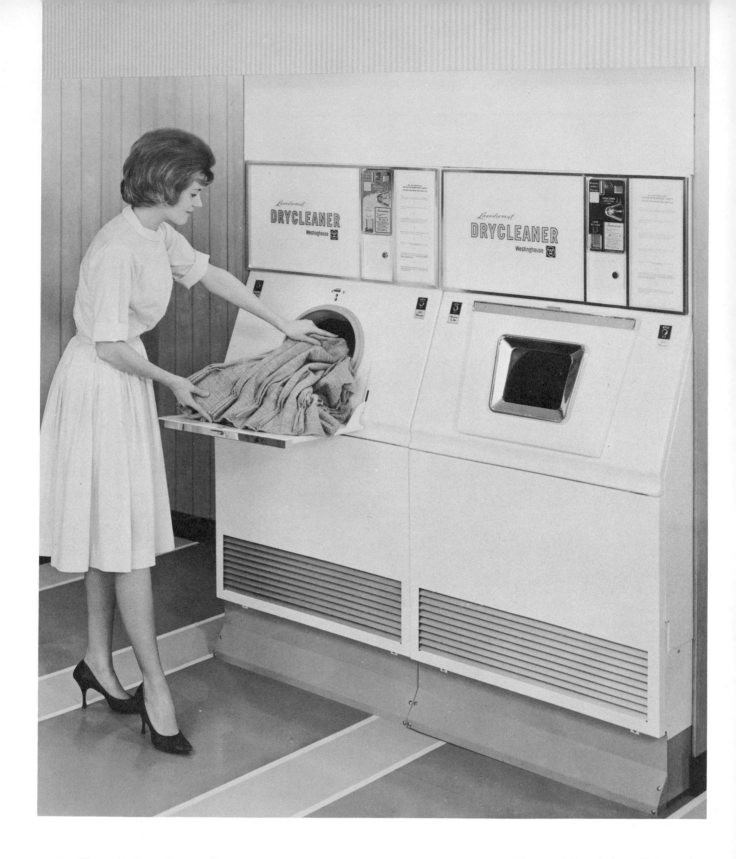

ordinarily made for other media.

Public-relations photos distributed to individual newspapers in major cities are almost invariably "exclusive in your city" or occasionally "exclusive in your area," as in the case of New York, Chicago, and Los Angeles papers.

Different photos on the same subject or theme may be distributed to competitive newspapers or to smaller papers in distribution areas of the bigger papers in New York, Los Angeles, Detroit, Chicago, etc.

Many public-relations firms maintain "A," "B," "C," and "D" mailing lists for the big cities, or employ a distribution agency which maintains such lists, to insure exclusive photo distribution to newspapers.

Different requirements. These Westinghouse Coin-Operated Drycleaner photos were made at different periods in the public-relations campaign. The photo at the left is informational. This type of photo is printed by trade publications and sometimes in new-product sections of newspapers and magazines. Once the product is no longer news, photographs must have an additional dimension of human interest, service, or both. The photograph at the right is one from a series about three secretaries who are enjoying additional income as owners of a Westinghouse Coin-Operated Drycleaner.

MAT SERVICES

Photographs to smaller dailies and weeklies are usually distributed through syndicates specializing in this service. Two or three of these mat services, such as Stamps-Conhaim and Metro, make no charge for this distribution, receiving their income from the papers which buy their feature services.

However, most mat photos are handled by services which receive their income from the client. Charges vary according to the size of the story and illustrative photo and the number of papers to which the particular mat is distributed. Newspapers pay no fee for these mats and are under no obligation to use them. These services maintain close contact with the editors and counsel their clients about story and photo quality and approach to maximize publication. Generally a mat feature, including illustration and caption or story, should not exceed two columns in width and seven inches in depth, nor include more than three people.

COLOR SERVICES

Color photos for newspapers are distributed by the public-relations practitioner in three ways: in original or duplicated 8 × 10 or 5 × 7 color transparencies "exclusive in your city"; by feature services; and in color mats.

"Exclusive in your city" placements are often preceded by phone calls from the public-relations practitioner to an individual editor to explain the subject and approach and to ascertain interest.

Certain syndicates, such as Wide World and NEA, accept public-relations color transparencies. Some-

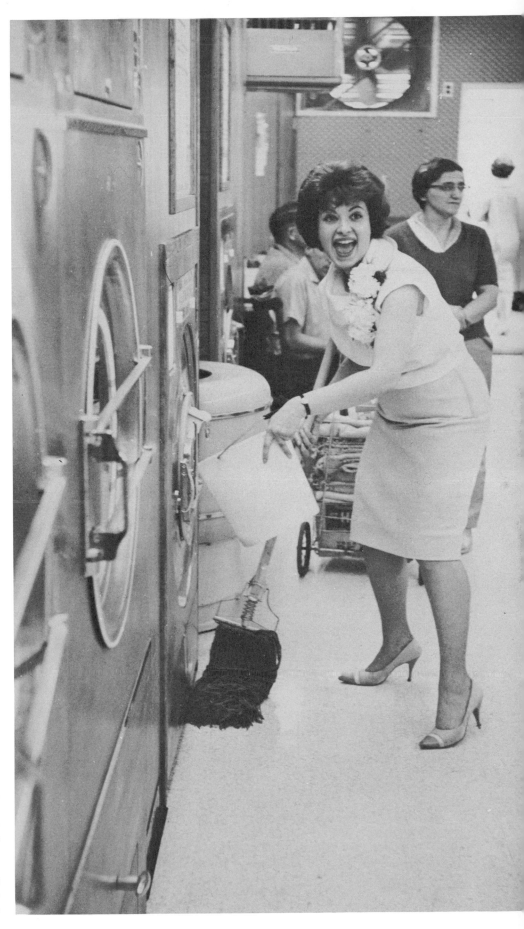

times color is shot exclusively for one service in response to an editor's request.

A recent development is the color-mat service. The *Milwaukee Journal* was a pioneer in this field, furnishing color mats to noncompetitive newspapers all over the country. The *Journal* accepts, without distribution charge, public-relations photos which measure up to its high standards.

A later development has been the color-mat distribution specialist, a service utilized primarily for women's-page placements in food, fashion, home furnishings and for tourism and travel promotion. Page proofs of one to four color photos and copy, set up on a standard newspaper-size sheet, are distributed nationally to some 450 newspapers which use color. The first paper from each city requesting one or all photos has exclusive rights in that city for the photos requested.

Suppliers of color photos and copy to these color-mat services pay a basic rate for the space occupied by their story and photo(s)—one-third to a full-page. Additionally, the supplier pays the the cost for each mat distributed to a newspaper.

WHAT EDITORS WANT

Different editors have different yardsticks for a successful public-relations photo. Fashion editors want news trends and themes. Food editors emphasize service. Business and real-estate editors want photos that are news, or provide reader service or human interest. All want visually appealing photographs.

Individual departments in a newspaper ordinarily select their own photos, making up their own pages in accordance with the over-all policy, but with the choice of each day's photos left to the responsible editor's taste and interests.

Photos for the general-news sections are the responsibility of the photo editor. News and human-interest photos are his first choices. One veteran editor commented, "There's nothing to beat a pretty girl, except maybe appealing children and pets. Sometimes you get all three in one picture."

A single picture ordinarily suf-fices to illustrate real or manufactured news within a public-relations program. Feature stories in magazines, Sunday supplements, and syndicates often require six or more photographic illustrations.

Newspaper travel editors and most magazines generally choose a single photo to illustrate a subject. Usually people will not be shown and, if they are, they are not identified. A travel magazine may illustrate the same story with several photos. If people are shown, they are rarely identified. A feature editor, covering the same subject, ordinarily wants several photos which combine to tell a story. The story may be developed around one or two real people, interesting in themselves or in what they are doing.

Except for the "how-to" article, where photos depict individual steps, a single photo customarily illustrates food or home-furnishing articles in newspapers and magazines other than those devoted exclusively to the home-furnishings field. On the other hand, newspaper fashion editors ordinarily prefer several photos on a single subject and frequently print three or more to illustrate each article.

Business editors of newspapers and magazines generally belong to the one-picture school, but occasionally either will present a photo story. However, even if only one picture will be published, editors like to make their selection from several.

The picture editor of Wide World Photos, an Associated Press service, sets this measure for a good public-relations photo: "Technical excellence. Top-quality print. Good composition. Eye-catching. Imaginative."

Recommending that client plugs be handled subtly, he urges, "Be honest in the photo, in the caption, and even with such information as to the full disposition that has been made with the photo."

Wide World prefers 8 × 10 black-and-white photos, one top-quality glossy print of each photo accepted. In color, Wide World's preference is for 4 × 5 transparencies, although it will accept 8 × 10, 5 × 7, and 2¼ × 2¼. In connection with spe-cial subjects, Wide World occasionally wants duplicated color transparencies.

The King Features Syndicate's photo editor says a successful picture "combines clarity, action, and human interest." King Features wants black-and-white 8 × 10 or 5 × 7 glossy prints and likes the negatives also. After King Features has distributed the photos, the negatives are returned to the supplier.

The photo editor of Central Press, headquarters in Cleveland, wants photos of national interest. He recommends the commercial plug be minimized but admits "more leeway is permitted if the subject is in the interest of science."

NEA services will accept black-and-white photos in 5 × 7 to 11 × 14 size, but prefers 8 × 10. NEA editors prefer 8 × 10 color transparencies. North American Newspaper Alliance wants 8 × 10 black-and-white glossy photographs.

Trans World Syndicate services black-and-white and color, primarily to overseas magazines and newspaper clients.

Most public-relations photos are placed with these services by a public-relations practitioner. On occasion, the photographer himself may place such a photo or photo story. These national syndicates make no payment for the public-relations photos they accept and do not charge for distribution of photos that meet their editorial standards. Some of these services also maintain commercial departments and make public-relations photos for a fee, supplying prints or negatives to their public-relations clients. Some of these photos subsequently may be distributed to member newspapers as a subscriber service; most are not.

SUNDAY SUPPLEMENTS

The Sunday supplements, including *This Week, Poise, Parade, Family Weekly,* and *Suburbia Today,* have standards comparable to any other national magazine.

Their interests vary according to their audiences. They use color and black-and-white; most of them like to see black-and-white prints in 11 × 14 size. Sometimes photographers are able to sell public-relations photos to these publications and occasionally public-relations photos are made specifically for a Sunday supplement.

NATIONAL MAGAZINES

Life occasionally accepts public-relations photos and pays the photographer its standard rate. More often *Life,* if it likes the story presented in a set of photos, will assign a staff team of one or more writers and photographers to do its own version.

Look, Saturday Evening Post, Time, Newsweek, and *Holiday* work in similar fashion. Public-relations photos rarely appear in these publications. More often they serve to stimulate editors to assign their own coverage of the particular subject or event.

Most other national magazines also do their own photography, using staff or free lance photographers of their individual choice. An exception often will be in the industrial area, where public relations photographs made by staff or free lance photographers are accepted regularly by national magazines.

The romance, fan, and "how-to" publications, and youth, baby, home economics, and other special-interest publications are important media for public-relations photos. The usual procedure is for a public-relations practitioner to approach an editor with a story or idea. If the editors approves it, he will decide what kind of photographic coverage he wants. His interest may range from a single black-and-white photo, to a photo-story, to color, including a cover. The photography then fits the editor's specifications.

"HOUSE" OR COMPANY MAGAZINES

Policies of company publications vary widely. Some make all their own photos, using staff or free lance photographers; some accept public-relations photos supplied to them exclusively by customer, supplier or noncompetitive companies or organizations. Some regularly use nonexclusive photos called to their attention by specialized feature services which send out monthly digests of currently available public-relations material. One to ten photos in black-and-white and/or

Corporate head, corporate symbol. This photo served a double public-relations purpose: 1) It put The Borden Company on the editorial pages of newspapers and business, grocery, dairy, ice-cream and ad trades through the device of presenting Elsie the Cow as an honorary member of Borden's Quarter Century Club. 2) The delighted participation of Harold W. Comfort, company president, indicated that the head of the nation's largest milk distributor is a warm and friendly man.

color are offered through these digests. Usually one or two photos are supplied to give a brief description of the story.

Editors request stories and photos that fit their publications. These requests are turned over by the services to the responsible client, who, in turn, supplies photos and stories to the publications. Newspapers and a great variety of magazines recieve material through these services in addition to the company publications.

Some public-relations campaigns

utilize photo-story distribution services every month. The services distribute their monthly digests to some 15,000 outlets. Fees vary according to the amount of space the client uses to present his story and photo in the digest.

TELEVISION

Local television programs, particularly women's-interest interview shows, often use public-relations still photography. Ordinarily, a single telop (photograph) illustrates a news, service, or other feature.

Identifying the product. The delicious association of chocolate and walnuts has been effectively promoted as "Cookin' Cousins" by the Nestlé Company and Diamond Walnut Growers Inc. Besides advertising, the promotion included widespread publicity, with assignments divided between public-relations representatives of the two corporations. These photos were made by Diamond Walnut Growers Inc. The handsome walnut-decorated linen, partly shelled walnut, and nutcracker add visual appeal to the California-walnut identification.

As the commentator talks, the camera shifts from commentator to telop and back again. The telop can be of any product of interest which is presented in a news or viewer-service context, or it might be of a celebrity in connection with an activity or event. Telops should be horizontal and matte-finished. While some are distributed in 8 × 10 or 5 × 7 size the 4 × 5 telop is the most commonly used.

Public-relations firms which offer aggressive television program promotion as one of their techniques will supply local stations with 35 mm glass station-identification slides promoting individual shows. About half of these start with a still photograph. Over a section of this, on acetate, will be the name of the show. Then, on occasion, there will be a second overlay on the acetate, this time with the call letters of the individual station that will carry the show locally. The advantage of the glass slide is that it is used with a projector and does not require a live camera. The glass slide with the single overlay costs about one dollar each, produced in quantity. The cost for the individual slide with station call letters is approximately six dollars each. The mass-produced 4 × 5 telop costs about ten cents each.

CLIENT REQUIREMENTS

Knowledgeable users of public-relations photography make only three demands of any public-relations photograph: 1) It must contribute to a public-relations objective. 2) It must meet standards of good taste. 3) It must be technically and stylistically acceptable to the media for which it is made.

THE PHOTOGRAPHER'S ROLE

The photographer should analyze each public-relations assignment in terms of six basic questions:

1) What is the objective of this assignment?

2) What basic idea am I trying to project or interpret?

3) What am I trying to sell?

4) To what type of people am I supposed to appeal?

5) For what medium is it?

6) How can I put over the basic idea photographically?

There are secondary considerations also, such as: How large is the photograph most likely to be used—one column, two columns, more? If it is an exclusive picture for one medium only, does the editor of that medium have any unusual prejudices? Does the client?

If it is color, what size transparency is preferred in the medium? What are preferences relative to settings and accessories?

Since public-relations assignments are rarely accompanied by a layout, standard with advertising assignments, it is essential that the photographer ask questions so that he understands clearly the nature and purpose of his assignment.

On occasion, the public-relations representative will simply state the objectives and leave execution to the photographer. In most travel and other international programs, particularly when a photographer is being retained overseas or sent from the United States, the assignment will be defined as closely as possible, with the ultimate execution left to the photographer who may or may not be supervised on the assignment.

Assignments to photograph personalities, food, fashion, and home furnishings are ordinarily closely supervised, with one or more public-relations representatives on hand throughout the shooting. Architectural and industrial assignments are more usually unsupervised.

In either situation, it is the responsibility of the photographer to insure that the equipment and techniques he employs meet client and media requirements.

Annual Reports

Annual reports now seek to humanize the company and dramatize its people, products, services, and resources. Photography has a large role in the majority of reports. While color is used occasionally, in the main it is avoided or confined to the cover as management has no desire to invite a charge of unnecessary extravagance.

In an annual report photography

Direct lighting emphasizes the texture of this cake made with walnuts in the batter. The coffee pot in the upper right fills a hole in the composition and reminds viewers that coffee and cake are a delicious combination. (Photo: Moss Photography)

may be used to:

1. Develop shareholder and financial-community appreciation of the scope of the company's operations, of the nature and advantages of its products, or services, and physical resources, and of the human element behind the machines, products, and services.

2. Encourage shareholder and financial-community belief that the company has a dynamic leadership.

3. Help create a theme that unifies and dramatizes the report.

Photographs of facilities, resources, and employees at work are occasionally used as full pages. Photographs, usually in silhouette, sometimes appear on pages traditionally restricted to statistical matter, such as the long-term financial review and consolidated income statement. Small head portraits of executives with traditional portrait-studio lighting have given way, for the most part, to more candid, less retouched situation portraits and action photos.

Occasionally the annual report is accompanied by a second publication showing in greater depth some facet of company operation—its research laboratories, new products, people, or physical resources. Here, text is sometimes subordinated to photographs.

Architecture and Interior and Industrial Design

Photographic assignments in design and architecture come from two sources: public-relations representatives for architects and designers or from representatives of the firms that retained the architects and designers.

Emphasis on good photography in newspaper real-estate pages, in motel and hotel publications, and in building and architectural magazines indicates an expanding future for this field.

Company Publications

Company publications, or house organs, are of two types: internal and external. Internal publications range from a weekly mimeographed sheet to a four-or-more-page weekly offset publication to a monthly or quarterly letterpress or offset slick-paper magazine. Distribution is limited to employees and except for the mimeographed publication, all

utilize photography, almost always in black-and-white.

There is a noticeable demand for better layout, design, and typography in internal company publications and most particularly for more, bigger, and better photographs—whether of an employee celebrating a special anniversary, a group at work, a winning softball team, or an employee wedding.

The primary objective of the external house organ is to increase sales. The production is usually the responsibility of public relations because the sell is ordinarily soft or indirect. External publications usually are bigger and more expensive than the internal magazine and use more and bigger photographs, frequently in color. While name photographers are rarely employed for an internal magazine, they are often called upon for the external publication.

Fashion Photography

Extremes of fashion photography are the "catalog" approach, which endeavors to sell the fashion by showing every stitch, seam, and fold against a white no-seam paper background, and the interpretative approach which might try to sell the very same fashion in a blur of motion or activity in a real or dream-life situation.

The great bulk of public-relations fashion photography falls between these two approaches, the individual look dictated by the style and instincts of the photographer, instructions from the public-relations practitioner interpretating or forming the client approach, and the requirements of the media for which the photographs are made.

Most wanted are fashions carefully accessorized and clearly and distinctively presented in a setting. Ordinarily, a natural setting is desired, such as a ballgown against an elegant backdrop, but occasionally a ballgown will be photographed against bales of cotton or a printing press, the incongruity expected to build memorability.

This approach is practical if the client controls the outlet, such as an advertisement or brochure. It can be costly in publicity, where usage depends upon the reaction of individual editors. Acceptance is most

likely when fashions and background are compatible and logical, while fresh and appealing.

If the public-relations practitioner or photographer wants to present fashions in a contradictory mood or setting, caution recommends discussing the idea in advance with one or more editors. The safest course is to interest one editor in the desired approach and make the pictures for that particular editor, if the editor's circulation or medium is valuable enough to justify the expense, and then it is preferable for the editor to be present during the sitting to assist in supervision.

Accessories for fashion photographs ordinarily are obtained by the public-relations representative, but some photographers retain a stylist to fill this function. Because of the rapid changes in fashion, photographers are not expected to stock a variety of accessories or props, although many maintain a selection of costume jewelry and unusual fabrics to be used for comparison purposes, if no other.

Food Photography

"I want the food close-up, sharp, and so realistic I taste and smell it!" The food editor of a major U.S. newspaper who set forth this yardstick for a food photograph reflects the majority opinion among the nation's food editors on newspapers, wire services, and magazines.

Texture, sensory appeal, and mood are the primary photographic concerns of most public-relations people—usually women and, increasingly, graduate home economists—who specialize in food publicity and public relations.

Because brand-name mentions are restricted by many editors, product identification and consumer interest are developed through the food, accessories, mood, and setting.

Food appeal in magazines has been increased by a trend from high-key to low-key photos, a technique denied the photographer whose work is destined for newspaper publication in black-and-white or color. The newspaper photograph must make its impact through skillful lighting and careful selection of accessory and background. Once banned, black backgrounds now occasionally appear in food-public-

ity photos. Color for newspapers must have sharp, clear backgrounds, offering great contrast to the food, such as white utensils against a red wall or no-seam paper.

There is a constant danger that the eye, beguiled by the appearance of the food in its natural or enhanced colors, fails to analyze the scene in terms of black-and-white. When a retake is necessary, the public-relations client ordinarily expects to bear the additional cost, since the photograph was made with his approval. When there has been an error in technique, such as poor lighting, the photographer is not paid for the retake, but the public-relations client bears the cost for food, preparation, and prop rental. To minimize retakes and encourage client satisfaction, some photog-

graphers shoot Polaroid tests before making the finished photo.

The photographer specializing in food must have the greatest variety of nonphotographic equipment. While there are some location assignments, in the kitchens and plants of food processors and public-relations organizations, the great majority of food photographs are made in a photographer's studio. The photographer who expects continuing food assignments needs an up-to-date, attractive, well-equipped kitchen, and a variety of props— china, serving dishes, cutlery, etc.

Even so, special props will be bought or rented by the public-relations representative or by the photographer's stylist, if he retains one, and occasionally by the photographer himself. In New York,

Los Angeles, San Francisco, and Chicago and other centers of food photography, the photographer is expected to have a maid on duty during a photographic session to wash dishes and otherwise assist and keep the kitchen in order.

The approach, theme, and props are usually agreed upon mutually by photographer and client. The food is prepared by a home economist or food specialist provided by the public-relations agency. The photographer is expected to make suggestions about the appearance and

presentation of the food.

Food photos for consumer publications are of three types:

1) Mood photo, showing a finished dish in a setting illustrating a theme of season or occasion.

2) Ingredient photo, with finished product and ingredients to create the product in the same photo.

3) How-to photo with model or real-life cook demonstrating one or a variety of points in technique.

Only rarely is the product shown in the photo in packaged form. In the ingredient photo, packaged or bottled items occasionally will be displayed, but only rarely with the label showing completely.

This photograph of the model wearing a winning entry in the Diamonds-International Awards was distributed to newspaper editors nationally on an "exclusive in your city" basis.

Trade photos focus upon the package, in close-ups for new products or close-ups of product and available display materials, and in-store situations where the product is featured in displays provided by the food processor or created by the retailer. The latter frequently illustrate "success stories" where the retailer reports an increase in sales through a particular promotion.

Government

The U.S. Government utilizes photography for informational purposes to develop public understanding of its departments, bureaus, and facilities, to attract recruits for the Armed Forces, to record historic occurrences and specific developments within the national life, and to encourage tourism to the United States.

Foreign governments utilize photography for the same purposes, and some also employ it within programs to stimulate demand for particular products and to attract foreign investment.

Tourism photography presents the same problems for all countries: to select places which are unique. A California seashore may be a major attraction, but except for Monterey Pines it looks very much like a French or Italian or Yugoslav seashore. Spain boasts salmon fishing and summer skiing, but how can these photographs be made to sing of Spain? How can the fisherman be enjoying himself in Spain and not appear to be in Oregon or Wisconsin? Or the skier be in the Pyrenees in July and not in Vermont in January?

The single scene is most in demand by newspaper travel pages. Magazines and feature editors of newspapers and syndicates require several photographs to illustrate or tell a story. Because of increasingly high photographic requirements of American media, foreign governments directing public-relations campaigns to the United States frequently find it necessary to bring U.S. photographers to their countries in order to make the type of pictures which will satisfy U.S. editors.

Home Furnishings

Except for new-product photographs destined for trade and design journals, home furnishings photographs must project an idea—of reader service, new usage, or design inspiration.

To work successfully in a field which encompasses table settings, textiles, wall coverings, rugs, floorings, furniture, and the multitude of accessories for home, office, and institution, the photographer should have a large, well-equipped studio or specialize in location work. A strong sense of design and color is essential.

Usual assignements include:

1) New product lines. Some companies introduce new lines twice yearly; most, annually. Informational pictures are distributed to home-furnishings editors of newspapers and magazines, trade publications in appropriate fields and to the "horizontal trades."

2) Photographs to show the new products in use: in room settings as photographed in actual rooms, or in vignettes created in the studio to give an illusion of an actual place.

3) Photographs to show old products in new uses or interesting situations.

4) Photographs of client products as displayed through activities or events—home and design shows, conventions, etc.

In these latter situations, the photographs are ordinarily for consumer publications, through national distribution on an "exclusive in your city" basis to women's-page editors, home-furnishings editors or newspapers; otherwise the photographs are prepared exclusively for a magazine.

The romance, baby, home-economics, and do-it-yourself publications accept photographs and give credits when photographs are made for their exclusive use. The big *shelter* magazines, such as *House & Garden, House Beautiful, American Home, Better Homes and Gardens* and the women's service magazines such as *McCall's* and *Ladies Home Journal*, and general-interest publications, including *Life* and *Look*,

This photograph was produced for trade-magazine and new-product column publication in newspapers and magazines to introduce Scripto's new Tilt-Tip ball-point pen. The objective was to produce a close-up that was sharp enough to show the tilted tip. (Photo: Carl Perutz)

will ordinarily make their own photographs.

Industrial

Many big industrial concerns, including those in the automotive and electronic fields, maintain their own photographic staff. A large share of the photographs they make are for internal viewing only. In textiles, for instance, photos can be used to study problems in manufacture.

Industrial photographs can require techniques of photojournalism, of macro- and microphotography and of the product publicist.

Institutions

Hospitals, schools and colleges, and foundations utilize photography in public-relations campaigns to dramatize achievements, encourage public appreciation of their activities, and to raise funds.

Photographs of medical operations, often in color, and research projects are used in medical journals and occasionally in national magazines and newspapers. Budget is often a very serious consideration, and photographers may be asked to accept less than usual fees or contribute their services without charge. But the area does offer outstanding opportunities, and a contribution of services by a photographer may have long-range benefits on a professional as well as a personal level.

Livestock

This field has produced reputations for only a few photographers. While it would seem that every photographer has photographed a dog, cat, or cow, few have learned to create selling photographs of livestock.

The greatest need is for an informational approach emphasizing points of superiority. Such selling photographs appear in farm journals, brochures, and catalogs. A second need is for photography that capitalizes on the personality of a particular animal—whether it be a prize jumping horse, a poodle, or a Black Angus bull.

MOTION PICTURES AND TELEVISION

No industries receive so much publicity as do motion pictures and

television.

The cheesecake photo was the brain child of a press agent working in the entertainment field. It has been an industry mainstay ever since, and its use has been adapted by the public-relations professional generally to sell everything from resorts to food, from automobiles to xylophones.

Every motion picture and some television spectaculars will have a still photographer on duty at all times of production. These photographers belong to the International Association of Theatrical Stage Employees. It requires many years to gain admission. Once accepted for membership, the photographer's assignments come from the union, although the producer or company can request particular photographers. If the producer wishes to hire a free lance photographer because of his particular abilities, reputation, or for some other reason a union photographer also must be hired at his normal day rate.

The photographs made on the set are of scenes or episodes in the production, behind-the-scenes situations, a variety of candids, and occasionally formally posed portraits. These, as well as portraits of stars, are published on the entertainment pages of newspapers and magazines including fan (movie and radio-TV) magazines, in general-interest and news publications, and in advertising.

Many motion-picture and television studios maintain their own portrait studios, but, increasingly, posed, off-the-set publicity portraits of the principals are assigned to the independent photographer. This trend stems from a demand for particular photographic techniques or quality, work by name photographers, and a desire for lower overhead. It is less expensive to hire as needed a photographer who pays for his own equipment, space, and assistants than a maintain photog-

raphers on staff and provide equipment, studio, fringe benefits, and so forth.

SELLING, FEES, AND RIGHTS

Unlike advertising, where photographic assignments and purchases are handled by art directors or art buyers, or magazines and photo syndicates where they are the responsability of a photo editor or art director, centralized buying of photos is virtually nonexistent in the public-relations agency.

In agencies, individual account directors decide what photographs are to be made and which photographer will make them. The account director's decision is guided by the assignment, the budget, and personal or professional preference. Most agencies use a particular group of photographers or photo services. They tend to choose a photo service for news photos and to insist upon individual photographers for more specialized assignments, such as annual reports, company brochures, food, fashion, portraits, tourism.

Many major manufacturers today have one or more photographers attached to the their public-relations departments and maintain elaborate studios. These photographers fill all or most of the manufacturer's needs for public-relations photography and very often serve in other areas—product and packaging research, for example.

Two approaches to a single object— attracting American tourists to Ireland. The photo of Blarney Castle at left was distributed to travel editors. The photo at right by Joe Long was sent to newspaper food editors.

While the account director in the public-relations agency almost invariably makes his selection of a photographer for each different job, the public-relations department for a company or institution is more likely to centralize its photographic purchases. One person may have responsibility for all, or different people for different media or different areas, such as industrial, trade, corporate, or consumer.

Obtaining the first assignment or even an appointment can be difficult. Public-relations practitioners usually give their assignments to people they know or whose work they like or because they decide the photographer's reputation will enhance editorial acceptance of resulting material. Agency and public-relations practitioners agree that a satisfactory or outstanding job is the best method of obtaining repeat assignments.

Generalist or Specialist?

The geographical location of the photographer can be an important factor in his decision as to whether he will become an all-around photographer or a specialist in one or two fields. Ordinarily, the photographer in the smaller community will find it practical to make himself knowledgeable in the broadest variety of photographic techniques and public-relations areas. In larger cities, many photographers consider specialization imperative. Others resist specialization on the theory that it results in loss of enthusiasm, perspective, and skills. Some resolve this conflict by specializing in one area, such as fashion, as a profession and then pursuing, as a creative outlet or hobby, a totally different form—perhaps sports, abstractions, or landscapes.

Fees

Twenty years ago, it was not at all unusual to pay $5 for a publicity photograph. Today in larger cities in the United States, $20 is considered a minimum. Many photographers, and some services, will make one location news photograph, or even three photographs within the same assignment, for as little as $25.

Fees for food photographs are usually decided by the situation.

Some photographers give a reduced price if more than one photograph is made on a single day. Black-and-white food photographs, generally made with an 8 × 10 camera or the less preferred 5 × 7, will pay $40 to $100, although these same photographers may receive $75 to $2000 for a comparable advertising photograph. Certain well-established photographers insist upon fees above the national average for public-relations food photographs— $150 for a black-and-white and up to $350 for a color photograph.

Public-relations fashion photographers charge from $25 to $100 per situation, but most will work by the day—$150 to $600 per day, depending upon available budget, the photographer's reputation, and sometimes a public-relations practitioner's plea for special consideration. In a days' shooting, as many as 12 to 15 fashion photographs can be made.

Home-furnishings photography customarily is by individual assignment, and fees will vary according to complexity—how long it will take to set up, construction and model requirements, and so on. Prices ordinarily are slightly above those for food and fashion. In color work, film and processing are often paid for above the basic fee.

Model fees are extra. While photographers have different scales for public-relations and advertising assignments, models do not. Their rates prevail for both. Models will scale their fees downward for magazines and newspapers.

Architecture, industrial, tourism, corporate, and a number of other forms of public-relations photography ordinarily are paid for by the day, week, or assignment. Fees are rarely below the $100 a day minimum established by the American Society of Magazine Photographers, and may run as high as $500 per day. A fee of $750 to $1000 per week is usual for photographers of established reputation and skill. Film, processing, travel, and other expenses are normal charges above the basic fees.

Rights

In most public-relations assignments, the fee covers full rights to the photographs. The photographer frequently provides the client with a set of contacts, one print each of selected photographs, and the negatives. The photographs may then be used for any public-relations purpose and even, occasionally, for advertising and direct-mail campaigns. Usually if a public-relations photograph is deemed suitable for an advertisement, the photographer is paid an additional fee for this usage.

An exception to this general full-rights rule often occurs when the subject is a personality. Then the free lance photographer ordinarily agrees to provide a certain number of photographs or situations, but retains the negatives and secondary rights to all photographs and full rights to some.

Another exception is the photographer who accepts a public-relations assignment only when the client will conform to his demands regarding rights. These photographers may prefer to copyright the photographs, retain the negatives, and provide the client with only a specified number of prints of a specified number of situations.

Under certain conditions, the photographer may have first rights. He is paid a predetermined rate by the day, week, or assignment but before the client has the right to make any use of the photographs, the photographer can attempt to sell them to specified editorial media. This arrangement may prevail in connection with coverage of a particular place or an unusual story, perhaps conceived by the photographer, relative to a product, service, or facility.

The above arrangement sometimes results because the public-relations practitioner decides the photographer may be able to place the photographs with a more important outlet for a fee than could the practitioner, even though he could give the publication the photographs without cost. If the photographer is unable to sell the photographs within a specified period, the public-relations buyer then has full rights to all photos or negatives, or full rights to a specified number and the right of purchase for others.

BOY WITH CHICKEN   **ROSS LOWELL**

This appealing human-interest photograph of a young boy with his chicken is made even more effective by the composition's emphasis on the isolation of the child and his pet. The woman at the left and the man at the upper right are only suggested as dark, out-of-focus shapes in the background, but the feeling of the flow of life around the subject is effectively conveyed. The high angle (an adult's-eye view) from which the shot is taken further emphasizes the poignant impression of a lonely child and his pet, who are part of but, somehow, withdrawn from the bustling adult world about them.

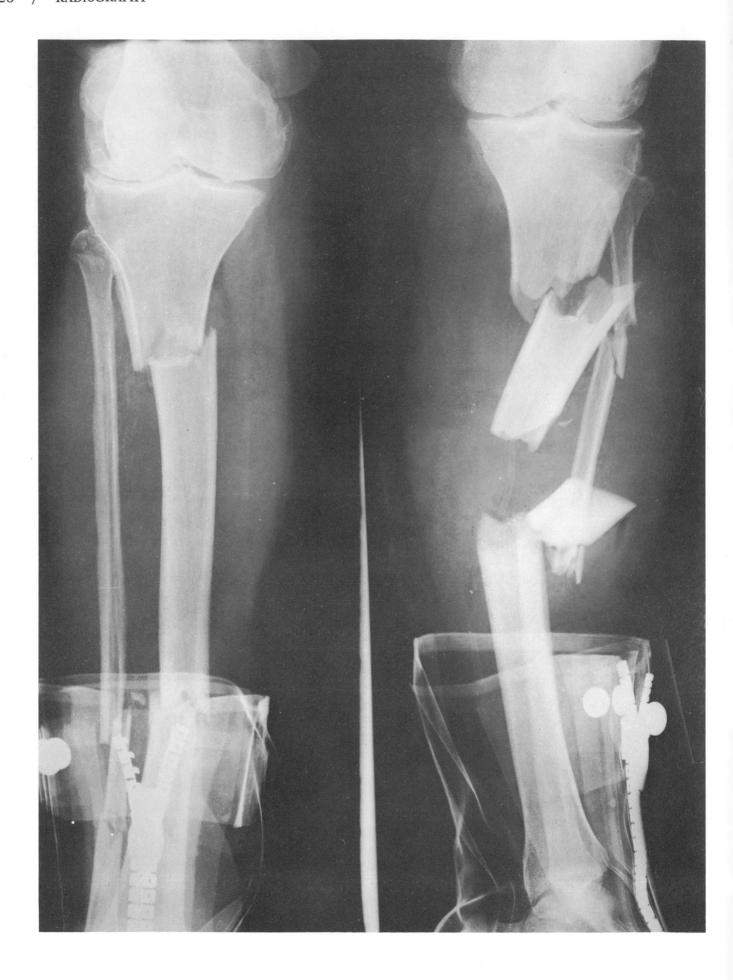

RADIOGRAPHY

OTHA W. LINTON
Public Relations Director,
American College of Radiology,
Chicago, Ill.

[The applications of X-ray photography extend into the fields of medicine, research, and industrial radiography. The historical background is given completely, together with a full explanation of the modern use of X-ray photography.]

• *Also see: Fluorography; Industrial Radiography; Medical Photography.*

RADIOGRAPHY IS THE TECHNIQUE OR art of using X-rays or electromagnetic radiation to penetrate an opaque object and affect a photographic-film emulsion or stimulate a phosphorescent screen. The partial absorption of the X-rays by the object or living tissue placed between the source and the sensitive film creates a pattern of light and dark shadows known technically as a roentgenogram, or less technically as an X-ray picture. This pattern, to a trained eye, is an accurate indication of the varying densities found within the object examined.

Modern uses of X-rays are highly significant in several areas of life. Best known are its uses in medical radiology, where the making of roentgenograms and the fluoroscopic examinations of patients are a routine part of diagnosis. Because X-rays affect the cells of a living body as they penetrate it, radiation is also used in medicine to treat disease conditions, notably certain forms of cancer. Radioactive isotopes, man-made radioactive substances, are used in small quantities to trace the function of body systems and in larger amounts as a treatment. The expanding uses of medical radiology have fostered the creation of precise and powerful X-ray sources, fluorescent screens, and films which allow sharp images with brief exposures.

Radiograph showing multiple fractures of lower legs with feet still contained in galoshes. (Photo: Eastman Kodak Company)

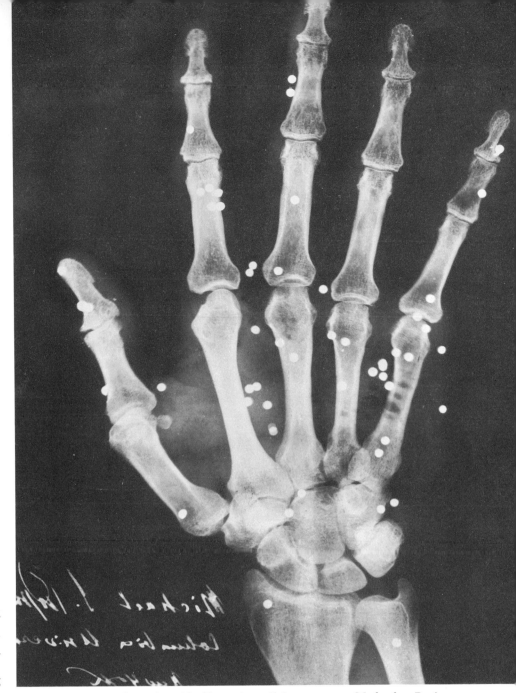

The first radiograph made with X-ray intensifying screens. Made by Professor Michael Pupin of Columbia University in February, 1896.

Dentistry and veterinary medicine use radiography as a prime tool in the detection and diagnosis of injury or illness. Radiography is also used by scholars to study old paintings, mummies and other artifacts.

Many types of industry now use X-ray films of castings and other metal parts, of assembled and packaged products, and of raw materials to test for strength and purity. X-ray films and the fluoroscope, which permits direct visualization of the image, offer a nondestructive method of inspecting boiler welds, regulating the uniform filling of containers, and making chemical analyses.

To use X-rays for any purpose requires a generator for electrical current, a tube to produce the X-rays, and a holder for sensitive film or for a fluorescent screen which transforms X-rays into visible light which can be observed or photographed.

In the instance of radiographs of thin or soft objects, films may be exposed directly from the X-rays, with the image being created by the

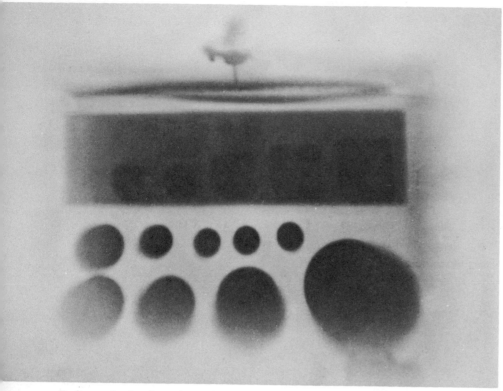

Radiograph of a box of metal weights made in 1895 by Wilhelm Konrad Roentgen, in his early experiments with X-rays. (Photo: Eastman Kodak Company)

X-rays passing through a subject onto the film in a light-proof holder.

For most techniques in medical and industrial radiology, the ability of the X-rays to affect photographic emulsion is enhanced by encasing the film in a holder also containing two fluorescent-intensifying screens. Thus the film receives the direct X-ray image plus the photosensitive response of the intensifying screens. Such combinations, coupled with devices for further intensifying the image by light or electronic refraction, make possible the viewing of X-ray images in a lighted room, their transmission by television, or their recording on motion-picture film. Radiographic tools have been developed or modified for uses in medicine and industry.

HISTORY OF X-RAYS

The discovery of X-rays was a product of the growing science of the late 19th century. Its immediate applications furnished a prime example of the practical uses of a scientific discovery even before its basic principles had been defined to the satisfaction of its discoverers.

The actual discovery of X-rays is credited to Wilhelm Konrad Roentgen, a German physicist working at Wurzburg University. His paper, published in late 1895, on a new invisible ray which could penetrate solid objects and flesh to expose photographic plates, caused tremendous excitement in the scientific world.

By the time a natural source of similar radiation, radium, was isolated three years later by Marie and Pierre Curie, physicists and doctors were using X-rays to take films of the skeletons of patients.

Roentgen's work was based, in particular, upon the work of Heinrich Hertz and Phillip Lenard and, in general, upon the development of high-tension currents and methods to achieve working vacuums. The Crookes tube, used by most researchers of the period, was a partially evacuated chamber into which an electrical current was induced.

In 1892, Hertz announced his finding that cathode rays given off by heating an electrical filament in a vacuum tube could penetrate metal

foil. Lenard, two years later, demonstrated that such rays could penetrate the walls of the tube and pass a short distance through air. Lenard also noticed that photographic plates were fogged by the Crookes tube rays and that they affected fluorescent substances.

It remained for Roentgen to make the definitive discovery of a new, unknown ray. His basic apparatus was a Rumkorff coil to generate electrical current, a Hittorf-Crookes tube, and a fluorescent barium-platinocyanide screen. In duplicating one of Lenard's experiments, Roentgen covered the tube with opaque paper and found that the cathode-ray impulses still stimulated the fluorescent screen. Then, he happened to place his hand between the tube and the screen and saw, not a solid shadow but instead, a shadow of the bones. This demonstrated that the rays were not a form of light but something entirely different.

He tried the same thing with opaque objects and found that he got shadows of their internal structure, rather than their exterior form. From the fluorescent screen to a photographic plate was a natural progression. A pattern similar to the fluorescent one developed, except that the areas of light and dark shadow were reversed.

As a scientist, it was natural for Roentgen to call his discovery X-rays, using the mathematical symbol for the unknown. His colleagues later called them roentgen rays but they are known more commonly by their original name.

Other scientists, reading Roentgen's report, duplicated his experiments. In a matter of months, Thomas A. Edison had begun building fluorescence intensifying screens which combined the direct exposure of the X-rays with the sensitivity of a photographic plate to the visible light caused by the X-ray striking the screen.

Using Edison's screens, physicist Michael Pupin began making exposures of patients upon the requests of their doctors. In Chicago, Emil H. Grubbe, also a physicist, claimed comparable experiments to locate fractures and kidney stones for doctors. In 1897, Grubbe also claimed to have been the first to suggest the therapeutic uses of X-rays after observing skin changes from holding his hand in an X-ray beam. American manufacturers began building equipment to make radiographs in 1896.

EARLY USES

The first uses for radiographs were in medicine, though Roentgen made other experiments using X-rays as a research tool. Many doctors induced commercial photographers to attempt the new kind of pictures. Soon they were experimenting with bismuth of nitrate and other chemicals found to be opaque to X-rays in an effort to visualize the stomach and other body organs.

By modern standards, the methods, apparatus, and results of Roentgen and his successors were crude. Images were vague and the time of exposure amounted to several minutes or more. The properties of the Crookes tube were undetermined and the static machines or other generators used were imperfect, too. Furthermore most early radiographers were more concerned with the possibility of electrocution than with the still unknown hazards of radiation.

IMPROVEMENTS

Edison's intensifying screens made shorter exposures and sharper images possible. Photoplate manufacturers began to modify their products for X-ray exposure. In 1896, John Carbutt of Philadephia made the first plate specifically for X-ray use. The same year, the Victor Electric Company of Chicago began making X-ray coils. Glass blowers in Germany and elsewhere modified the shape of the vacuum tubes. Other researchers found that the X-rays were stronger if the cathode rays were projected against a metal target or anode, rather than the wall of the tube.

In short, the making of X-ray plates stimulated research in the several disciplines upon which their production and use depended. Instead of the partial vacuum of the Crookes tubes, X-ray tubes were

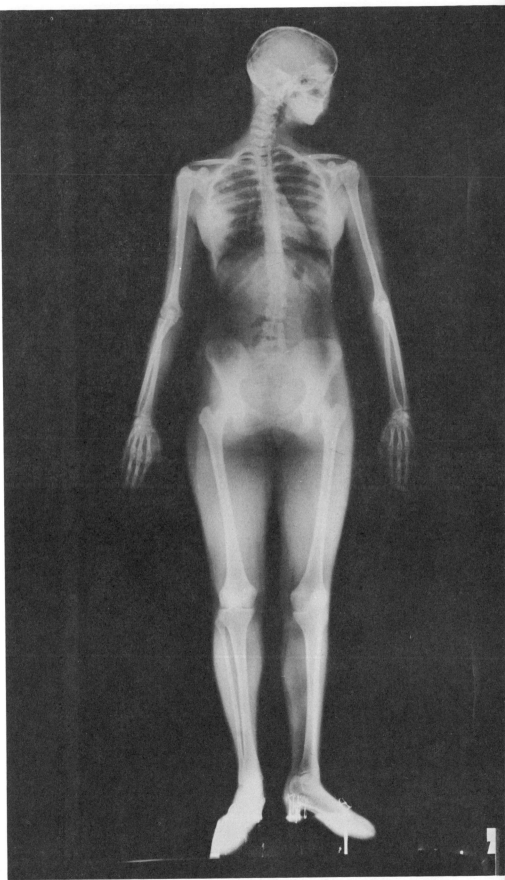

Full-body skeleton radiography made by Arthur Fuchs of Eastman Kodak in single exposure with special apparatus on 32×72-inch film. (Photo: Eastman Kodak Company)

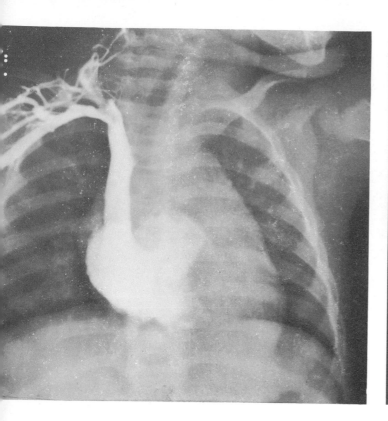
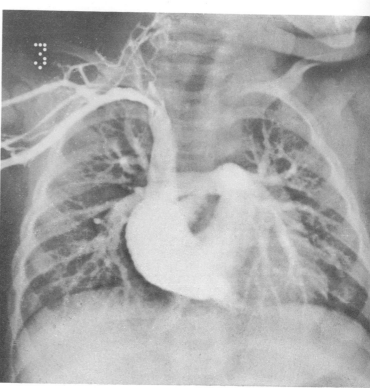

A series of spot-film radiographs of an angiographic examination of an infant's heart. The films were made rapidly to trace the course of the media after it was placed in the heart chamber through a hollow catheter inserted through the brachial artery of the arm. The normal beating of the heart causes the media to be carried along with the regular flow of blood into the chambers of the heart, into the coronary circulation which supplies the walls of the heart, and out into the aorta or great vessel which supplies the body trunk. (Photos: Department of Pediatric Cardiology, Cook County Children's Hospital, Chicago)

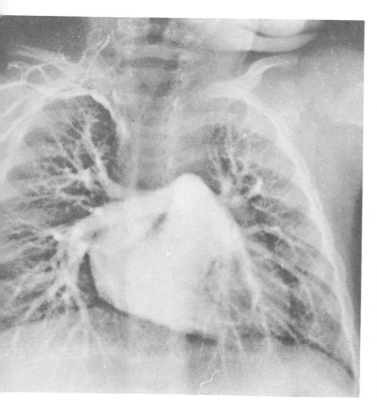
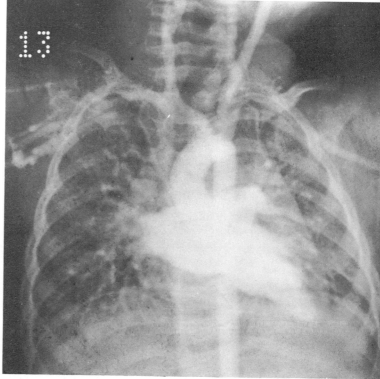

filled with an inert gas. The anode was positioned variously and finally located at an angle to the cathode, where it has remained. X-rays were found to be more penetrating when higher voltage currents were used to excite the cathode.

During World War I experiments with photographic emulsions for X-rays led to a workable single-coated film which had an effective sensitivity to the blue-violet portion of the light spectrum in which X-ray fluorescence is found. Improved emulsions reduced the exposure time necessary for a readable film.

MORE PROGRESS

Intensifying screens progressed along with emulsions. The first successful high-speed calcium-tungstate screen was offered in the United States by Dr. Herbert Threlkeld-Edwards in 1912. Its principal drawback was that the size of the fluorescent crystals caused a grainy appearance. As exposure requirements for films were lowered, a problem of a time lag in the fluorescence of screens arose and was solved, along with the elimination of the coarse grain of the crystals.

A major problem in getting clear plates was overcome by a German and an American radiologist working separately. Their joint discovery was based on the phenomenon that although X-rays cannot be refracted like visible light, the rays are scattered in passing through a solid object. The scatter radiation thus created caused considerable blur by striking the film at a tangent to the original rays.

In 1913, Dr. Gustav Bucky of Berlin reported on a grid of alternating strips of wood and lead which stopped much of the scatter. The grid was placed between the patient and the film so that the strips were parallel to the direct rays. The fixed grid left an exact pattern of the lead strips on the film. Dr. Hollis E. Potter of Chicago, improved on the fixed grid by devising a moving grid. The movement of the strips blurred them out of the film and stopped the scatter even more successfully than

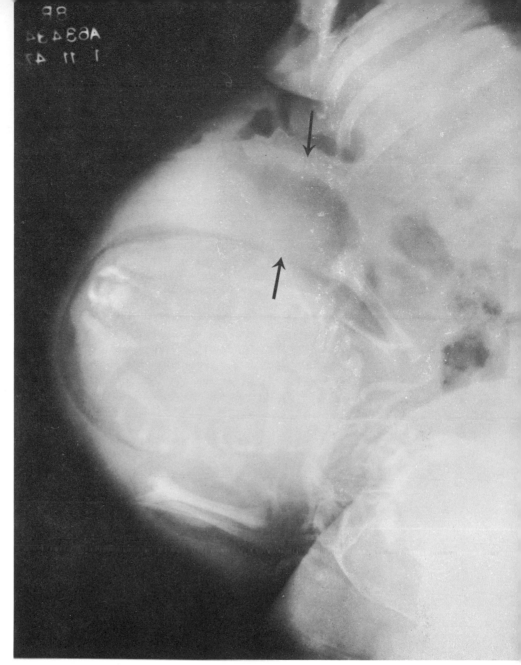

Lateral radiograph of a pregnant uterus with the fetus near term. (Photo: Department of Radiology, Duke University Medical Center)

the fixed grid. Thus, the Potter-Bucky diaphragm came to be standard radiographic equipment.

The X-ray tubes themselves posed a serious handicap to improved results. The gas-filled tubes were generally unreliable and completely unstandard. There was no way to measure the output of a tube from day to day, or even from minute to minute. In 1913, William D. Coolidge announced a hot-cathode vacuum tube which could provide a steady, reliable source of X-rays. Three years earlier, Dr. Coolidge had succeeded in making tungsten ductile. Besides its adaption for fila-

ments in incandescent lights, it was also used for the cathode in the Coolidge tubes.

NEED FOR PROTECTION

By the early 1920's, X-ray workers had learned that repeated exposures to radiation were injurious. Some of the earliest pioneers, who had worked with unshielded tubes, began to develop skin disfigurements and several forms of cancer. The problem of protecting the operator and patient against unwanted radiation led to the development of shielded tubes of lead glass plus metal casings with

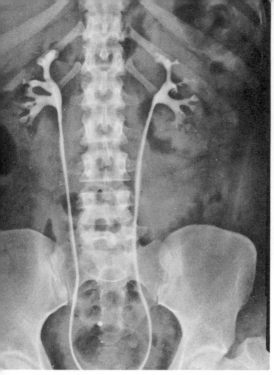

Above: *X-ray film showing the injection of contrast media into the ureters leading from the kidneys to the bladder. The film represents a normal urogram.* (Photo: The American College of Radiology)

Below: *An X-ray film of the lower colon containing a barium-sulphate mixture for contrast. A cancer of the colon (small arrows) is indicated at the lower right of the picture. The dark areas of the colon outline are trapped air.* (Photo: The American College of Radiology)

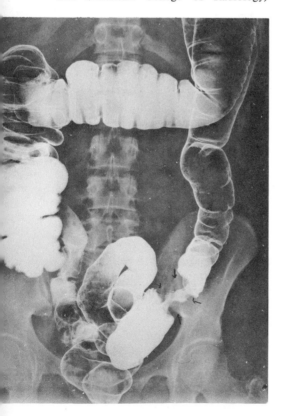

only a small aperture to expose the film. Lead shields and metal filters to block the soft portion of the X-rays were introduced while international and national bodies of physicians and physicists began to devise standards for the safe use of X-rays in medicine, industry, and research.

X-ray film manufacturers adapted the cellulose-nitrate base film (originally developed for motion pictures) to X-ray use, as it became apparent that breakable glass plates were unsatisfactory and uneconomical. In 1918, the first duplitized film was made available and by the early 1930's cellulose-acetate safety base was standardized.

The achievement of better film, more intense and reliable sources of energy, and better protective means led researchers to devise new uses for X-rays. Early in the 1920's, the first industrial units were offered for the nondestructive testing of metal castings. The need for high-energy sources to penetrate thick metal parts led to the first million-volt generators for X-rays.

Others began working on timing. Soon, the flight of a bullet was stopped halfway through a target on X-ray film. Like other modern photographic films, modern X-ray film requires exposure times measured in fractions of a second. These shorter exposures coupled with other advances tend to provide clearer films. Medical procedures requiring repeated rapid exposures became possible as film changes were devised.

It was only a matter of time before better image intensification (beyond the X-ray sources) was achieved by using visible light to enhance the quality of the image. The image created by X-rays on a fluorescent screen was picked up and intensified by refraction of the visible light.

The photoroentgen device was developed as a way of using smaller-size film for mass X-ray film programs. Because X-rays cannot be refracted with lenses, it was necessary to transform the X-rays into visible light by means of a fluorescent screen. The image on the screen could then be reduced

in size to perhaps 35 or 70 mm film, such as is used in chest-survey units. A viewer could project the film back to normal or enlarged size to study the X-ray image to his best advantage. Such *minifilms* generally lack the clearness of standard-size X-ray films but they are adequate for many uses.

The need to study soft-tissue body systems and body functions sparked the continued exploration of image intensification. Soon researchers went beyond visible light to enhance the sharpness of X-ray images by electronic means. The quality of image necessary for television viewing in a lighted room required either a tremendous level of radiation or else an enhancement of the image several thousandfold by other means. The safety of the patient and X-ray workers prohibited increasing the energy level, so that development had to come through image intensification.

With sufficient brightness, it became possible to take motion pictures of the fluoroscopic process for later study. Such systems did not see wide use until the 1950's but experiments with X-ray motion pictures began as early as 1925. Modern equipment combines developments in X-ray apparatus, film, electronics, and photographic techniques.

RECENT DEVELOPMENTS

In recent years, experimenters have begun to use other sources of radiation besides X-rays to make radiograms with some success. A cobalt or other isotope source for therapy gives an indistinct film which is useful in the placement of a radiation field for cancer treatment. Other isotopes with relatively long half-lives and stable handling qualities have been tried as the source for portable units for use in locations where a supply of electric current is not available. One of the most recent attempts to achieve usable films involved the isotope ytterbium which has a half-life of 30 days.

THE PHYSICS OF X-RAYS

The generation of X-rays by

man-made apparatus has been highly systematized since Roentgen's discovery of the unknown by-product of cathode-ray production.

A cathode made of tungsten or other metal is implanted in a vacuum tube to receive a high-voltage electric current. The current passes through the cathode which is heated to the point where electrons are freed, or boil off in an electron cloud. The electrons, having a negative charge, are hurled away from the cathode at a speed which has a direct relation to the level of electric voltage passed through the cathode.

By shaping the cathode, a good proportion of the free electrons can be made to strike a tungsten-and-copper anode or target. The electrons enter the material of the anode and cause molecular collisions which release the radiation called X-rays. This radiation may be caused by a simple collision between a free electron and the electrons of the target material, or it may result from multiple collisions. However, unless the electron displaces target matter, no X-rays are formed.

Actually, less than one percent of the energy in the electron beam becomes X-rays. The rest becomes

heat. Modern X-ray tubes are built with anodes which rotate at speeds up to 10,000 revolutions per minute to dissipate the heat created by the electron bombardment.

Electrons striking the anode cause X-rays to be thrown off in all directions. The surface of the anode is leveled at an angle to the cathode so that the strongest part of the beam may be directed to the object to receive the radiation. Early glass tubes had no shielding so that all within range of the X-rays shared equally in their radiation.

Modern X-ray tubes have been made of lead glass and are enclosed in shielding so that only a desired arc of radiation is released through a window specially ground to cut down filtration.

A remote-control center for the doctor is shown in this new X-ray system developed by Westinghouse Electric Corporation. The doctor can perform fluoroscopic and spot-film radiographic examinations while seated in a control booth window of lead glass overlooking his patient on the X-ray table. Closed-circuit television transmits a live fluoroscopic image to a TV monitor in the booth.

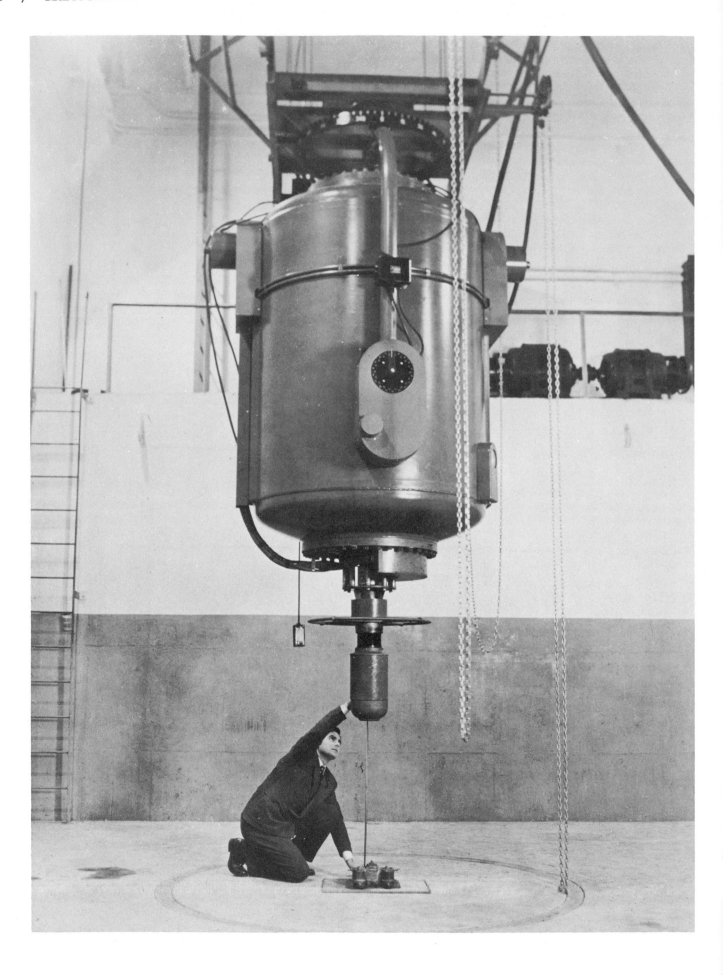

SPECTRUM OF RADIATION

X-rays contain a spectrum of radiation ranging from soft to hard, roughly comparable to the range from alpha radiation to gamma rays found in nature. The softer rays have less penetrating power, and alpha radiation can be stopped by a single piece of paper. Beta radiation is more powerful but can be stopped by a thin aluminum or other metal filter placed over the opening in an X-ray tube. Beta radiation is unwanted in most medical and other uses because it contributes to the total exposure while lacking the capacity to pass through the subject and aid in recording an image on film or a fluorescent screen.

For the most part, the harder rays are desired. Their penetrating power depends upon the level of electrical energy used. X-ray generators of several-million volt capacity are needed to make X-ray film of thick metal castings. In another application of the same principle, high-energy radiation in the million-volt range can be passed through living tissue with fewer unwanted effects than radiation in the orthovoltage range of up to 250,000 volts.

The production of usable X-ray films depends upon a satisfactory coordination of energy exposure and the density of the subject matter through which the X-rays must pass to expose the film. The amount of energy needed to penetrate ten inches of steel is much greater than the amount of energy needed to penetrate an adult chest to get a comparable image on X-ray film. As noted, the brightness of the image itself may be enhanced enormously by the use of intensifying screens and other devices which combine with the film's reaction to radiation.

Unlike light rays, X-rays cannot be deflected by reflectors or refracted by lenses. However, the shaping of the cathode and the position of the anode can be arranged to provide a small focal spot. X-rays emerging from a tube diverge in straight lines from a point source and the area to receive radiation may be defined by shutters, cones, or other devices which block all but the desired field—that is, that portion of the object which can be recorded on a film or viewed fluoroscopically.

Because the X-ray can be partially deflected by its collision with the atoms of the subject matter before penetrating to the film or screen, this reflected, or scatter radiation tends to blur the image produced. The Potter-Bucky diaphragm, and modern variations of it, were produced in efforts to block all but the rays which continued to travel in a straight line until they reached the film. Thus, a clear image is preserved.

RADIATION PROTECTION

In the early days of X-rays, detractors of the new discovery based their objections upon moral grounds and claimed an undesirable invasion of privacy. Current objections to X-rays and radiography are not so common but they are based upon the problem of protecting the users and subjects of X-rays from the harmful effects of radiation.

Several international committees of physicists, physicians, and other scientists were created in the 1920's and subsequently, to develop standards for the uses of X-rays in medicine, industry, and elsewhere. Permissible levels of exposure for patients, radiologists, and X-ray technicians were designed to prevent somatic or genetic damage from exposure.

Almost as soon as Roentgen's contemporaries noted that X-rays affected tissue in passing through it, lead-foil wrappings, leaded glass, and metal screens were used to block unwanted radiation. X-ray tubes were shielded, filtered, and the beam was limited by a cone or shutter device. Radiologists and technicians working with repeated exposures began to use lead aprons to protect their bodies and lead gloves for their hands. Rooms in which X-ray machines were located were lined with lead or heavy materials to block erratic radiation. Regular checks were instituted to guard against the buildup of radiation. Personnel were given film badges or other measuring devices to record the cumulative exposure to their bodies.

Knowledgeable estimates, made in 1962 by a representative of the American College of Radiology, indicate that the average body dose of radiation received in medical procedures by residents of the United States and other urban nations amounts to between 25 and 50 milliroentgens a year. This figure compares with an average background-radiation level of about 150 milliroentgens yearly from cosmic rays and radioactivity in the soil and water.

MEDICAL RADIOLOGY

The most commonplace use of X-rays is in medical diagnosis. Based upon the National Health Survey, the U.S. Public Health Service estimated that in 1960 Americans made 85-million visits to a physician, hospital department, or clinic for X-ray services. All but three million of these visits were for diagnostic procedures.

Since 1934, physicians wishing to specialize in medical uses of X-rays and be certified as radiologists have been required to complete a three-year program of supervised training beyond their internships and then pass a qualifying examination administered by the American Board of Radiology. More than 6000 American physicians are currently so qualified.

The basic tools of the modern radiologist are highly sophisticated versions of Roentgen's fluorescent screen and photographic-plate exposing device. By distinguishing between the relative densities of bone, fatty tissue, water, and air space in the body, medical radiologists have gone far beyond the "bullets, bones, and kidney stones" first found on X-ray plates.

For body systems or organs lacking sufficient contrast on X-ray films, radiologists devised radiopaque media which could be ingested or injected to permit study of the stomach, blood vessels, and even

A two-million volt X-ray unit is used to make X-ray films of large or small metal castings. (Photo: The American College of Radiology)

the brain and heart. A barium-sulfate mixture which can be swallowed is used to examine the gastrointestinal tract. A special halogenated oil may be used as an aerosol mist to trace the alveoli of the lung. Other media can be injected into the blood vessels, the lymphatic system, or into body organs. Certain abdominal procedures can be performed by the injection of air or carbon dioxide into the abdominal cavity to provide contrast between the trapped air and the greater density of surrounding tissues and organs.

Laminography.

Because all the structures of a body cross-section show up their varying densities on an X-ray film, it was necessary to work out a method of focusing, as it were, on a particular layer in the body. This technique, called laminography, involves an X-ray tube and film holder driven in opposing arcs so that only the area to be studied is shown clearly at focal length and structures on either side are blurred and translucent.

Procedure.

Most medical X-ray films are taken in doctor's offices or hospitals on machines which function between 40 and 125 kilovolts (thousands of volts) of energy. For simple work with hands or soft tissue, direct exposure of the X-ray film may be made. For the large majority of films of thicker body sections, a film holder containing two intensifying screens is used to contain the X-ray film. Where necessary, a diaphragm is used to block scatter radiation between the patient's body and the film holder. The beam of radiation itself is filtered as it leaves the tube and its area is confined by a cone device.

Fluoroscopy, or the visualization of body function on a phosphorescent screen, has gained increasing use in medicine as a method of studying the actual function of the body organs by X-rays. To enhance the sharpness of the image, fluoroscopy is done in a darkened room. Most fluoroscopes have an attachment with which X-ray films may be made during the fluoroscopic examination High-speed film chan-

However, large body vessels and the heart may not be accessible to direct puncture. For media placement in them, a small flexible tube, called a catheter, is threaded into a vessel in the arm, leg, or neck along the supplying arteries to the point to be studied. By careful manipulation, the catheter tip can even be inserted to study defects in the chambers of the heart. Catheters are placed under fluoroscopic examination and spot films usually are made.

Chest surveys.

One of the most common adaptations of the fluoroscope principle is found in the photoroentgenographic unit and is used for mass chest surveys. It allows the use of smaller film by photographing the visible-light image of a fluorescent screen.

Electronic image intensification has made possible the coupling of motion-picture cameras and television to a fluoroscopic unit to make a permanent record. For such filming, a much higher order of sharpness is necessary than for routine spot films or viewing in a dark room.

Image-converter tubes were developed which allow brightness gains of several-thousands times normal. The intensified image takes the form of a glass envelope. At one end, shaped like a dish or curved mirror, is the fluoroscopic screen which converts basic X-rays into visible light after they pass through the patient.

Adjacent to, but separated from the fluorescent screen by a clean shield of glass or plastic is a sheet of material which emits electrons when exposed to light. Because of the close contact between the two screens, the electron pattern is faithful to the fluoroscopic image. The electrons travel across the tube under high-energy impetus and impress themselves upon a layer of phosphor at the opposite end. Because of electron acceleration, the output phosphor is brighter than the input. A reduction in size by refraction through an electron lens also adds brightness to the image.

Reproduced again as visible light, the image can be magnified to viewing size by a series of optical

gers make possible the taking of a series of films at split-second intervals to record media flow in blood vessels and the heart.

To place necessary radiopaque media in position to outline soft-tissue systems, radiologists have had to devise methods of spotting the media precisely. In some cases, this can be done by tapping an artery or vein and allowing the natural blood flow to carry the media into position.

lenses or mirrors. For simultaneous film recording and viewing, a mirror can be used to split the image.

Besides medical procedures, X-rays are also basic to dental practice. The Public Health Service reckoned 49-million dental visits for X-ray services in 1960. Similarly, radiography is of considerable use in veterinary medicine. A speciality of veterinary radiology is taking form in the ranks of veterinarians.

RADIOGRAPHY IN INDUSTRY

From experimental beginnings in the 1920's, industrial uses of radiography have become widespread in numerous industries. As Roentgen discovered, the X-ray has the same ability to distinguish varying densities in inanimate objects as it does in living tissues.

X-rays were first used industrially to inspect castings for hidden flaws which could weaken the product. In the construction of Boulder Dam, the 80 miles of welds in the pipe installed in the massive structure were inspected for weak points. By contrast, fluoroscopic units can now be used to scan food products for the presence of foreign objects, such as a metal hairpin in a loaf of bread.

Steel, brass, concrete, or other types of material have a characteristic structure of sufficient density to be examined on radiographic films. Besides serving as inspection devices for finished products, X-ray and fluoroscopic units in industry serve as a means of checking the manufacturing process.

The need to penetrate several feet of metal in a brief time provided an impetus to the development of multimillion volt X-ray generators and tubes. Some of these operate on

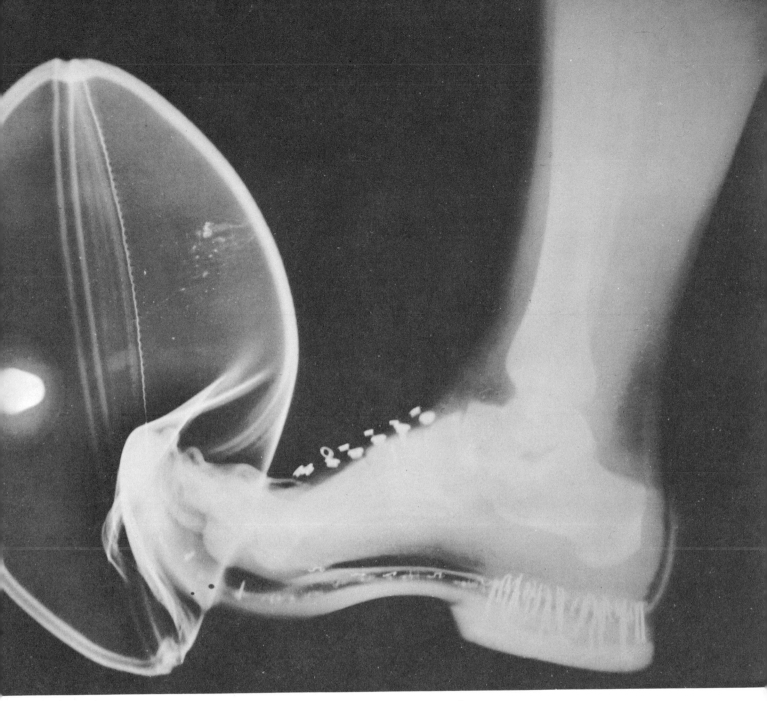

High-speed X-ray at 1/1,000,000 second showing football at point of impact, made with special X-ray tube developed by Westinghouse X-ray Corporation.

the cascade principle developed by William Coolidge. This is actually a series of tubes in which the energy level is raised progressively as it is passed along—the final voltage being equal to the sum of all the boosts.

For situations where radiographs are needed immediately, a process called xeroradiography, or dry processing electrostatically charged plates, bypasses the time needed to develop standard X-ray film. In addition, films which can be developed in less than 60 seconds with-

out a darkroom are available for X-ray use.

X-RAY IN RESEARCH

The X-ray has been used to depict the frail structure of a flower and to penetrate the wrappings of an Egyptian mummy, as well as to unmask a fraudulent "old-master" painting. Biologists, botanists, geologists, metallurgists, physical chemists, engineers of all varieties, and physicians have made X-rays a standard-research tool.

The field of microradiography

has opened new insights into many chemical and physical processes. Again, such efforts have been possible because of the coupling of X-ray apparatus with electronic devices which can be magnified or minified.

Roentgen's discovery in 1895, has had a large role in the evolution of modern medicine, science, and industry. The technology of radiography has drawn from and contributed to modern instrumentation, photography, electrical physics, and nuclear energy. The role of radiography in the future promises even more uses of its unique capacity to see the structure of opaque objects.

RAILROAD PHOTOGRAPHY

ANDREW P. WITTENBORN

[Making photographs of trains and railroads is still an active hobby for many amateurs. Here the writer gives a report on the change from steam to the Diesel and what it means in terms of pictorial angles, record views, and equipment. Museum railroads and short lines are also described.]

• *Also see: Action Photography.*

ALTHOUGH THE FIRST USE OF THE steam engine in 1830 marked the historic beginning of modern railroading, only a few pictures recorded the progress of the "iron horse" for the next thirty years.

Not surprisingly, Mathew Brady is recognized as the father of railroad photography. Brady, in the

The natural curve helps to give this full-length view of the Denver & Rio Grande Western (narrow gauge) at Cumbres Pass dramatic power. Three engines are used on the 13-mile climb at Windy Point. Remember, high altitudes require less exposure than at sea level. (Photo: Andrew P. Wittenborn)

course of making a pictorial history of the Civil War, included many scenes of locomotives and trains. During the ten years following the War a considerable number of railroad photos were made. One of the most outstanding records of this period is to be found in the photographs of Colorado and Rocky Mountain railroads by William H. Jackson. Many of the Jackson views compare favorably with the best of those made today.

RAILROAD PHOTOGRAPHY COMES OF AGE

Although a few scattered "rail fans" took pictures during the early 1900's, it wasn't until the late 1930's that the amateur photographer gave serious consideration to

this field. The demise of steam, starting in the late 1940's, brought about an interest which has been mushrooming over since. Few areas of photography have attracted so many followers in such a short span of time.

Railroad photographers have seen many changes during the last decade. The steam engine has disappeared from class-1 railroads and is to be found today only on short lines, tourist lines, and in museums. The Diesel-electric, gas-turbine, and Diesel-hydraulic locomotive now rule the right-of-way in this country, and the railroad photographer who is not satisfied with the Diesel has had to turn elsewhere for his pictures of steam engines.

RAILROAD PICTURES

Some photographers specialize in one type of engine, collecting them from all the different roads where they are in use. Others concentrate on one railroad and attempt to photograph all the principal types and classes of engines it may have in service. Still others are interested in mechanical details and may use the photographs they take as a guide to the construction of miniature engines.

There are some specialists who photograph and collect views of cars, coaches, odd types of rolling stock, trolleys and interurban cars, and miscellaneous scenes of signals, towers, and other structures. Pictorialists have found the railroads a fertile field for unusual scenes.

Today many railroad fans belong to clubs which help them find subjects for the pictures they want. Fan trips, with planned photo stops along the line, are popular and rewarding. Many organizations not only furnish the photographer with his subject, but also collect railroad equipment and produce books, pamphlets, and magazines. The following list mentions some organizations and publications useful and interesting to the railroad photographer:

Organizations.

Railroad Enthusiasts, Grand Central Terminal Building, New York, New York.

Railroad Boosters, Los Angeles, California.

Railroadians of America, San Francisco California and New York, New York.

Railway and Locomotive Historical Society, Cambridge, Mass.

Rocky Mountain Railroad Club, P. O. Box 2391, Denver, Colorado.

Electric Railroaders, New York, New York.

Canadian Railway Historical Association, Toronto, Ontario, Canada.

Publications.

Iron Horse News, Box 641, Golden, Colorado.

Railroad Magazine, 205 East 42nd Street, New York 17, New York.

Railway Age, New York, New York.

Steam Locomotive & Railroad Tradition, 203 Main Street, Susquehanna Pennsylvania.

Switch Lamp, Iowa Chapter NRHS, 704 East Charles Street, Oelwin, Iowa.

Trains magazine, 1027 North 7th Street, Milwaukee 3, Wisconsin.

INSIDE THE RAILROAD YARD

The yards and terminals of railroads are interesting for photographers, when detail and still shots of equipment and structures are desired. Unfortunately, there is the added complication of permissions to be obtained, rules and regulations to be followed, and objects which may not be photographed.

Permission may be obtained either by writting ahead of time to the railroad's operating department or by seeing the person in charge at the yard office. Almost always the photographer will be requested to sign a release so that the railroad will not be held liable in case he gets hurt. In very congested and complex yards, the photographer must sometimes be accompanied by a guide. One cardinal rule in the yard is to keep off all equipment, as it may move unexpectedly.

The photographer who chooses the railroad yard for his photog-

Georgia Pacific No. 19, a Shay, in West Virginia woods. People help to make this photo more interesting, as the crew oil up before returning to the mill. (Photo: Andrew P. Wittenborn)

raphy must be alert for moving engines and cars. Although it is sometimes possible to get equipment moved for better pictures, the photographer should not expect such consideration.

RECORD VIEWS

For a record shot of an engine or car, the three-quarter front view is the best. The waist-level shot is the most commonly used but a near-ground or elevated shot may be more dramatic. A broadside view is often good, but hard to get in congested yards. Many photographers are growing weary of the stereotyped three-quarter angle views and are using a fresher approach to the subject. Shots of men servicing equipment are always good, as is the use of other objects to frame the subject or give it depth. Detailed close-up pictures are especially effective for the model-train hobbyist, or for the artistic patterns, light shades, and composition they yield.

The ideal background is a clear sky. Watch for poles, trees, or towers that may protrude above the locomotive, detracting from the shot. See that no extraneous matter, such as piles of rails or ties in the foreground, obstructs the lower portion of the wheels. Be on the lookout for any tools, ladders, or other equipment used in servicing and repairing the engine, as they may hide a portion of the subject.

Views made on the turntable at a roundhouse are often quite convenient, as the table can be swung until the engine is in the best position. Generally, however, turntables have girder sides or hand rails which obstruct a portion of the view. Wash racks, inspection pits, or coal docks are sometimes the only places in the yard where an engine can be photographed—but unless the photographer wishes to picture these areas and their functions, he should look for more satisfactory locations.

For best results, a locomotive should be photographed either in the early morning or late afternoon. The low sun at these periods fully illuminates the under-carriage and drive wheels. At midday these parts are buried in deep shadows, making it almost impossible to give a correct exposure. Snow on the ground aids considerably in reflecting light to the under portions of the engine. Cloudy days are excellent, as the light will be much less contrasty; however, a tripod may be required to get the correct exposure. Tripods are not especially welcome in and around busy railroad yards and terminals, and should be avoided whenever possible.

RAILROAD LORE

Most photographers like to find out when the engine was built, by whom, its construction number, and its road classification. In the case of steam engines, a cast-iron plaque situated on the smoke-box gives the builder, construction number, and date (example: Baldwin Locomotive Works, Philadelphia, 10-1929, #637512). On the side of the cab, beneath the engine's number, is its road classification, which could refer to type of engine, year built,

A three-quarter rear shot that is interesting and dramatic. Buffalo Creek & Gauley No. 14, at Widen, West Virginia. (Photo: Andrew P. Wittenborn)

The maze of tracks in and around stations and yards offers the photographer exciting and varied compositions. In this picture, made just before the departure of the Santa Fe's San Francisco Chief, the train (a four-unit diesel) slips into the old Dearborn station in Chicago to couple onto the waiting train. (Photo: R. Ball)

Yard activity and varied motive power on today's railroad challenges the photographer with many different shapes and sizes. This busy scene is at New York Central's Harmon, N. Y. shops. (Photo: R. Ball)

road service, or wheel arrangement. Diesel engines have similar plaques on the frame.

PICTORIAL ANGLES

Studying photos in print, as well as using your imagination, will help greatly in composing a good railroad photograph. As previously mentioned, be sure that no distracting objects are in the way, so that the train does not appear to be sprouting trees, poles, or houses.

Of course, in shooting fast-action shots, a high shutter speed must be used; in this day and age most cameras are fully equipped to handle such speeds.

Smoke and steam blowing back over the train help give an illusion of speed, although at times they block the sun or hide the train. Pictures in the snow are interesting, too, and shots of trains in action made at night can be quite spectacular, with the use of electronic

flash or large flashbulbs in series.

A little imagination will sometimes result in shots of extraordinary interest. An increasingly popular technique shows the engine as it has just passed the camera, three-quarters rear, so to speak. Panning with the engine gives an impression of tremendous speed. Care must be taken to shoot at a speed that is not too slow, and to follow through with the camera as the picture is taken. This may be troublesome at first, but practice will perfect your technique.

Some photographers make pictures from moving cars; again, as mentioned in the yard section, it helps to use trees, houses, and people to frame the picture, or give depth and liveliness to it. There are many other angles to shoot from, as the photographer will learn from experience. Curves, heavy grades, bridges, tunnels, and so on help to dress up the photograph.

SPEEDING LOCOMOTIVES

Accuracy, plus considerable practice, are required to photograph the train at just the right moment and also to stop its movement on the film. That right moment needs plenty of practice, but stopping can be more easily calculated. It must be remembered that head-on shots require the least amount of shutter speed, that three-quarter shots must be about two times faster, and broadside shots even faster.

Since most cameras today have high-shutter speeds $1/500$ to $1/1000$ the following rules may be used:

$1/100$ for slow action (10-20mph), head-on only,

$1/250$ for 30-50mph range, three-quarter view,

$1/500$ plus for three-quarter view, 50mph plus, or broadside.

The speeds suggested above are for a $2\frac{1}{4} \times 2\frac{1}{4}$ reflex camera. Larger size cameras require higher shutter speeds, as the subject travels over more negative area. Slower speeds may be used with smaller cameras, such as 35 mm, which have less negative area.

EQUIPMENT

Most amateur railroad photographers prefer the less bulky cameras in the $2\frac{1}{4} \times 2\frac{1}{4}$ or 35 mm size, although where weight and room are not a problem, the 4×5 press-type camera is still widely used. As a general rule the rectangular negative is more suitable for railroad pictures; with the square negative, there is a tendency not to use the negative to its fullest

degree. Today inexpensive cameras with fast shutter speeds, combined with fast lenses, have made picture taking easier, and interchangeable lenses provide even more margin for creativity.

In addition to improved camera equipment, a wide variety of panchromatic films have come into use. Color film is also used extensively by railroad photographers, accounting for at least one half of the pictures taken. Color slides, arranged for slide shows, can be shown to fellow fans. Films in this category also have a wide range of speed and are very easily adaptable to high-speed photography.

Filters should be used whenever and wherever possible. The yellow filter is the most commonly employed; it has a low factor, and brings out the sky and clouds more effectively. A polarizing filter, which can be used with either black-and-white or color films, will cut reflections down to a minimum and bring out richer shades in the scenery and sky. A UV or skylight filter may be advisable for color films, although the special coating on most modern lenses usually make it unnecessary.

The usual line of accessories will be found useful for railroad photography. A good exposure meter is a necessity, either built into the camera or used separately. A tripod should be employed wherever convenient, as shots can be more easily composed, and lower shutter speeds will provide lower f-stops and more depth of field. A sunshade will help considerably in producing clean, brilliant negatives and a flashgun, of either the bulb or electronic type, is also a very handy thing to have along.

Great Western Railway engine No. 90. Here is a good detail-record picture made with a sky background to avoid distracting objects. A tripod was used for greater depth of field and a yellow filter served to darken the sky. (Photo: Andrew P. Wittenborn)

MOVIES

Movies are being used more and more in railroad photography as they can recreate so vividly the movement of trains in action. Better pictures are produced with 16 mm cameras, but 8 mm machines are more commonly used because they are about half the cost of the 16 mm. Most of the angles and ideas used for still shots can be applied to movie photography. Pan shots, mentioned earlier, are standard fare in this field, since a movie camera can follow the train's approach and its recession into the distance. Excellent shots of trains in motion can be readily made from a moving car with a movie camera.

MISCELLANEOUS

Along with many a railroad photographer goes his portable tape recorder, 12-volt batteries, and an inverter for converting 12-volt DC to 110-volt AC. What could be more enjoyable, when looking over your photographs, than to hear a steam engine blast and whistle over the hi-fi? Good tape recorders and microphones should be used and can be bought quite reasonably. For those photographers who don't want to bother with making their own tapes, commercial recordings on long-playing records are obtainable from companies specializing in railroad recordings.

The presentation of photos to railroad officials and employees is well worth a mention here. If you want to show your appreciation to someone who has gone out of his way to help you—say with a little more smoke at a preselected spot, or an engine moved around, or a whistle at a crossing for your tape recording—you'll find the distribution of a few pictures a tremendous help. You'll often be the recipient of letters of appreciation—and a welcome visitor when you return. You can also pave the way for other photographers who are looking for the same special attention you received.

THE MUSEUM RAILROAD AND SHORT LINES

Since steam is becoming part of the past, many groups have set up operating museums all over the country. The engines may be so "overdressed" as to be ridiculous, but nevertheless they do provide steam for photographers and fans. Also many amusement parks feature operating steam engines.

There are also museums displaying steam engines and equipment. Many towns and cities throughout the country have a steam engine sitting in a local park. And there are even a few individuals who own their own standard-gauge steam engines and run them on fan trips.

Some short lines refuse to succumb to the Diesel and persist in using steam. Eventually, one assumes, they will either abandon operations or adopt Diesels—but for the present they provide the photographer with another chance to photograph steam in action. Most short lines take good care of their power and welcome railroad fans. Some of the lines—even those which are Dieselized—use steam to run fan trips or even regular tourist runs during the summer.

A Monon time freight races north through Greencastle, Indiana behind four diesel units. The station agent is handing up train orders under a threatening sky background. (Photo: R. Ball)

RANGEFINDERS

Most camera rangefinders are based on a system of measurement known as *triangulation,* which depends on the geometric fact that a triangle can be completely defined if either the length of two sides and the value of one of its angles, or the value of two angles and the length of a single side is known.

In the case of a right-angle triangle, one angle is necessarily 90 degrees. This being known, it is obviously necessary to know only the length of one side, and one of the remaining angles in order to draw the entire triangle. Thus, in Figure 1, if we know the length of the side B and the value of the angle x, y, or z, we can calculate the length of the vertical side (respectively X, Y, and Z for the three angles given).

In the case of a camera rangefinder, this is accomplished by providing two mirrors, M_1 and M_2 respectively (Figure 2). M_1 is either partially silvered or split, depending on the construction of the rangefinder, and is fixed in position at 45 degrees to the line of sight, as shown. Mirror M_2 is mounted on a pivot and can be tilted through a known angle less than 45 degrees. The distance between the two mirrors is accurately known and corresponds to base B of the triangle in Figure 1.

Looking through the eyepiece, we seen the object either through the half-silvered mirror, or over the top if it is a split or half mirror. In the mirror itself, we also see a reflection of the subject as seen by mirror M_2. Now, by tilting mirror M_2 on its axis, we can get the image of the subject to overlap the image as seen through or over mirror M_1.

Knowing the distance between the two mirrors and measuring the angle to which we have tilted mirror M_2, we can easily calculate the distance to the subject. But since the base length is fixed, the mirror M_2 will always tilt to a given angle for a given subject distance. We can, therefore, mark the mirror's tilting mechanism, not in degrees but in actual subject distances. This, then, is the essence of a rangefinder.

TYPES OF RANGEFINDERS

Most rangefinders are of one or two types. If mirror M_1 is partially silvered, the reflection of the subject as seen in M_2 will be superimposed over the direct view. However, because of the distance to mirror M_2, its entire area will occupy only a small part of mirror M_1 and we will see its reflection as a small circle in the middle of the field. If the mirror is not set at the correct angle, two images of the subject will be seen inside this circular area and displaced sideways from each other, as in the upper left of Figure 3. When the mirror M_2 is tilted to the proper angle, the two images will be exactly superimposed and only a single image will be seen inside the circle.

To facilitate the use of this type of rangefinder, the left-hand window is often covered with a yellow filter. Here the reflection of M_2 appears as a white circle against a yellow field, and the double images are respectively white and yellow. When they combine, they form a stronger white image.

The alternative construction uses a half-mirror for M_1 instead of one that is only partly silvered. Through the eyepiece a round field is seen, split into two halves by a horizontal line. The image of the subject is likewise split into two halves, somewhat displaced from each other. When mirror M_2 is tilted to the correct angle, the two halves of the image join together to form a single unbroken image, as in the right-hand part of Figure 3.

COUPLED RANGEFINDERS

As long as the base of the rangefinder is known, the amount of mirror tilt needed is constant for any distance. Similarly, the amount of a given lens must be racked in or out in order to focus at different distances is constant for any one distance. A mechanical coupling can be devised so that operating the focusing mechanism of the lens also operates the tilting mirror of the rangefinder. Thus the lens can be focused while watching the subject through the rangefinder; when the two images merge, the lens is cor-

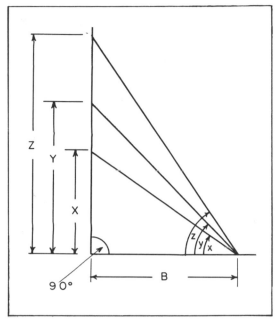

Above: *Figure 1. The basic operating principle of the rangefinder is based on the right-angle triangle. See text.*

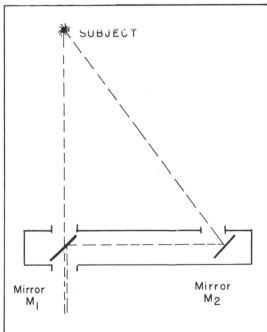

Below: *Figure 2. Mirror M_1 is fixed at a 45-degree angle while mirror M_2 is mounted on a pivot and is adjustable for determining the angle and the distance to the subject.*

rectly set for the same distance.

For press cameras using only a single lens, the coupling between lens and rangefinder is relatively simple, and rangefinders for these cameras are often sold as accessories. But for 35 mm cameras it

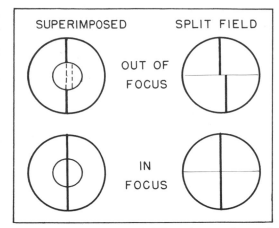

Above: *Figure 3. When the superimposed or split-field image is brought into alignment, the camera lens will be automatically in focus.*

Below: *Figure 4. There are no moving mirrors in this fixed-prism rangefinder. See text.*

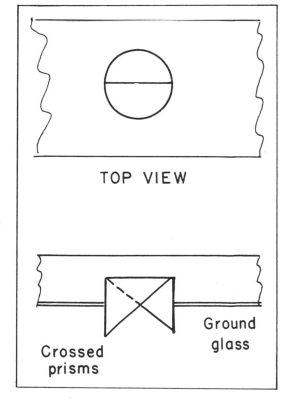

TOP VIEW

Crossed prisms   Ground glass

is usually necesary to fit the various interchangeable lenses with a cam, so that the different focusing movements of the lenses can be translated into a single motion that will operate a single rangefinder correctly for all lenses, whatever their focal length.

Certain rangefinders produce the same result with a pair of fixed mirrors. The movement of the

image is accomplished by an auxiliary prism placed in front of one of the windows, and rotated to different positions by the movement of the camera lens.

Another type of rangefinder is often used on the 35 mm single-lens reflex. In this type of rangefinder (Figure 4) no moving mirrors are used at all and the measurement is not by triangulation. Instead the groundglass is fitted with a pair of fixed prisms in the center of the field. These two prisms have opposite slopes, and the crossing point is exactly in the plane of the ground surface of the glass. If the camera lens is not focused exactly in the plane of the groundglass, the image as seen through the two prisms will be displaced respectively left and right, and it will appear split, just as in the ordinary split-image rangefinder. Properly focused, a single image, exactly like that of an ordinary split-field rangefinder, will be seen in the groundglass.

This system simply indicates whether or not the image lies exactly in the plane of the groundglass, and since it needs no coupling to the lens itself, it is particularly suited to cameras with interchangeable lenses. This type of rangefinder is usually not so sensitive as the tilting-mirror type of rangefinder, since the movement of the image depends on the focal length of the camera lens. Wide-angle lenses will show very little doubling of the image even when far out of focus; long-focus lenses will show a greater doubling and more movement.

This type of rangefinder is usually used with the single-lens reflex fitted with zoom lenses, and in this case, maximum sensitivity can be attained by shifting the zoom lens to its greatest magnification before focusing.

ACCURACY OF RANGEFINDERS

Returning to the triangle diagram, Figure 1, it is fairly obvious that the greatest movement of the mirror will be required when focusing at close ranges; the movement of the mirror becomes less as the subject gets farther from the camera.

This would seem to imply that the accuracy of a rangefinder is

greatest at close range, and least at the greatest distance. However, if we examine the focusing scale of a lens, it will be found that the lens requires its largest motion for focusing close-up, while the movement rapidly diminishes at greater distances until from 50 feet to infinity it is very small indeed. Obviously, then, the accuracy of setting required is greater at closer ranges. Since this is exactly the condition existing in a rangefinder, the two effects cancel each other. It will be found in practice that a rangefinder is equally accurate at close and far distances, in terms of the permissible error (or depth of focus—*not* depth of field) of the camera lens itself.

□

RAPID-PROCESSING METHODS

Grant Haist
Research Laboratories, Eastman Kodak Company
[There are times when the fast processing of photographs is extremely important. Newspaper, industrial, commercial, and military photographers require this speed on numerous occasions. Here the author carefully explains the basic steps in rapid processing and also gives certain cautions for obtaining quality results. Even the average photographer will find useful information that can be applied in his work.]
• *Also see: Drying Negatives and Prints, Photofinish Photography*

There are five distinct operations in normal photographic processing: 1) development, 2) stopping development, 3) fixing, 4) washing, and 5) drying. Shortening the total time of this cycle can be achieved if one or more of the steps can be completed more quickly, or if two or more steps can be combined, or if some of the steps can be eliminated or delayed until a later time.

Of the five operations needed to secure permanent photographic images, the last three, fixing, washing, and drying, are the most time-consuming. The greatest saving in time will result, therefore, from procedures that will speed these slower operations rather than from efforts to reduce the relatively short times of developer and stop-bath treatment. In some cases, where requirements permit, elimination of part of the normal cycle, such as washing, can result in a substantial speeding up of the process.

Processing for maximum rate starts first with the selection of a suitable photographic material, preferably one having a thin, super-hardened emulsion layer. The extra hardening is often needed to withstand the effect of the application of liquids at elevated temperatures, as heat is often used for its powerful activating force upon chemical reactions. In addition, turbulent agitation is used many times to supply active solution continuously to the emulsion surface and to sweep away reaction products.

The nature of one processing step can have a profound effect upon the efficiency of the subsequent steps, such as the type of fixing upon the rate of washing. Because of the number and importance of these interrelated factors, rapid processing is usually considered from a systems viewpoint so that every accelerating influence can be coordinated for maximum efficiency. A brief discussion of these basic principles is given in the next section as a guide to better understanding of fast processing.

FUNDAMENTAL FACTORS IN RAPID PROCESSING

Development

Rapid development requires fast-acting, highly energetic solutions with large concentrations of the developing agents. Selective reducing agents that are active as neutral or low-charged negative ions, for example Metol or Phenidone, initiate development rapidly but must be combined with density-building compounds, usually hydroquinone, to produce the desired contrasts. Sodium isoascorbate is sometimes used to speed image formation. Antifoggants, often more than one, are needed in most cases to restrain the production of fog from unexposed silver-halide grains. Potassium bromide is a restrainer commonly used in combination with benzotriazole, 5-methylbenzotriazole, or 6-nitrobenzimidazole nitrate.

To insure that the developing agents are present in their most active ionic form, strong alkalis, generally sodium or potassium hydroxide, are added to make a very alkaline developing solution. Sodium carbonate, or other similar buffering compounds that require a high salt

The Kodak Versamat Film Processor automatically processes and dries sheet and roll films in only six minutes, utilizing the wringer-roller principle to produce top-quality negatives without any hand operations.

concentration, are of limited utility for this purpose as the effect of the salt prevents the minimum swelling of the gelation needed for rapid diffusion of the developer constituents.

Increasing the temperature of the developer is a universal method of speeding chemical reactions and diffusion in emulsion layers. According to Ives, Russell, and Crabtree, "the rate of development increases by a factor of about two for each 15 F rise in temperature up to 125 F, at which point it is eight or ten times that of 68 F. There is a limit, however, to the useful temperature rise, usually around 150 F with existing emulsions, because of the rapid growth of fog that must be offset by the addition of increasing concentrations of antifoggants which, in turn, cancel most of the gain in rate." These investigators reported that the use of a high-activity developer at elevated temperatures may increase the development rate as much as 50 times.

The rate of development may be limited by the nature of the photographic emulsion layer, especially when ultrarapid treatment of the fractional-second type is desired. The rate of diffusion of the developer components throughout the emulsion thickness was stated by Ives to be a major factor when the development time was about one second. Developing time may be twice as long for the thicker, coarse-grained emulsion layer as for the thin, fine-grained layer. By studying the distribution of the developed silver image throughout the thickness of the emulsion layer, the net rate of development has been shown to be largely influenced by the rate of developer diffusion as the processing temperature increased, shortening the time of treatment.

Stopping Development

Probably one of the most critical but least appreciated steps in photographic processing is the stop-bath treatment after development. Because rapid developers are maximum-activity solutions of the most potent developing agents, image formation does not stop when the film is removed from the developer but continues at a high rate until all the developer is removed or deactivated. An appreciable drain time during

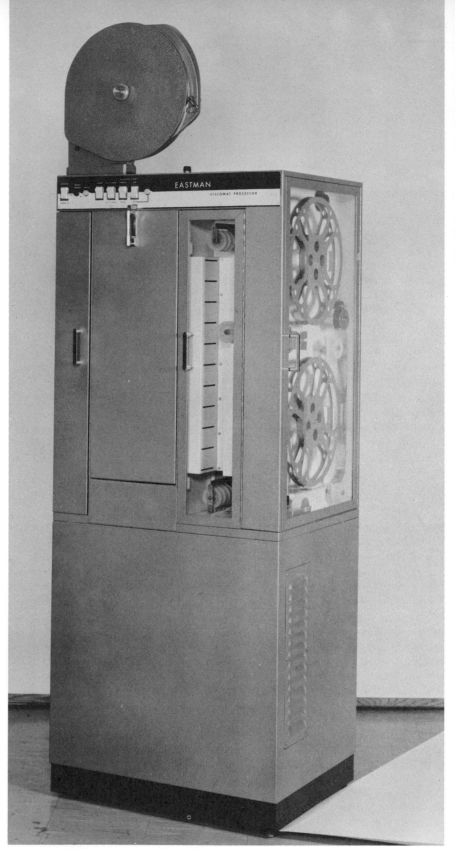

By applying first a viscous developer and then a viscous-fixer layer to the film surface at 125 F, the Eastman Viscomat Processor can process recording films at 16 mm motion-picture camera speed.

transfer from one solution to another will often result in poor image uniformity. And simply immersing the film in an acid bath does not instantly stop the developing action which still may continue during the neutralization reactions.

Ideally, it would be an advantage, as a means of speeding the processing cycle, to omit the stop bath and put the film directly into the fixing bath. Unfortunately, placing a film emulsion swollen with a very active developing solution into the fixing bath may cause dichroic fog on the film and sludging in the bath. Water rinses can be used but must be sprayed on forcefully to be effective. Rinsing with water may cause excessive emulsion swelling before the hardener of the fixing bath can take effect.

Well-designed rapid processors have efficient squeegee action to reduce the carry-out of developer, very short crossover times between solutions, and a means of providing strong agitation in the stop bath. Acid stop baths of about three-percent acetic acid are often used with very vigorous agitation for about 15 seconds. Strong acid baths cannot be used if the developer contains sodium carbonate, because the gas released during the neutralization of this compound may blister the emulsion layer.

Fixing

The purpose of rapid fixing is not only to solubilize the undeveloped silver salts but also to keep the emulsion layer from swelling. Fresh, acid hardening baths should be used. Fresh solution is needed to secure maximum silver-solubilizing activity. By starting with unused solution, the concentration of the silver thiosulfates is kept to a minimum, reducing the danger of having these unstable, image-attacking compounds becoming trapped in the gelatin of the emulsion layer. The hardening action of the bath suppresses the swelling of the gelatin. This action will help speed the final drying step since less water will be absorbed during the washing period.

Ammonium thiosulfate has been suggested by Crabtree as the most satisfactory fixing agent for rapidly clearing film. The fixing rate was found to increase only about 20 percent when the ammonium thiosulfate concentration was increased from 15 to 30 percent. The addition of 500 grams per liter of ammonium thiocyanate to a 15-percent ammonium-thiosulfate bath reduced the fixing time to about one-third the time taken by the thiosulfate bath alone. Thiocyanate is a gel softener, however, so only super-hardened emulsions can be used with it at high temperatures.

Crabtree and Russell found that raising the temperature from 68 to 80 F reduced the time of fixing by about 20 percent. At 125 F only one-third the normal time at 70 F was needed. These investigators also reported that rapid fixing was not conducive to good emulsion-hardening. Hardening action was slow, not being entirely effective until after three minutes, even at 80 F. Acid hardening-fixing baths should still be used even at times shorter than three minutes. The limited hardening of rapid fixing is helpful in limiting the water retention of the emulsion layer, making drying just that much easier.

An ammonium-thiosulfate fixing bath reaches its maximum effectiveness when the high-temperature solution is applied forcefully to the emulsion surface, as both temperature and agitation combine to speed reaction and diffusion rates. However, it was noted by Ives that there is only an approximate doubling of fixing rate in going from moderate to very strong agitation. Diffusion of the thiosulfates throughout the emulsion layer appears to be the limiting factor for ultra-rapid processing times.

Washing

Removal of the thiosulfate compounds by washing with water is a process of dilution controlled by the diffusion rate of these compounds from the emulsion layer. This process is accelerated by having fresh water sweeping the emulsion surface free of any of the diffusion products. With very vigorous application of water, such as by spray or jet impingement, the rate of the washing process can be increased 25 to 100 times. By these techniques, negative film can be washed thoroughly in 15 to 45 seconds, and photographic paper without a baryta coating in 30 seconds.

There is evidence that small quantities of the thiosulfates are still strongly held in the gelatin, baryta, or paper fibres even after considerable washing. Reducing the concentration of these last unstable chemical compounds considerably lengthens the washing period. Certain constituents of the fixing bath have been found to increase the difficulty of removing the silver and sodium thiosulfates. Potassium alum, often present as a hardening agent in fixing baths, causes high retention of residual thiosulfates. Highly acid fixing baths have the same effect. Nonhardening baths, or those containing chrome alum as the hardener, do not promote retention. Chrome-alum solutions are little used because of their sludging tendencies. Hardening the film or paper before the fixing step or starting with superhardened emulsions would be beneficial in shortening the washing time by allowing more suitable fixing baths to be utilized.

Two successive fixing baths have been recommended as a technique to cut down on the quantity of silver thiosulfates retained, as it is these compounds that decompose to produce staining. "For a fixed time of washing," Crabtree, Henn and Edgerton reported, "three times more hypo and seven times more silver were retained by prints fixed in a bath containing three grams of silver per liter than by prints fixed in a fresh bath."

The undeveloped silver halide is solubilized during immersion in the first fixing solution. The second, relatively fresh bath then helps to remove the remaining silver thiosulfates. Since these compounds are much more soluble in the fixing bath than in water, washing can be more effective as many of the silver thiosulfates will already have been extracted from the photographic film or paper. Two-bath fixation is also economical since it permits 200 prints per gallon to be processed to the same degree of image permanence compared with only 50 for the single-bath procedure.

Other methods have been studied as aids to help reduce the prolonged periods of washing necessary for archival permanence. The use of salt solutions as immersion baths between fixing and washing has been known from the early days of photography as a means of shortening wash times. Only in the last

20 years, however, has this effect been examined systematically. Eaton and Crabtree found that the removal of thiosulfates was accelerated by washing in sea water, which contains approximately 3.5-percent salts, mostly sodium chloride. Films and prints washed in sea water need only one-half the usual time, but a five-minute wash in fresh water was necessary to remove the sea salts. Increasing the temperature of the sea water cut the treatment time considerably. But sea water at 50 F removed thiosulfates more rapidly than fresh water did at 70 F.

Later, Crabtree and co-workers studied the effect of salt-bath compositions upon the elimination of absorbed thiosulfates. Usually, the salts are present in a separate bath after fixing. Polyvalent anions (citrates, phosphates, sulfates, and sulfites) were found to be more effective in displacing the thiosulfate or silver thiosulfate bound to alum-hardened gelatin than were monovalent anions (acetates, bromides, chlorides, and nitrates). Two-percent sodium sulfite was especially efficacious as a bath for either film or prints. Bathing 30 seconds in a balanced-sulfite solution, followed by a two-minute wash, lowered the thiosulfate content of Kodak Micro-File Film to archival levels of permanence. For spray treatment, a 15- to 45-second application of the balanced-sulfite solution and a 60-second wash were recommended for motion-picture films.

Rapid washing is thus intimately linked with fixing. High rates of residual thiosulfate removal—the aim of rapid washing—are achievable only by the combination of suitable fixing-bath chemistry coupled with turbulent agitation of a large volume of water at temperatures as high as the hardness of the thin emulsion layers will allow. Washing aids further increase the speed of washing, because these salt baths effectively displace silver thiosulfates that are bound to the gelatin so strongly that removal by water alone is almost impossible without a long treatment.

Drying

The last step in the processing cycle must eliminate surface water and reduce absorbed water to a level suitable for storage of the photographic material. The techniques of rapid drying somewhat resemble those of rapid washing as both require strong surface agitation. In the case of drying, vigorous air flow is necessary to remove the exaporating water. Drying also requires large quantities of heat to vaporize the water.

Every precaution during the processing cycle should be taken to reduce the final drying time needed, since photographic materials have limited ability to withstand high temperatures. The water absorption of the emulsion layer is directly related to the gelatin content, so low-gelatin, thin-layer films and papers are most advantageous, especially those highly hardened in manufacture.

All processing steps should be kept to the minimum times. Prolonged liquid treatment can result in absorption of water by some film-base materials and so-called waterproof or water-resistant paper bases. Surface application of the processing liquid to the emulsion side only of the photographic film or paper entirely avoids absorption of the solution by the base. The surface-application technique, coupled with thin, low-swelling emulsions layers, is an ideal method when rapid drying is necessary.

Loose surface water can be removed by efficient squeegees or pinch rollers. Surface drainage can be accelerated by treatment with a photographic wetting agent after washing. The remaining absorbed water is often removed by forcing air of low relative humidity continuously past the surfaces of the film or paper. Air of sufficiently low humidity can be obtained by heating the available air to a high temperature.

Hot air also supplies the heat for the evaporation of the water. In many cases, this heat may be provided by pressing the photographic material in contact with a heated drum or platen, or through the use of radiant-heat lamps.

Saturated air near the emulsion surface needs to be swept away continuously for the most efficient drying. High air velocities directed from jets or nozzles provide impinging streams of air that are much more effective than passing large volumes of air past the film or paper.

RAPID PROCESSING FOR THE PHOTOGRAPHER

Conventional processing of photographic films and papers is the most practical method of obtaining a lasting silver image of the highest quality. The activity of each solution has been adjusted so that times of immersion are long enough to minimize the effects of minor deviations in time, temperature, and agitation. And acceptable image uniformity results from the normal procedure of immersing the photographic material in the developer and then stopping development by a water rinse or acid bath.

Amateur and professional photographers would appreciate a shortening of darkroom sessions to provide more time for creative activities. However, satisfying this desire to speed processing poses real dangers for the working photographer. Conventional developing and fixing times have already been reduced to the minimum consistent with maintaining the finest results. Although activating the processing solutions by raising their temperature will reduce the total time required, serious injury may result to regular roll and sheet films which are not sufficiently hardened to withstand the treatment at higher temperatures.

The phenomenally short processing times of the more specialized uses of photography are usually achieved by using the highly hardened, thin-layer films, with precisely formulated chemical baths and with ingenious but complicated (and costly) automatic-processing machines. When the photographer, without the advantages of these films, chemicals, and machines, attempts to shorten the normal processing cycle, he runs the risk of obtaining poor image uniformity, increased graininess, emulsion softening, and inadequate image stability.

However, it may still happen that the photographer, more from necessity than from choice, must shorten his processing times. He should try the proposed rapid-processing solu-

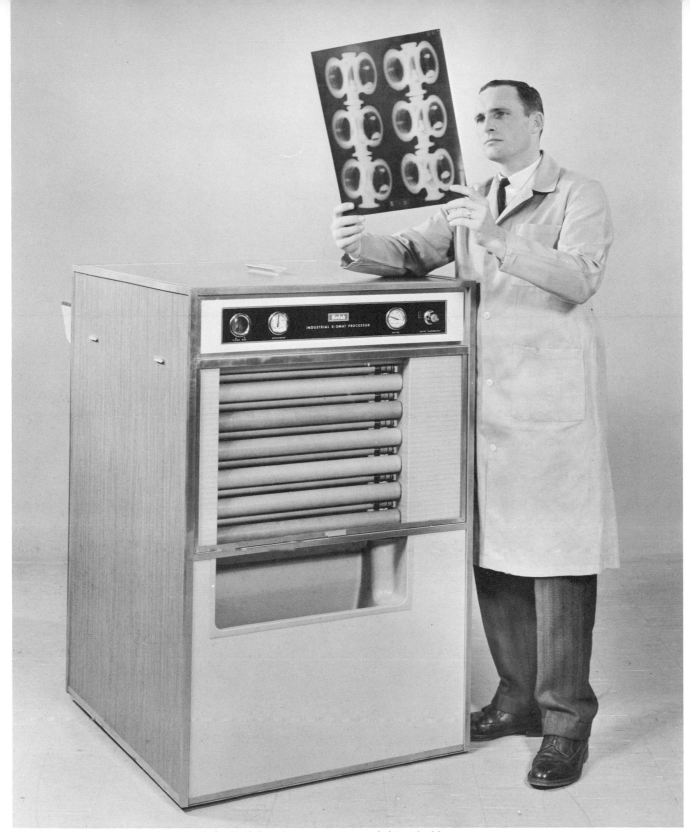

The wringer-roller transport system of the Kodak X-Omat processes and dries double-coated X-ray films in six minutes, resulting in a saving of about one hour over conventional procedures.

tions and procedures first to determine whether the resultant image has the quality and stability needed for his purpose. For those working photographers and technicians who must adapt commercially available films and chemicals to their specific needs, a brief review is provided of practical rapid-processing materials and techniques.

Fast Development

Today's standard developers are extremely quick-acting when compared with those of only a few years ago. Immersion times can be shortened even further by using somewhat higher temperatures with increased or continuous agitation.

In some cases, less dilution of the working solutions or the use of highly energetic developers, such as those normally employed for processing papers, can reduce development time for films to about one minute. A rapid-development system combining all these features may be used to secure the shortest possible wet time.

The emulsion technology incorporated in the latest photographic film has done much to provide good-quality results with a very short development time. The lower-silver, thinner emulsion layers often respond best to processing in low-solvent, high-activity developers rather than in the slower-acting, high-solvent types used for many

The Consolidated Electrodynamics Corporation 5-123 Recording Oscillograph produces superior print-out images on a special recording paper that is heated during the second light (print-out) exposure.

years. Developers now recommended for regular processing require short immersion times. For example, Kodak Developer HC-110, supplied in a concentrated-liquid form, is a highly active developer for black-and-white films, producing sharp images with moderately fine grain. With the 1:15 dilution, the developing time at 68 F is only 4½ minutes for Kodak Tri-X Pan Film (35 mm) and three minutes for Kodak Panatomic-X Film (35 mm). Acufine Film Developer (Baumann Photo-Chemical Corporation) is another rapid developer with similar times for these films. Other competitive products offer short development times.

For developing sheet film, Kodak Developers DK-50 and DK-60a have long been used to provide developing times of five minutes or less at 68 F. For more rapid treatment of sheet films like Kodak Royal Pan and Kodak Super Panchro-Press, Type B, an energetic developer, such as Kodak D-72 or Kodak Dektol, needs only 60 to 90 seconds at 68 F with continuous agitation. Milt Freier, at the Leica School in New York City, applied this same type of rapid development to Kodak Plus-X Pan Film (35 mm). This film was developed in undiluted Dektol for one minute, rinsed in water, given a quick fix, another rinse in water, and the negatives were printed while still wet. The prints were said to be quite satisfactory for newspaper reproduction.

Most commercially available rapid developers are proprietary products, and their composition has not been revealed. Of course, D-72 Developer is an exception, since its formula has long been published. Another rapid-acting formula was published by Dickerson who thought that the bromide resistance of Amidol made it well adapted to rapid development. The Amidol developer, pH 9.0, has the following formula:

Demineralized water 900 ml.
Sodium sulfite 25.2 grams
Amidol 19.7 grams
Sodium metaborate 56.4 grams
Potassium bromide 5.9 grams
Demineralized water to make
1 liter

Sparkling, fine-grain negatives were said to have been obtained by a 60-second, 68 F development of popular roll films. The unused developer was found to show little deterioration after six months in completely full and tightly stoppered bottles. However, once it has been used to develop film, the solution begins to deteriorate rapidly, even under the best storage conditions.

The trend in photographic processing is to use higher solution temperatures to gain shortened immersion times. In processing both color and black-and-white films, the standard temperature is usually 75 F. Some color films have their standard cycle set at 80 F. Although the exact time saved is dependent upon the nature of the developer, raising the temperature from 68 to 75 F in processing black-and-white films will generally reduce the development time by one quarter to one third.

Most manufacturers of black-and-white films are reluctant to recommend developing temperatures higher than 75 F because of the possible degradation of image quality. However, some manufacturers of film developers do list times of treatment as high as 80 and 85 F. For example, Acufine Film Developer, which required 4¾ minutes at 70 F for Tri-X Pan Film (35 mm), needs only 2¼ minutes at 85 F. And the two-minute, 70 F developing time of Panatomic-X is reduced to only one minute at 85 F.

As times of developing are shortened because of the higher solution temperatures, the method of initially immersing the film, the agitation in solution, and the stopping of development become more critical if image uniformity is to be maintained. One widely used procedure requires a 15-second gentle agitation immediately after immersion in the developer and five-seconds' agitation every 30 seconds thereafter. Other rapid developers call for ten-seconds' agitation after every 30 seconds of developing time. When working at high temperatures, it is necessary to follow closely the recommended agitation instructions, since even small departures can cause considerable difference in the quality of the developed image.

Image formation does not stop as long as there are residual quantities of active developer within the emulsion layer. Even though the film has been removed from the developer solution, image formation continues during the draining period, and for a time in either a water rinse bath or an acid stop bath. Because of the energetic nature of rapid developers, the activity of conventional stop baths may be inadequate to prevent poor uniformity.

To minimize these effects, it has been recommended that a stop bath, such as Kodak Bath SB-5, be used at double strength for 15 seconds, with vigorous agitation of the solution. The double-strength bath contains 64 millilitters of 28-percent acetic acid and 90 grams of dessicated sodium sulfate in a liter of working solution. There may be blistering of the gelatin if the developer contains sodium carbonate.

Fast Fixing, Washing, and Drying

These steps are grouped together because the nature of fixing has a large effect upon the rate of washing and drying. Acid hardening fixing baths prevent excessive swelling, which, in turn, reduces the amount of water retained after washing, and hence makes quicker drying possible. Most quick-fixing baths are of the ammonium-thiosulfate type, the kind found to be most effective for rapid fixing. Two-bath fixing is especially efficient with photographic prints on paper base to permit removal of residual silver thiosulfates in reasonable washing times and to insure image stability.

Commercially available salt baths, such as Kodak Hypo Clearing Agent, can sharply reduce the washing time with image permanence superior to that produced by normal long-time washing. After fixing, black-and-white film is given a 30-second rinse in water, followed by a one- to two-minute immersion in the clearing bath. The total washing time is only five minutes with a normal water flow. Photographic prints can be transferred directly to the clearing bath after fixing. Single-weight prints are immersed for at least two minutes; double-weight prints for at least three minutes. Single-weight prints are washed for ten minutes and double-weight prints for 20 minutes, using normal conditions of washing. Although addition of an extra bath may seem to lengthen the processing time, the longest part of processing, washing, is cut to one-sixth its normal time, a saving of about 45 minutes for single-weight prints.

Turbulent agitation is ideal for rapidly washing out the residual thiosulfate salts. Commercially available turbo washers, such as the Miller Hurricane, for roll and 35 mm films need not be complicated or costly to achieve rapid washing. The Hurricane, which is connected to an ordinary water faucet, has two water jets in the base which spin the film reels as well as change the water every few seconds. The makers claim that films can be completely washed in only three minutes.

Low-gelatin, thin-emulsion films with low water retention dry rapidly when warmed air is forced past their surfaces. Bathing a film in ethyl alcohol to remove the water is still recommended as a means of rapid drying, as it was in 1936 by Parker and Crabtree. The film should be immersed for only a brief period in ethyl (not methyl) alcohol containing at least ten percent water, then dried at temperatures not greater than 80 F.

Today's recommendations for rapid film drying also include the use of a saturated solution of potassium carbonate to dehydrate the emulsion. Not mentioned is the fact, pointed out by Parker and Crabtree, that it is necessary to rewash and dry the negative, or it will become sticky or full of carbonate crystals. The carbonate treatment is therefore not the most desirable rapid-processing technique.

HIGH-TEMPERATURE PROCESSING

High solution temperatures are often used in specialized systems to secure ultrarapid processing. Photographers might reason that processing at really high temperatures, not just 80 or 85 F, would also help provide rapid processing. Unfortunately regular photographic materials, especially film, cannot be subjected to such conditions without softening of the emulsion layer.

However, it should not be concluded that regular photographic films and papers cannot be proc-

essed in solutions as high as 100 or 110 F. They can, provided suitable precautions are taken to minimize swelling. One method is to add large quantities of a neutral salt, usually sodium sulfate, to the developer. For securing rapid development, it is unfortunate that the salting effect slows the rate of development so that the immersion time at the higher temperature is about equal to that at normal temperatures.

The amount of sodium sulfate to be added for some Kodak developers is shown in the table on

All processing solutions and the wash water should be within five degrees of the same temperature. It is recommended that the developed film be treated for three minutes in a freshly prepared hardening bath, such as Kodak SB-4, before it is immersed in a fresh acid hardening-fixing bath. Two minutes in such a fixing bath, followed by a 10-15 minute wash, completes the processing.

Hardening before development is often used to protect photographic emulsions against damage at high temperatures. An alkaline formaldehyde prehardener, such as the Kodak SH-5 bath, requires ten minutes with moderate agitation at normal temperatures. This is followed by a brief drain, a 30-second rinse in water, and another drain, before development can begin. However, prehardened film can be processed at temperatures up to 110 F without damage to the emulsion. Some developers may require the addition of antifoggants to reduce fogging tendencies above 95 F.

Times of development are decreased from normal approximately as listed.

EFFECT OF TEMPERATURE ON TIME OF DEVELOPMENT

Processing Temperature	Developing Time (percent normal developing time at 68 F)
80 F	85
85 F	70
90 F	60
95 F	50
110 F	25

Processing is completed by using the normal processing cycle with a fresh acid hardening bath.

Because effective hardening is a slow process, some of the time saved by rapid development and fixing is lost. Ideally, hardening during development would eliminate the extra bath and handling procedures. Aldehydes are good hardening agents but infortunately are unstable in the presence of many developing agents. Certain aldehydes have improved stability but may have other disadvantages, such as tendency to stain. Completely satisfactory hardening developers would indeed be most useful for high-temperature processing but such solutions are not currently available.

For the photographer requiring rapid-access treatment, processing standard photographic films at higher temperatures does not result in striking savings of time. Possibly a better method, as suggested by Ives and Kunz, would be to avoid high temperatures entirely and employ instead all the other techniques of rapid processing, especially quick-acting baths and vigorous agitation. These investigators used a highly active, clean-working developer, called Kodak Rapid Developer SD-26, of the following composition.

Kodak Developers	Sodium Sulfate Addition		
	75 -80 F	80 -85 F	85 -90 F
D-11, D-19, D-16a, D-76	50 grams per liter	75 grams per liter	100 grams per liter
DK-50, DK-60a, D-72 (1:1), Dektol (1:1)	100 grams per liter	125 grams per liter	150 grams per liter

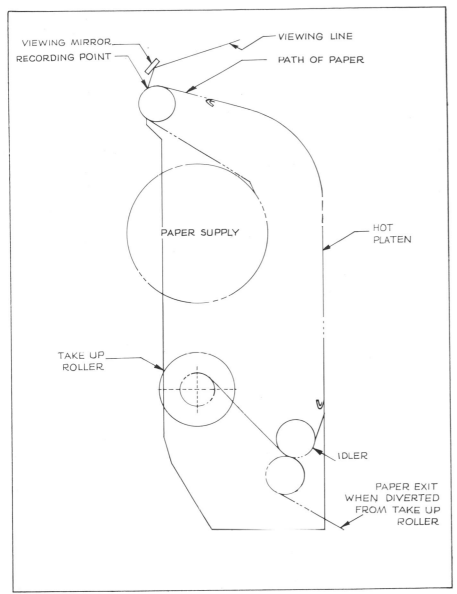

Schematic drawing of Consolidated Electrodynamics Corporation's Recording Oscillograph.

Kodak Rapid Developer SD-26
Water, about 90 F (32 C) 750 ml.
Kodak Elon Developing
Agent   20 grams
Kodak Sodium Sulfite
(desiccated)   60 grams
Kodak Hydroquinone   20 grams
Kodak Sodium Hydroxide 20 grams
Kodak Potassium Bromide 10 grams
Cold water to make   1 liter

High-speed negative films were processed in four minutes' total time at 70 F: one minute each for the developer, for the Kodak Rapid Liquid Fixer with Hardener, for spray washing, and for impingement warm-air drying, with a two-second spray rinse with water between development and fixing. If suitable spray equipment and impingement dryers are not available, the rapid developer could be adapted to other systems, but this would have to be determined experimentally.

RAPID MONOBATH PROCESSING

The simplicity and convenience of single-solution processing make desirable the use of combined developer-fixing baths for fast treatment of photographic films and papers. Early investigators of this technique found that the concentration of the fixing agent must be sufficiently low to permit satisfactory image development. This low rate of fixing led Crabtree and Russell in 1944 to conclude that "no time is gained by the use of a combined developer and fixing bath as compared with the use of separate solutions." This statement was in accord with the opinion of Richmond, the founder of monobath processing, who, in 1889, said, "...I should say that the separate solutions would do the work in a shorter time."

However, with the introduction of new, rapid-acting developing agents, such as Phenidone, with the manufacture of lower-iodide, thin-layer emulsions, and with a fuller knowledge of the chemical mechanism of simultaneous development and fixing, monobaths have found specific uses in rapid processing. Keelan, in 1953, even claimed that modern monobaths provided the advantage of speed of processing over three-step methods, citing his Monobath 290, in which he developed and fixed Kodak Azo Papers F-2 and F-3 in ten seconds.

Seymour studied several processing methods before monobath treatment was selected for a side-looking radar-mapping application. An experimental film was completely fixed in 18 seconds at 130 F after the solution was applied just one-half inch from the exposure plane.

In 1958 Drumm, in a sensitometric study of the effect of a number of rapid-processing solutions upon a variety of photographic films, found that image formation by monobaths was highly dependent upon emulsion characteristics. Certain combinations of monobath formulations and films did provide more rapid processing than the multi-step processing. The very thin emulsion films, Kodak Micro-File and Ansco Telerecord, responded most favorably to single-solution treatment.

Ansco Telerecord Film was also used by Goldhammer, Kelly, and DuPree in a portable 16 and 35 mm processor. Combined development fixing of this film for five seconds at 60 F produced a gamma of 1.0 and a maximum density of 2.5. Telerecord Film was reported by Duffy to have a resolving power of 100 lines per millimeter and

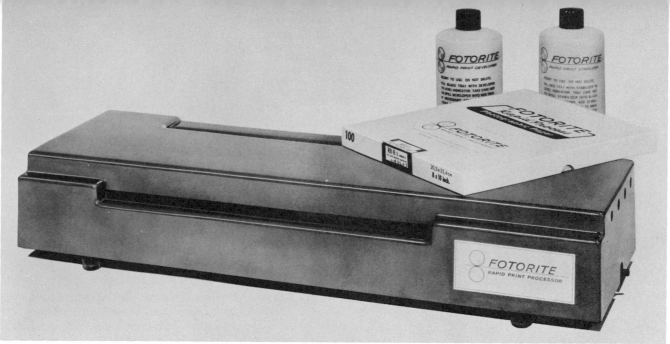

Fotorite rapid print processor gives prints and enlargements up to 11×14 in from 5 to 15 seconds. Two premixed photochemicals are used. Also duplicates any original from its own paper negative.

slightly coarsened grain when this film was processed for ten seconds at about 90 F in a commercially available monobath and processor.

Nevertheless, Smith, in devising systems for processing Autopositive Paper for office copying, selected a two-solution system after attempting to adapt monobath processing to a simple immersion-processing machine. Sufficiently high processing speed could not be attained to provide the desired ten feet per minute rate.

From the references just given it is evident that monobaths can provide rapid processing in certain situations, especially in systems where photographic material, solutions, and processor can be made compatible as a unit.

RAPID- AND ULTRARAPID-PROCESSING SYSTEMS

Rapid and ultrarapid are descriptive terms applied to normal times of processing. Crabtree attempted to restrict rapid to any procedure that reduces the normal processing time to $1/10$ or less, and ultrarapid to $1/50$ or less. Although such a rigid approach is not entirely satisfactory, it does emphasize that modern processing techniques have reduced the time needed to a few minutes or seconds, or even a fraction of one second. The emphasis is usually on access time, the interval after exposure needed to provide a record for examination. In this section only a few of the

recent developments in the various fields of rapid-access processing will be described.

Ideally, it would be desirable to have the recorded image available without any chemical treatment, so-called dry processing. Print-out materials available for such use are, for example, Du Pont Lino-Writ 5, or Kodak Linagraph Direct Print Papers which are used to record oscillographic traces photographically. The latent image is made visible by a second over-all exposure to light. Jacobs has described a method of heating the exposed paper during this second exposure to light, resulting in the appearance of the image in just under one second. Better trace definition, contrast, and resistance to fading were claimed for this technique compared with those produced by nonheated light exposure. After the image has been printed-out, it can be made permanent in special processing solutions, but this need not be done until a later time. In some cases, these images are dried after fixing without washing. This procedure is widely used in rapid-access processing and has been given the name *stabilization processing*.

Rapid dry development of oscillographic traces has been reported by Stewart, Bornemann, and Kendall, using a photographic paper containing all the necessary devel-

oper chemicals incorporated in the emulsion layer. A visible image results when the paper is heated and moisture is driven from the emulsion layer and paper base. Condensation of this moisture upon the surface of the cool emulsion layer entering the processor initiates development. Complete image formation was obtained at paper-travel rates up to 35 feet per minute. The processed paper, however, will continue to develop and print-out slowly, especially under high humidity. Image degradation can be halted by fixing.

Another rapid-access method involves applying a developer to the film or paper, then drying it rapidly to form the image and stop development. As originally proposed by Levenson, the recording paper was first soaked in the developer, exposed, and then dried on a drum. Flash processing, as commercially adapted by Jacobs, consisted in the application of a very thin layer of developer to the surface of the exposed silver-halide recording paper. The paper was then heated on the back to give rapid development and drying. With a paper-travel speed of 25 inches per second, the Datarite Magazine Processor (Consolidated Electrodynamics Corporation) has an access time of 0.8 second for the developed and dried paper. The processed record is resistant to print-out but needs fixing eventually, if permanent images are needed.

Arrested development was used by Mertz as a method of processing a cathode-ray tube recording film (Ansco Hyscan Recording Film) for airborne processing. A highly concentrated, highly alkaline developer required a minimum time of five seconds at 50 C, and was followed by a one-second, 50 C treatment with an acid stop bath. No fixing was used. The film was then available for viewing on a white backlighted panel.

A quality equal to that of normally processed film was claimed for Hyscan Film when it was treated with a developing-clearing-rinsing cycle that permitted the photographic image to be viewed only eight seconds after exposure.

WRINGER-ROLLER PROCESSING

There are many photographic applications that require complete but rapid processing with no sacrifice in quality or stability of the image. Wringer-roller processors do this by combining film transport and film agitation in roller mechanisms that have opposed or staggered rollers. Russell credits Sherwood with designing the first such unit for processing dental X-ray film. In this unit the film passed through a series of wringer rollers arranged around a large gear wheel which drove the rollers. A sufficient number of units were interconnected to provide the necessary processing cycle.

The wringer-roller transport system was adapted by Russell for rapid processing of X-ray films up to 14 × 17 inches. The commercial version, called the Kodak X-Omat Processor, processes and dries double-coated X-ray films in six minutes, a reduction in processing time of about one hour from the normal procedures. Active solutions are used at 80 F, with the wash water at the same temperature. The high degree of agitation and squeegee action of the rollers provides excellent image uniformity. Drying is accomplished by heated jets of air impinging on the film as it passes between rollers. The success of the drying is largely dependent upon the hardening-stop-bath and fixing-bath formulas which provide mini-

Since the information contained in aerial photographs is usually needed quickly, especially in wartime, various forms of rapid processing are used.

In order to meet deadlines, newspapers frequently use rapid-processing techniques. Often, seconds are so precious that the print will be made from a wet negative. This humorous photo was taken during the presidential campaign of 1956. (Photo: Lewis McLain / Miami Herald)

mum swelling and tackiness of the emulsion layers.

The outstanding advantages of roller-transport processing can be adapted to films other than X-ray. As indicated by Kunz and Russell, the self-threading feature of roller systems should be adaptable to processing lengths of roll film or sheet films, provided film curling and emulsion sticking can be overcome. Processors designed to handle roll or sheet films, such as the Kodak Versamat Processor, have been introduced commercially.

DRUM PROCESSING

For rapid treatment of film or paper, it is often desirable to wet only the emulsion side, as this great- ly simplifies the washing and drying stages. The Lumostat L-25 developing machine, a product of Lumoprint Zindler K. G., West Germany, consists of a 120 revolutions-per-minute rotating drum whose lower section is immersed in a monobath solution. The high rotation speed

of the drum causes a layer of solution to be carried on the surface of the drum. This solution wets the emulsion side of a photocopy paper as it passes over a segment of the drum surface. Because of the high speed of the drum, vigorous agitation occurs at the paper-emulsion surface, resulting in a 20-second processing time.

Multiple-drum processors were studied by Hersh and Smith. Triple-roller applicators, driven opposite to the direction of film travel, were used to apply developer, fixer, and wash water to the surface of the film. This processing technique was said to reduce processing time to one-half that of immersion processing under the same temperature and bath conditions.

Processing times of five seconds with some films and reversal processing in eight seconds were claimed by Barnes and Fortmiller, using a multiple-drum processor with as many as ten drums. Because the 30-feet-per-minute processor was operated at solution temperatures of 120 F, only thin, hardened films, such as Recordak Micro-File Film, Type 7455, and Eastman Television Recording Film, Type 7374, could be used. High temperature was found to be the most important factor in processing for minimum times, the effects of agitation and chemical formulation being relatively minor. No deterioration of quality was claimed for a three-second development of the Micro-File Film compared with a two-minute normal development.

VISCOUS-LAYER APPLICATION OF PROCESSING CHEMICALS

Processing solutions can be thickened by suitable thixotropic agents so that they can be coated on the surface of the photographic material. Such "non-slop" processing is especially desirable for use on shipboard, in airplanes, and in satellites, as well as normal earth-bound uses. Henry described the Fairchild Camera Equipment and Instrument Corporation's EH-33A processing machine which uses the application of a viscous layer. A layer only 0.002-inch thick is applied to the film surface. A thin, transparent Saran film is laid on top of the viscous processing fluid to form a sandwich which can be viewed immediately. The Saran overlay can be stripped away later and the film washed to remove the adhering viscous layer. Applied to Ilford BY Film, a monobath viscous liquid produced a gamma of 1.0 and a maximum density of 2.5 in 60 seconds at 90 F.

In the Eastman Viscomat Processor, Model 10P, a thin layer of a viscous developer is applied to the surface of the film from an extrusion hopper. After development for 2½ to 7 seconds at 125 F, the viscous layer is flushed off with jets of water at 130 F. Viscous fixer is then applied from another hopper. After fixing is complete, a hot-water spray is used to complete the wet processing. One frame of 16 mm film is said to be completely processed in one minute. The processing rate of 36 feet per minute for positive and television-recording films corresponds to 16 mm motion-picture camera speed.

SPRAY PROCESSING

Spray application of processing solutions is widely used in rapid processing, especially in processing motion-picture films. Ives reported that spray techniques could reduce washing time by a factor of 50 by continuous forceful spraying of the entire surface with fresh water. An acceleration by a factor of 100 compared with the rate by conventional drying was attained by using heated air with high velocities.

Townley has described an atomized jet-spray applicator system, controlled by compressed air, called the Kelvin-Hughes Rapid Processing Photographic Projector (35 mm RP3). Development and fixing each require two seconds at 40 C, which provides an access time of only five seconds. Other photographic systems using this jet-spray technique have also been devised.

WEB PROCESSING

For those uses where spillage of solution cannot be permitted, as in airborne processing, impregnating a web of absorbent material with suitable processing chemicals, and bringing it into contact with the exposed photographic film, has several advantages over conventional systems. Schreck has used a fine-fibre paper laminated to a nonabsorbent plastic backing as the chemical carrier. The 35 mm Rapromatic magazine processor, utilizing such a web presaturated with monobath chemicals, is reported to have performed satisfactorily up to

John Rawlings.

simplified technique for obtaining stable images quickly. For producing black-and-white reproductions by this process, the exposed silver halide is developed in a highly solvent solution, and the unexposed and undeveloped silver halide is then solubilized so that it may diffuse or migrate to a superposed receiver sheet. Here, the silver is precipitated on suitable nuclei to form the positive image. This process has been employed in the office-copying field, but its most spectacular application is the ten-second Polaroid black-and-white print and the 50-second Polacolor print.

An excellent review of the diffusion-transfer process has been compiled by Newman, starting with the 1857 work of Lefèvre, who is thought to be the probable inventor of this technique. The basis of most present-day transfer processes, including those of Land and others, was the work of Rott, who, in 1939, patented the essential features of diffusion transfer.

☐

JOHN RAWLINGS
Biography

In photography, the name John Rawlings is synonymous with elegance. His fashion photographs for *Vogue* magazine, his advertising illustrations and, of course, the famous Rawlings nudes have earned him his reputation as one of the world's master photographers.

John Rawlings was born in Marion, Ohio in 1912. He attended Ohio Wesleyan University where he studied fine arts. Later he served an apprenticeship in the hotel business and then came to New York City to study decorating. Several jobs designing displays for well-known department stores followed. While working as decorator for the Hammacher-Schlemmer store in New York he also managed to photograph many of the famous customers who came there. Some of these candid photographs were seen by the late Condé Nast (publisher of *Vogue* and other magazines) who invited him to come for an interview.

At Condé Nast's urging, Rawlings left his job as a decorator to work (for one-quarter the salary) as a prop man in the famous *Vogue*

camera speeds of 80 frames per second. The photographic quality is said to be as good as that for material processed in any other manner under similar limitations.

A somewhat different approach was taken by Tregillus, Rasch, and Wyand. Nonabsorbent carriers, such as cellulose acetate or polyester films, were coated with gelatin or other absorbent layers. The web was then saturated with the necessary processing chemicals and physi-

cal development nuclei, for example, Carey-Lea silver. After saturated web and an exposed photographic-emulsion layer are brought into contact and then stripped apart, a developed negative image is obtained and the nonexposed silver halide has been transferred to the web material.

SILVER-DIFFUSION TRANSFER

The formation of positive images by diffusion transfer represents a studio. While there, he had the opportunity to work with many of the great photographers of the day, including Hoyningen-Heune, Cecil Beaton, and Edward Steichen.

After six months with Condé Nast, his career took a major step forward when he was sent to London to build a new studio for the English *Vogue* and to be head photographer there. For five years Rawlings worked in the London and Paris studios of *Vogue,* shooting travel pictures, portraits, fashion, and anything else that the magazine required. When the war broke out, he returned to the United States, and in 1945 opened his own studio in New York City.

Perhaps because he had worked for so many years in studios in which photographers used multitudes of lights, Rawlings' own concept of a studio was in complete rebellion against this idea. His was a "daylight studio." Located on the top floor of a New York office building on East 55th Street, it had an immense skylight and white-tiled walls to reflect the light. While in the earliest days of photography pictures were taken by natural light, there had been a long period in which artificial lighting was the rule. Rawlings, in a sense, had rediscovered the beauty and simplicity of natural studio lighting.

Although Rawlings has since moved to a more elaborate studio, the bulk of his pictures are shot on location and by natural light. He comments, "To me, the natural light of the sun, whether brilliant or overcast, direct or reflected, is preferable for all photographs."

Even perhaps more than on his

John Rawlings.

mmercial and fashion work Rawlings' fame in the photographic world is based on his superb photographs of the nude. His first book on the subject *100 Studies of the Figure* has become a classic in the field and he still continues to work on this type of photography in his spare time. Of his work in this area he has written, "It was, of couse, inevitable that photographers should try the figure—and for the same reasons that had always made the subject so attractive to painters. Here was human grace in all its infinite variety. In a nude photograph, the props are secondary. Interest doesn't depend on clothes or background, but on body and facial expression.

"Because of these rigid limitations, the subject offers the photographer a wonderful chance to come to grips with the essentials of his craft. Most professional photographers have one field which is considered their specialty (my own happens to be fashion photography). Working with the nude offers an escape from the rut of specialization; at the same time, it brings the sort of knowledge which is invaluable in solving any photographic problem."

Rawlings is one of the few photographers who has been able to do equally outstanding work in both black-and-white and color. In either he feels that what is of ultimate importance is not how literal the picture is, but what is expressed by it. Of his color work he says, "Too often we photographers try to achieve a red or blue which is the 'real' red or blue. In this we act as though there were a whole set of proper colors put away in some official bureau of standards, which have to be followed as rigidly as the butcher's scale follows the official definition of the pound. But fortunately photographers don't have to be such literal tradesmen. We are free to use hundreds of different reds and blues and the camera lens is waiting to discover them for us. It is only up to us to make the most as artists of this miraculous third eye which science has given us." It is this constant desire to discover the unique way in which the medium can express his message which gives a characteristic freshness and originality to Rawlings work.

In addition to his editorial work for such publications as *Vogue* and *McCalls,* Rawlings has done advertising photography for General Motors, Dupont, and almost every major cosmetic manufacturer in the United States including Revlon, Max Factor, Tussy, and DuBarry.

His wife, Babs, also has a wide knowledge of the fashion field, having been employed as a fashion editor by Condé Nast Publications in Paris, London, and New York. The Rawlings share a passionate interest in theater and opera and are collectors of fine books on costume through the ages.

John Rawlings is an active member of the American Society of Magazine Photographers and in 1949 served as president of the Society of Photographic Illustrators. In addition to his editorial and advertising work, he serves as a visual consultant on many television commercials and is preparing a new book of photographs of the nude.

—Charles R. Reynolds, Jr.

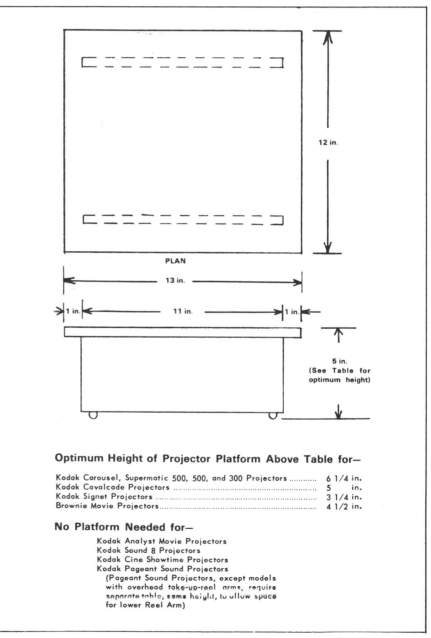

Optimum Height of Projector Platform Above Table for—

Kodak Carousel, Supermatic 500, 500, and 300 Projectors	6 1/4 in.
Kodak Cavalcade Projectors	5 in.
Kodak Signet Projectors	3 1/4 in.
Brownie Movie Projectors	4 1/2 in.

No Platform Needed for—

Kodak Analyst Movie Projectors
Kodak Sound 8 Projectors
Kodak Cine Showtime Projectors
Kodak Pageant Sound Projectors
   (Pageant Sound Projectors, except models with overhead take-up-reel arms, require separate table, same height, to allow space for lower Reel Arm)

Platform for single-mirror cabinet.

The single-mirror cabinet used for rear projection.

REAR-PROJECTION TECHNIQUES

[This article gives a thorough analysis of rear-projection techniques. Also discussed is the construction and operation of the single- and triple-mirror projection cabinets.]
• *Also see: Backgrounds, Painted and Photographic; Projectors and Projection for Still Pictures; Projection Screens.*

REAR PROJECTION ON TRANSLUCENT screens is often a good way of presenting either slides or motion pictures. Because of the high efficiency of the translucent screen, it

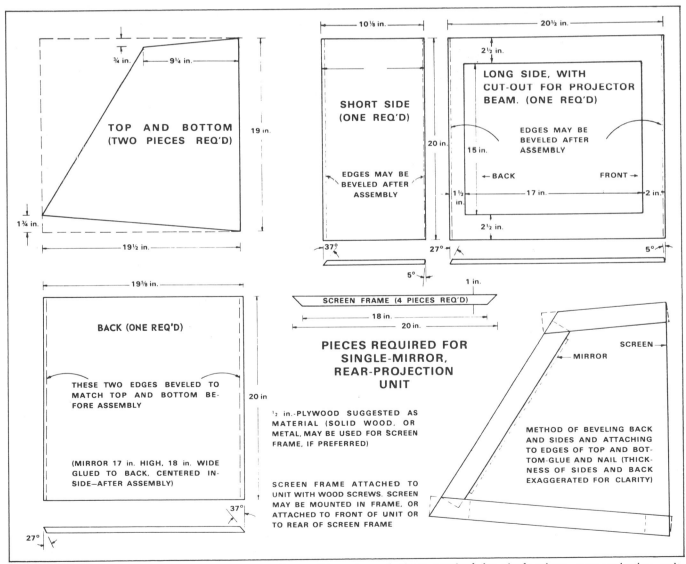

Above: *Dimensions of pieces required for single-mirror, rear-projection unit.*

of motion-picture film, or with special and modified projectors. Other cabinets can be used with a variety of projectors.

This article contains plans for building two rear-projection cabinets. One is a single-mirror, general-purpose unit that can be used with a variety of projectors. The other is a more specialized, three-mirror unit designed primarily for the Kodak Carousel Projector, Model 550. Either unit can be built in almost any woodworking shop, and construction is simple. Both cabinets provide an 18×18-inch image area. Both can be used on table, desk, or counter top.

The single-mirror cabinet can be inverted, so the projector can be located on either side. This kind of cabinet is convenient when the projector is in a corner location, with its beam paralleling a wall. A slide, filmstrip, or motion-picture projector can be used. The single-mirror cabinet is an appropriate unit to use when providing programmed (self-directed), instructional A-V materials for individual students.

For screen-filling images, moderately short focal-length projection lenses will give a compact arrangement when the projector is near the cabinet. Lenses of standard focal length (four or five inches for 2×2-inch slides; two inches for 16 mm; three-quarters or one inch for 8 mm) require slightly more space between the cabinet and projector if the

The three-mirror cabinet can be used with the Kodak Carousel projector equipped with a four-inch lens. 81 slides can be projected continuously.

is not necessary to have the room completely dark for adequate projection.

For successful use of a rear-projection screen, the space behind the screen must be dark; otherwise the contrast of the projected image will be lessened. In addition, it is often difficult to secure sufficient projection distance unless mirrors are used. The best way to solve both problems is to build the screen, and often the projector as well, into a cabinet which provides the necessary darkening for the rear of the screen, and houses the mirrors

required to increase the projection throw.

Usually an odd number of mirrors is used as this avoids the necessity of laterally inverting the slide in the projector. It is especially important to use an odd number of mirrors in the case of sound films; since the film has perforations on one edge only, it cannot be reversed in the projector. This rule also applies to projectors using 8 mm film.

Excellent commercial rear-projection cabinets are available. Some are special-purpose units for use with repeating projectors, with magazines

Position of slides for proper projection when used in the three-mirror cabinet. Note that slide is right-side-up and right-way-around when viewed from the rear of the projector.

screen is to be filled. Slides or filmstrips being projected in this unit are oriented just the way they are projected on a regular reflection-type screen.

An auxiliary platform is suggested for use with low-profile projectors.

The three-mirror cabinet is designed primarily for use with the Kodak Carousel Projector, Model 550, equipped with a four-inch lens. The Kodak Projection Ektanar Lens, four-inch, $f/3.5$, can be supplied with the Carousel Projector on special order, or can be purchased separately. The Kodak Projection Zoom Lens, 3¾- to 6¼-inch, $f/3.5$, can also be used.

This cabinet is useful for exhibit, display, or other purposes for which a standard set of up to 81 slides must be used, whether continuously or at intervals. It provides equipment protection and security in exhibit and display used, and also keeps the mechanics of projection from being visible. The screen extends to the front of the cabinet body, so the cabinet can be concealed in a wall or behind an exhibit background.

The space above the screen can be used for a printed message or for a small loudspeaker. A tape recorder with the Kodak Cavalcade Programmer can be used with either projector to add synchronized sound to a visual presentation.

There is provision for obtaining 18-inch images from any one of the four common sizes of 2×2-inch slide masks. This is achieved by providing three locations for the rear mirror. Changing the position of the mirror changes the length of the projection beam without having to move either the screen or the projector. A single-mirror position suffices. If the Kodak Projection Zoom Lens is used.

MATERIALS AND CONSTRUCTION NOTES

Screens

Suitable screen materials (flexible plastics, rigid plastics, or glass-supported screen surfaces) are available from a number of manufacturers. A dark screen material will enhance image contrast and color saturation if the cabinets are to be used in a lighted room. Here are

a few sources of supply: Eastman Kodak Company, Special Sensitized Goods Division, 343 State Street, Rochester 4, New York; Polacoat, Inc., 9750 Conklin Road, Blue Ash, Ohio; Bodde Screen and Projector Company, 11541 Bradley, San Fernando, California; Edmund Scientific Corporation, 101 East Gloucester Pike, Barrington, New Jersey; Commercial Picture Equipment, Inc., 5137 North Broadway, Chicago 41, Illinois; Raven Screen

Corporation, 124 East 124th Street, New York 35, New York; Trans-Lux Corporation, 625 Madison Avenue, New York, New York; Da-Lite Screen Company, Inc., Warsaw, Indiana; Stewart-Trans-Lux Corporation, 1161 West Sepulveda, Torrance, California.

Many materials for rear-projection screens are matte on one side and glossy on the other. If the cabinet is used in a lighted area, placing the matte side toward the

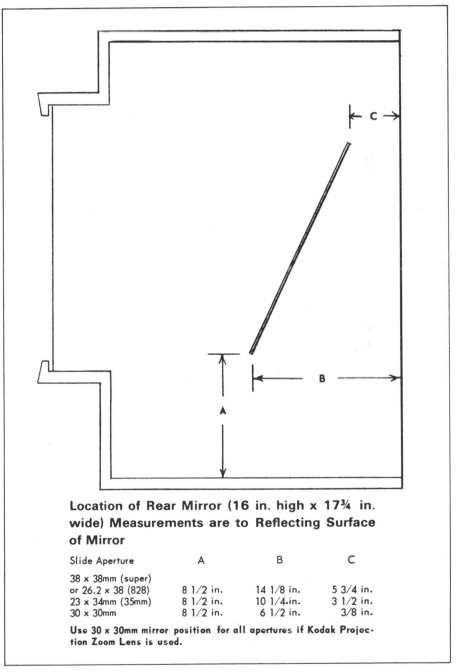

Location of Rear Mirror (16 in. high x 17¾ in. wide) Measurements are to Reflecting Surface of Mirror

Slide Aperture	A	B	C
38 x 38mm (super) or 26.2 x 38 (828)	8 1/2 in.	14 1/8 in.	5 3/4 in.
23 x 34mm (35mm)	8 1/2 in.	10 1/4 in.	3 1/2 in.
30 x 30mm	8 1/2 in.	6 1/2 in.	3/8 in.

Use 30 x 30mm mirror position for all apertures if Kodak Projection Zoom Lens is used.

Side elevation of the three-mirror cabinet.

3160 / REAR-PROJECTION TECHNIQUES

viewer will make any specular reflections from bright objects in the room less evident. Makeshift screen materials, such as, ground glass, cloth, and matte acetate seldom give good results.

Three different types of screens are available. Type I is white and transmits twice as much light at a viewing angle of three degrees as ground glass, under the same conditions. Type IV is rather black, which improves image contrast substantially at high ambient-light levels. Type IVR is green in color, which is restful to the eyes in applications where continuous viewing over long periods is required. Kodak Day View Screens are available in all three types in sizes up to 30 × 40 inches.

The screen material can be mounted in wood or metal frames, which in turn can be attached to the cabinets or inserted into suitable grooves. Aluminum-frame channels and corners provide a simple means of making frames for both flexible and rigid screens.

Mirrors

Mirrors of good-quality glass are suggested for the single-mirror cabinet and for the two large mirrors in the three-mirror cabinet. Mirrors that reflect a good visual image, relatively free from waviness, will be satisfactory. The mirrors should be unmounted so that they can be held by edge clips, or mounted with a contact adhesive directly to the supporting plywood or chip-board mounts of the cabinets.

Rear-surface (regular) mirrors will produce slight secondary images on the screen. These are seldom objectionable (and often not noticed), except when projected material consists of white lines, white lettering, or specular highlights against a dark background.

The alternative to rear-surface mirrors is front-surface mirrors. These eliminate the secondary images but are much more expensive and more easily damaged in service.

A high-quality, rear-surface mirror can be used for the small mirror in the three-mirror cabinet, but a good-quality, front-surface mirror is preferable. Because of its proximity to the projector lens, the image-quality advantage with a front-surface mirror is greater here. Its relatively small size keeps the cost low.

Small front-surface mirrors can sometimes be found at local optical-supply houses or at mirror and glass suppliers, or they can be ordered from optical suppliers.

Materials for the Cabinets

The dimensions given in the drawings are based on the use of ½-inch plywood for the single-mirror unit and ¾-inch plywood for the body of the three-mirror

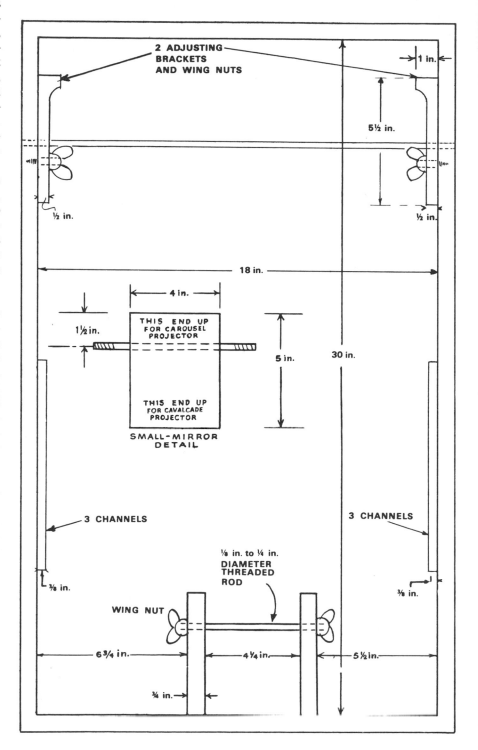

Rear elevation of three-mirror cabinet.

cabinet. Materials of other thicknesses will require minor modifications in dimensions to preserve the inside dimensions of the cabinets. Chip board ½-inch thick is suggested for mounting the mirrors in the three-mirror cabinet. The interior of the cabinets should be finished in matte (dull) black to subdue internal reflections. Rubber feet can be added to protect table surfaces.

ADJUSTMENT AND USE

Single-Mirror Cabinet

The projector lens should be approximately the height of the center of the screen (ten inches above table surface) and should be aimed through the side aperture to the

Side elevation of the three-mirror cabinet showing positions of the mirrors.

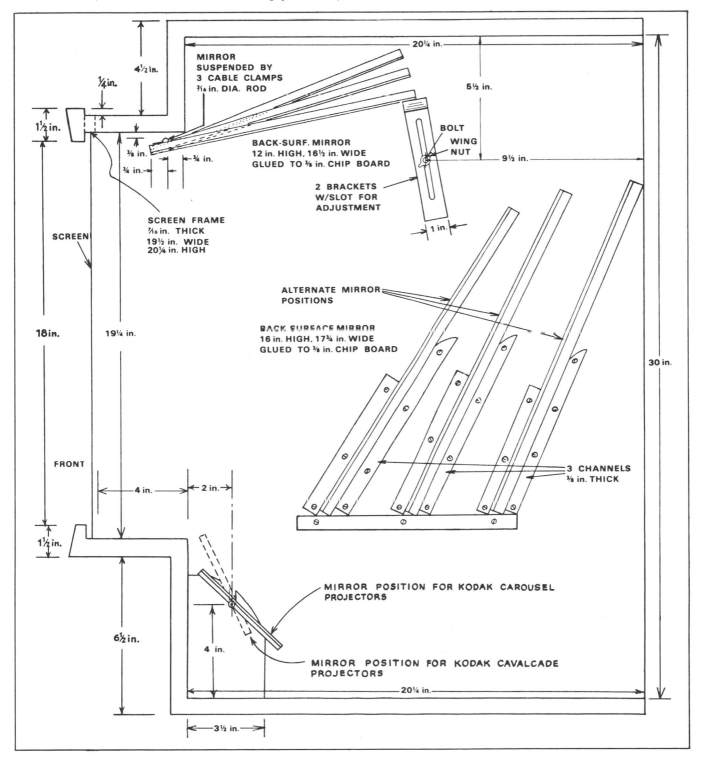

This Bolex titling stand can be used for rear projection and front illumination when making titles.

mirror. Move the projector from side to side or up and down, or realign the cabinet, until the edges of the image match the sides of the screen. If the projector is too far off-center, the image will be objectionably askew.

Three-Mirror Cabinet

Place the back mirror in the position required for the size of transparency mask to be used. When this cabinet is used, slides must be oriented in a particular way. Each one should be inserted into the slide tray so that the bottom of the transparency image is toward the bottom of the tray. Place tray in projector, and projector in cabinet, with the lens directly behind the small mirror. Turn the elevation knob full counterclockwise (no elevation) and the leveling knob to level position.

Swivel the small mirror until the projector beam centers on the top mirror, and then tighten the small mirror. A piece of paper held against the top mirror will help make the beam visible. Finally, tilt the top mirror until the image is centered in the screen.

Touch-up adjustments can be made by a slight repositioning of the projector (the leveling knob being used if the image is angled) and by a slight readjustment of the mirrors if necessary. If the image is too large or small some adjustment can be made by moving the projector a short distance forward or back, or by readjusting the mirrors. If the image is too small, tilt the smallest mirror so that the beam falls toward the front of the top mirror. If the image is too large, tilt the small mirror so that the beam falls toward the back of the top mirror. Then readjust the top mirror to center the image vertically.

Mark the projector position on the cabinet bottom to simplify realignment after the projector is moved for changing slide trays or cleaning mirrors. Small blocks of wood can be attached to the cabinet floor to position the projector positively.

The back of the cabinet is open for ventilation. The cabinet should not be placed against a wall or other surface which will restrict air flow. Hardware cloth, an open metal grill, or another grid that will not unduly restrict air flow can be used over the back of the cabinet. If the cabinet is used in areas where dust and dirt are problems the back can be closed, but an auxiliary blower will be needed for forced ventilation. There should be an air outlet near the top of the cabinet. An intake at the bottom can be covered with a furnace-type air filter. An exhaust fan or blower at the top or an intake fan or blower at the bottom will provide air circulation. If power ventilation is used, the screen should be of rigid material so that it will not bulge in or out.

A 90-degree "ell" of downspout pipe can be used to duct exhaust air from the front of the Carousel Projector, either through the floor of the cabinet or to the side. This is not necessary, but will slow air movements within the cabinet and reduce dust problems in some locations. (Most of the text and illustrations used with permission from the copyrighted Kodak pamphlet, T-47, on this subject.)

NIGHT WORKERS   CLYDE HARE

A diagonal shaft of light with strong interior shadows gives this photograph of oilmen at St. Mary's, Virginia, its dynamic composition, while the dramatically backlighted figures of the men and their long black shadows serve to define the visual center of interest. The tension of the composition is further heightened by the large imprisoning areas of black in the lower-left and upper-right segments of the picture.

RECIPROCITY LAW AND EXPOSURE

Exposure in photography is defined as the product of light intensity and time. Thus, $1/25$ of a second at $f/11$, $1/50$ of a second at $f/8$, and $1/100$ of a second at $f/5.6$ are all considered the same exposure, for, as the time is halved, the aperture (or, in effect, the light intensity) is doubled. The reciprocity law states that equal exposures affect a film equally.

Photographers have long taken this rule for granted, since it holds true for the general run of exposures. However it breaks down seriously at the extremes of the exposure scale—at speeds shorter than $1/1000$ of a second in very bright light and longer than five seconds in dim light. The reasons for the failure of the reciprocity law are obscure and the phenomenon will probably not be fully explained until science knows more than it does about the chemistry and physics of latent-image formation.

Through a process of trial and error it has been found that the calculated exposures must be doubled or even tripled with very fast shutter speeds, or with those types of electronic flash working at $1/20,000$ of a second and faster. The calculated exposure must also be increased considerably for long time exposures. In astronomical photography, where exposures run into hours, reciprocity failure is a very serious problem indeed, and effective-exposure indexes are a great deal lower than the ASA ratings of the film.

It is interesting to note that at both extremes the effect of the reciprocity failure is an apparent loss of film speed. The extent of speed loss differs with different emulsions and no general rule can be given. Required exposure compensation for reciprocity failure must be found by experiment for each emulsion. Often the film manufacturer's consumer-service department can supply this information on request.

Reciprocity Failure With Color Films

Since reciprocity failure varies with different emulsions, it can be expected to have a particularly marked effect on color films where the coating consists of three differently sensitized emulsion layers. Reciprocity failure changes not only the effective speed of the film, but also its color balance, since the three layers will not necessarily be affected to the same extent. Thus, for very short or very long exposures on color film it may be necessary not only to give additional exposure, but also to use color-compensating filters to correct the shift in color balance due to the different speeds of the different layers at these exposure times.

It is not possible to specify a given correction for all color films, since all are different in this respect, but the manufacturer can sometimes make recommendations for a given filter set for a known exposure level. A special case in point is to be found in the two types of Ektacolor Sheet Film, which instead of being named by their color balance, are specified as Type L (long exposure) and Type S (short exposure).

The Type L film is balanced for tungsten illumination and the speeds of the layers are adjusted for reciprocity balance at exposures ranging from $1/5$ of a second to 60 seconds. Even over this range, the exposure index varies from 25 for $1/5$ of a second exposures to 10 for 60-second exposures. This means that for exposures approaching 60 seconds, $2\frac{1}{2}$ times the calculated exposure must be given, if the normal speed is considered as 25. For exposures shorter than $1/5$ of a second or longer than 60 seconds the film cannot be used because layer speeds and contrasts both change to such an extent that it cannot be corrected either by filters or variations in printing.

Type S film is balanced for daylight at exposure levels of $1/10$ of a second or shorter; again, it cannot be used for time exposures longer than $1/10$ of a second because the color balance will change to a point where it cannot be corrected in printing. Thus, while the film can be used with tungsten light and the proper light-balancing filter, this is only possible if enough light is available for exposures shorter than $1/10$ of a second.

RECORDING PHOTOGRAPHY

The use of photography as a recording medium in industry is a specialty field that is growing in importance.

The earliest practical application of recording photography involved the use of a simple camera to read large groups of meters such as telephone-message recorders. These messager recorders consist of small counters, arranged on panels in rows, and they keep track of the number of calls made from each telephone. The task of reading thousands of these counters each month for billing purposes was simplified by photographing groups of meters with a simple fixed-focus camera. The negatives are then sent to the billing department, where the data is entered directly on the bills.

The first camera used for this purpose was a modification of the fingerprint camera; a simple fixed-focus, $2\frac{1}{4} \times 3\frac{1}{4}$ device with built-in lighting. The modified camera was known as the Factograph and since a full-size image was not necessary the camera was designed to cover a larger group of meters at each exposure.

Later, recording photography was applied to the reading of aircraft instruments. Today most test aircraft are fitted with cameras focused on the instrument panel. These cameras are operated by an intervalometer which trips the shutter at preset intervals and each picture shows the readings of all the instruments on the panel.

Many other uses for instrument-recording cameras are readily apparent. Today cameras are used for data collection in many scientific and engineering projects and business systems.

In any new project of this sort, there are several factors to be considered. The basic factors are described here as well as a complete system which will serve to explain just how the whole method is thought out.

CAMERA

The cameras needed for recording work vary depending on the job in question.

The size of the image to be

Robot 24 Recorder with transformer rectifier and automatic timer.

recorded is the first problem. If the panel to be covered is relatively small and the meters few, the desired information may be gathered on 16 mm movie film, using any type of movie camera that can be focused at the desired distance and operated either at very slow speeds or one frame at a time. Many recording systems using 16 mm film have been built around Army-surplus GSAP cameras which hold 50 feet of 16 mm film, are electrically operated from 24-volt d-c circuits, and are easily modified for single-frame exposures.

For larger areas, single-frame 35 mm cameras can be used. If the period of interest is short and can be covered with about 25 to 35 pictures, a ready-made camera like the Robot is adaptable. The old DeBrie Sept Camera which held 16½ feet (five meters) of 35 mm film, made 250 single-frame exposures on a roll. It operated at single-frame settings and its spring motor could expose the entire 250 pictures at one winding.

If longer runs are needed, the

35 mm movie camera, such as the Bell & Howell Eyemo or the DeVry newsreel camera, can be adapted. Since the spring motors of these cameras are not adequate to run the entire length of a 100-foot roll, they are usually replaced by an intermittent electrical drive or the

unit is attended and rewound at intervals.

The Graflex Photorecord camera, no longer manufactured, is also adaptable to this work. It has the advantage that its film transport can be easily shifted from single-frame 35 mm (¾ × 1 inch) to double

Right: The automatic-recording camera is invaluable for recording meters, counters, and similar changing subjects. Here is an example of meter numbers recorded by a Robot camera.

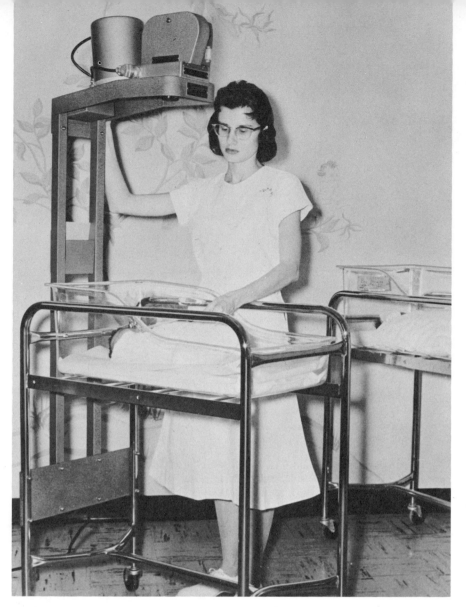

The Beattie-Coleman Nursery recording camera for photographing newborn babies in hospitals.

single frame 35 mm film. This, then, established the image size.

SELECTING A CAMERA

The desired picture interval was five minutes, that is, 12 pictures per hour or 288 per day. The unit had to operate unattended, but could be reached once a week for checking, so that established a total of $7 \times 288 = 2016$ pictures. Since 100 feet of 35 mm film will hold only 1600 pictures, some revision was necessary at this point and it was decided to have the unit attended every five days instead of once a week. This meant that the total number of pictures would be 1440 per roll and left some leeway on a 100-foot roll if the attendant should be late in arrival.

Thus, a 35 mm movie camera with 100-foot film capacity was to be used. The spring motor was removed from a DeVry newsreel camera and replaced with a rotary solenoid, which turned the camera one frame at each current impulse. A contact wheel was built into the camera, which made a quick contact at the shutter-open position. The purpose of this modification will be seen later.

DESIGNING A TIMER

Next, it was necessary to know not only the total readings of all the dials, but exactly when each picture was taken. For this purpose a clock was placed on the panel, so it would be photographed on the same frame as the meter dials. This was a specially built clock which showed the time of day, a.m. or p.m., and the date and day of the week. The clock was spring-wound, with an eight-day movement and the spring was wound by the attendant each time the camera was reloaded.

In addition to its indicating feature, the clock contained several sets of contacts. One set was arranged to "make" every five minutes; this tripped the rotary solenoid on the camera. A second set of contacts was designed to "make" once every

($1 \times 1\frac{1}{2}$ inches) simply by changing the aperture mask and shifting a lever.

When a still larger format is required, there are cameras using 70 mm film, such as the Beattie Portronic. There are also available a variety of specially built 70 mm cameras which are supplied in various modifications by the manufacturer for the exact job intended.

Sometimes a really large picture is required and the one way to solve this problem is to adapt an Army-surplus aerial camera. The old K-24 camera, for instance, made negatives $4\frac{1}{2} \times 4\frac{1}{2}$ inches on a roll of film sufficient for 180 pictures.

DESIGN OF A PHOTOGRAPHIC-RECORDING SYSTEM

There is more to making a photorecording system than merely setting up a camera to photograph a panel full of dials. The complexity of the system depends on a number of factors, such as how often the pictures are to be taken, how the data is to be used, and what supplementary information is required.

One such system, built a few years ago, exemplifies nearly all the problems in one single case, and a schematic description of it will outline the type of thinking necessary to meet such a design problem.

The basic problem was to photograph a bank of 24 counters, each starting from zero at a given time and progressing irregularly to various numbers. The 24 counters had figures about one fourth of an inch high, and were mounted quite close together; a preliminary picture made of the entire panel showed that the numbers would be adequately legible in a microfilm reader if the panel were photographed on hour; its purpose was to reset all the counters on the panel to zero, so the count progressed from zero during the hour and started over again at each subsequent hour.

Next, some safety devices were needed. First, the matter of illumination had to be solved, and it was decided that the best and most convenient light source for the battery-operated outfit was a strobe light. This was triggered by the contact

that was built into the camera shutter.

A photocell relay was mounted on the panel to be photographed and another counter added. Each time the camera light flashed, the photocell trigger operated and advanced the counted one number. This counter was placed just under the clock. It was also photographed on the film and provided an automatic way of numbering each negative.

This photocell trigger had a second job. It was connected to the

"make-each-hour" contact of the clock in such a way that if a picture was missed at any time during the hour, the clock contacts would not reset the panel dials but would permit them to continue counting during the following hour. This prevented the loss of data if a picture was missed due to failure of the strobe light.

SUMMARY

Thus a system was designed which photographed the necessary data and the time-of-day and date

Examples of Robot oscilloscope recordings that can be made at fixed time intervals.

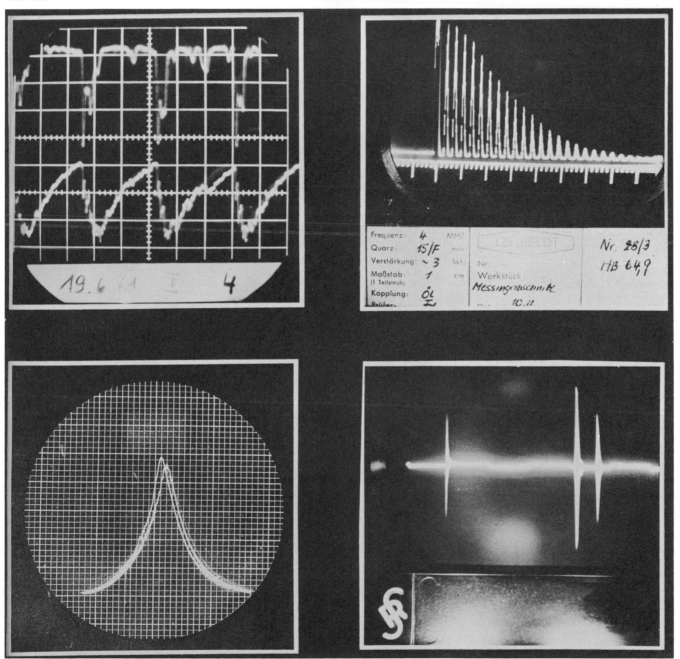

Above: *Robot Electro-Automatic recording system Recorder 24-e. A hinged tube with observation window and built-in light attaches to the Robot camera and to the oscilloscope, offering simultaneous-screen photography.*

Below: *Beattie-Coleman Hi-Speed Oscillotron Recording System. This is a dual recording system using Polaroid roll film and 35 mm film. The Polaroid camera permits the making of a test exposure before making the run on 35 mm film.*

information needed to interpret it. In addition, it kept a running record of the number of pictures taken and numbered each negative in sequence.

Finally, failure to take a picture would not result in the loss of all data. Only failure of the entire camera circuit could do this, and even then, the service man could still obtain the grand-total figures from the dials, for they continued to accumulate the information even if no pictures were taken.

Almost any data-recording system that has to be established will require one or more of the above factors. There are, of course, differences from one case to another —where electric power is available, electric clocks or electronic timers can be used in place of the spring-wound clock. If the camera runs steadily and no strobe light is used, it may be possible to omit the safety device, or the device may not be necessary where the loss of an occasional picture will be unimportant.

It should be understood that recording photography is more than just taking pictures of a set of dials or gauges. Usually it involves the engineering of an entire system to assure that all the required data will be obtained, and that none will be lost.

The color photographs appearing on the following eight pages were all reproduced from original Polacolor prints. *Courtesy the Polaroid Corporation.*

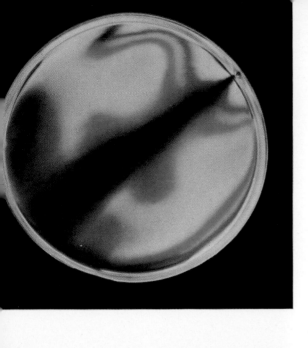

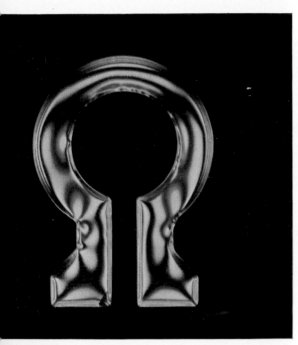

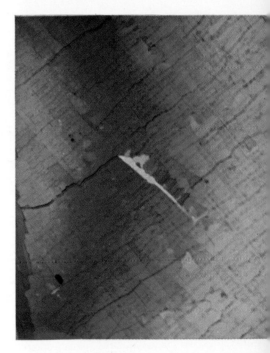

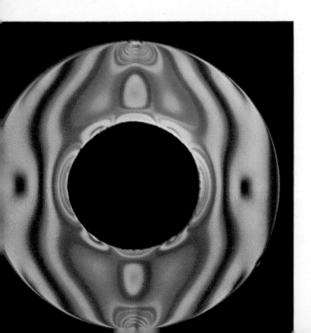

REDUCTION AND REDUCERS

ROBERT TAFT, PH. D.
Author "Photography and the American Scene"
[Reducers are often used on negatives when fog is to be removed, contrast improved, or generally whenever part of the silver deposit is to be removed. The three major types of reducers, subtractive, proportional, and superproportional, are covered, with formulas given for each. Local reduction and reduction of prints are also discussed.]
• *Also see: Chemistry of Photography; Intensification; Retouching Negatives and Prints.*

ANY PROCESS THAT REMOVES SOME of the image from a negative or print is called reduction. The reduction may be mechanical, that is, some of the image may be rubbed off by the use of a suitable abrasive, or, as is most frequently the case, effected by chemical means. Chemically, photographic reduction consists of the conversion of some of the black silver image into a silver compound and then dissolving the silver compound.

Reduction may be desirable for a variety of reasons—where overexposure or overdevelopment has produced too dense a deposit; to improve the photographic contrasts by increasing or decreasing them; to remove traces of fog; to prepare line illustrations.

Cutting or Subtractive Reducers

With an overexposed negative in which the light contrasts are small to begin with, the resulting negative will have densities in both highlight and shadow that tend to approach each other. This negative will not only be dense but flat as well. If a reducer which removes a larger proportion of the silver deposit in the shadows than in the highlights is used, printing quality will be improved considerably. Such reducers, which remove a larger proportion of silver from less dense areas of the image (actually the *total* reduction is the same at all densities in such reducers), are called cutting or subtractive reducers.

Superproportional Reducer

If a correctly exposed negative of a contrasty subject is overdeveloped, the negative can be improved if a reducer is used that removes a larger fraction of the silver deposit from the areas corresponding to highlights of the subject (the darkest areas of the negative and therefore those containing the most silver) than from the shadows. Such a process reduces the contrasts of the original negative and the solution producing the change is called a superproportional reducer.

Proportional Reducers

If a correctly exposed negative of an ordinary subject is overdeveloped, the error calls for a reducer that will remove an equal fraction of silver from all areas of the negative, thus decreasing the contrasts of the negative. Such reducers are called proportional reducers.

A negative that is to be subjected to chemical treatment subsequent to its initial development and fixation should be hardened to prevent softening and frilling of the gelatin. A suitable hardening bath has the formula:

Formalin (37 percent formaldehyde solution)
2½ drams (10 cc)
Sodium carbonate, desiccated
73 grains (5 grams)
Water to make
32 ounces (1 liter)

The negative is placed in this bath for three minutes, then in a fresh acid-fixing bath, and finally washed thoroughly in water before reduction.

SUBTRACTIVE REDUCERS

Farmer's Reducer

This process, originated by Howard Farmer, is one of the most extensively used of all reducing procedures. Variation of the formula produces variation in its rate of action and, to some extent, in its effects. The action of the reducer consists of converting the original silver in the image to silver ferrocyanide and the subsequent solution of this compound by the familiar hypo solution. Prepared chemicals for this reducer are also available. Since the materials necessary to produce these effects do not keep well together, two stock solutions are necessary:

Solution A
Potassium ferricyanide
2½ ounces (80 grams)
Water to make
32 ounces (1 liter)
Solution B
Sodium thiosulfate (hypo)
10 ounces (300 grams)
Water to make
32 ounces (1 liter)

In use, one part of *A* is mixed with three parts of *B* and 30 parts of water.

The negative is immersed in the mixture and carefully watched. Reduction in a shallow white tray facilitates inspection and is carried out until the desired density is obtained (one to five minutes). Since reduction continues after the negative is removed from the bath, allowance should be made for the continued reduction. After removal from the reducing bath, the negative is thoroughly washed. If sufficient reduction has not been secured, the process may be repeated, but a fresh bath should be used. Farmer's reducer should be discarded as soon as the negative is removed from the bath.

Although Farmer's reducer contains hypo, it is essential that the original negative to be reduced be thoroughly washed before the reduction is begun. This reducer may be used, however, with somewhat less washing than is the case with practically all other reducers, where the last traces of fixing bath must be completely removed before reduction begins.

Belitzki's Reducer

This subtractive reducer is made as a single solution, keeps well in the dark, and may be re-used.
Ferric chloride (crystals)
96 grains (6.5 grams)
Potassium oxalate
186 grains (12.5 grams)
Sodium sulfite
59 grains (4 grams)
Water to make
7 ounces (200 cc)
After the above ingredients have completely dissolved, add:
Oxalic acid (crystals)
44.5 grains (3 grams)
The mixture is shaken until it

turns green, allowed to settle, and the clear liquid poured off. To this clear liquid add:

Sodium thiosulfate

$1^3/_4$ ounce (50 grams)

When solution is complete, the reducer is ready for use. Immerse the negative in the mixture until the desired reduction is obtained and then wash well.

Haddon's Reducer

Another single-solution reducer of the subtractive type is made as follows:

Potassium ferricyanide

22 grains (5 grams)

Ammonium thiocyanate

44 grains (10 grams)

Water to make

10 ounces (1 liter)

As in previous cases, reduction is judged by the eye; when reduction has been completed, thorough washing is necessary. If deposition of a white substance on the negative occurs during reduction, it can be removed by bathing the negative in an ordinary fixing bath.

Permanganate Reducer

Almost as extensively used as Farmer's reducer, the permanganate reducer tends toward being a proportional reducer, rather than a strictly subtractive one. It is a very useful reducer for most images showing slightly heavy densities. It is also used for reducing heavy prints.

Solution A

Potassium permanganate

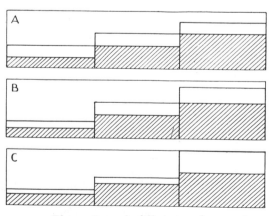

The action of different reducers gives varying results. The shaded area represents the silvers deposit; the blocks above represent the removed silver. A, subtractive; B, proportional; C, superproportional.

$1^3/_4$ ounce (2 grams)

Water to make

32 ounces (1 liter)

Solution B

Sulfuric acid (conc.)

1 ounce (10 cc)

Water to make

32 ounces (1 liter)

Great care should be used in preparing Solution B. The sulfuric acid should be measured out in a perfectly dry graduate and added very slowly, a drop at a time, to the water. The solution becomes very warm and if the acid is added rapidly, solution may take place with explosive violence. When this solution becomes cool, mix equal volumes of *A* and *B* for use. The stock solutions should be kept separately, as they do not keep well when mixed.

After the desired reduction, the negative is removed from the bath and washed in either a plain hypo, a fresh acid fixing bath, or in a five-percent sodium-bisulfite solution to remove the brown stain left by the permanganate solution. The negative is then washed in water.

Iodine-Cyanide Reducer

An exceedingly valuable and clean-working reducer of the subtractive type is made from a solution containing iodine and potassium cyanide. Like all solutions containing cyanide, great care must be exercised in the use of such materials because of their poisonous character. Direct contact with the reducer should be avoided (the use of rubber gloves is highly desirable), and the hands, trays, and graduates employed in its use must be thoroughly washed after the process has been completed. Solutions containing cyanide, when discarded, should be washed down the drain by the use of liberal quantities of water, special care being taken that no acid is present.

The iodine-cyanide reducer is mixed as follows:

Solution A

Potassium iodide

150 grains (10 grams)

Iodine

45 grains (3 grams)

Water

1 fluid ounce (30 cc)

Solution B

Potassium cyanide

1 ounce (10 grams)

Water

10 ounces (100 cc)

The reducer may be kept in stock as these two solutions. For use, mix as follows:

Solution A   30 minims (6 cc)
Solution B   5 minims (1 cc)
Water to make   1 ounce (100 cc)

As the mixture does not keep well, it should be discarded after use.

PROPORTIONAL REDUCERS

Both Farmer's reducer and the permanganate reducer can, by altering their proportions, be used to remove an equal fraction of the silver image from both highlights and shadows, and under these conditions are proportional reducers.

Proportional Farmer's Reducer

In this use, Farmer's reducer is a two-step process, as this process permits greater control of the reduction than in a single-solution process. For the two-step process use the solutions listed below.

Solution A

Potassium ferricyanide

1 ounce (7.5 grams)

Water to make

1 gallon (1 liter)

Solution B

Sodium thiosulfate

27 ounces (200 grams)

Water to make

1 gallon (1 liter)

Negatives are immersed in Solution A from one to four minutes (depending upon the reduction desired) and then in Solution B for several minutes. After treatment, the negative is well washed.

Proportional Permanganate Reducer

If acetic acid is substituted for sulfuric acid in the permanganate formula given above, proportional action is very nearly obtained. The reduction is otherwise carried out in exactly the same manner as already described.

Ferric-Sulfate Reducer

This reducer is of the proportional type. The negative to be treated should be completely free of hypo and silver salts. Since softening of the gelatin is produced by its use, hardening of the negative in a formalin bath is necessary. Still another disadvantage of the process is that staining will occur if the negative comes in contact with air during reduction. The reducer is slow in its action, from five to eight minutes being required. It is prepared as follows:

Ferric ammonium sulfate (crystals)
0.5 ounce (15 grams)
Sulfuric acid (conc.)
0.3 ounce (10 cc)
Water to make
32 ounces (1 liter)

Add the acid to most of the water as described under the permanganate reducer. Use more water to bring the volume of the solution up to one liter (32 ounces).

After reduction, the negative is removed as rapidly as possible from the bath and washed in water.

Nietz and Huse Reducer

Essentially this proportional reducer is a mixture of a substractive reducer with a superproportional one. It should be kept as two-stock solutions which are prepared as follows:

Solution A
Potassium permanganate
30 grains (0.25 gram)
Sulfuric acid (10% solution)
0.25 ounce (15 cc)
Distilled water to make
35 ounces (1 liter)
Solution B
Ammonium persulfate
0.75 ounce (25 grams)
Distilled water to make
35 ounces (1 liter)

For use, one part of Solution A is mixed with three parts of Solution B (use immediately).

After reduction, which should be watched and carried to the desired point, the negative is bathed in a one-percent solution of potassium metabisulfite to remove the brown stains left by the permanganate. The negative is then finally washed in water.

SUPERPROPORTIONAL REDUCERS

The only reducer in common use which removes a larger fraction of the denser areas of the image than it does of the less dense areas is a solution of ammonium persulfate.

Unfortunately, this reducer is uncertain in its action, but with care in its preparation and use satisfactory results can be obtained. Traces of impurities in both the ammonium persulfate and in the water used to dissolve it are largely responsible for the difficulties attending its use. The purest possible persulfate (Analytical Reagent grade) should be used and stoppered tightly after a sample is withdrawn. Stock solutions of the persulfate should be prepared as need arises. Distilled water is essential in preparing the reducer, and all vessels used should first be rinsed carefully with distilled water. The mixture is prepared as follows:

Ammonium persulfate
2 ounces (30 grams)
Sulfuric acid, c.p.
¾ dram (1.5 cc)
Water to make
32 ounces (500 cc)

The acid is added carefully to the water a drop at a time, the acid solution cooled, and then the ammonium persulfate is added to the acid solution.

The negative to be reduced is placed in a bath consisting of one part of the above solution and two parts of water. After immersion in the reducer, the negative should be watched carefully, as reduction proceeds more rapidly with time. It is best to remove the negative from the bath before reduction has proceeded to the desired extent. The negative is then bathed in a five-percent solution of sodium sulfite. Athough not necessary, it is preferable to refix the negative after treatment in the sodium-sulfite solution, as the negative can then be further treated if necessary. If the action of the reducer is too vigorous, its action can be decreased by diluting the stock solution with distilled water.

Eder's Harmonizing Reducer

This reducer produces a superproportional effect in a different manner. It is actually a reducer and an intensifier combined; while reducing the heavier densities, it intensifies the weaker ones. This tends to reduce the contrast of an underexposed and overdeveloped negative.

Water
25 ounces (750 cc)
Hydrochloric acid (conc.)
1 ounce (30 cc)
Potassium bichromate
146 grains (10 grams)
Potassium alum
1 ounce, 292 grains (50 grams)
Add water to make
32 ounces (1 liter)

Bleach to completion. Wash thoroughly until all the yellow stain has disappeared. The removal of the stain can be speeded up by first washing two to three minutes, then immersing the negative in a two-percent solution of sodium bisulfite for a few minutes, and then continuing the wash. When washing is complete, redevelop in Kodak D-72, DuPont 53-D, or Ansco 125, diluted 1:5. Then fix in a hardening-fixing bath, and wash as usual.

DICHROIC-FOG REMOVAL

Negatives which have dichroic fog (green on the surface, red by transmitted light) can be cleared by treatment in the following solution. Note that this differs from the usual permanganate reducer in that no acid is added; thus it does not attack the image, it only attacks the fog.

Solution A
Potassium permanganate
7½ grains (0.5 grams)
Water to make
16 ounces (500 cc)
Solution B
Potassium metabisulfite
73 grains (5 grams)
Water to make
16 ounces (500 cc)

Treat the negative in Solution A until the fog disappears. Then remove the permanganate stain by treating in Solution B until all the stain disappears. Wash thoroughly.

LOCAL REDUCTION

Local reduction can be carried out in the same manner as local intensification (see *Intensification*). Farmer's reducer will usually be found the most useful for such a purpose. To keep the reducer from spreading to undesired areas, work with a small brush moistened with the reducer, taking up all surface solution with a sponge.

Frictional or mechanical reduction is also carried out locally. A small quantity of a metal polish applied to a chamois skin can be worked with the finger tip for larger areas, and a round-pointed match stick for working down small detail. The negative, of course, sould be worked dry in these mechanical methods of reduction but should be washed in water after the process is completed. Abrasive pencils and erasers are also used for mechanical reduction (see *Retouching Negatives and Prints*).

Abrasive reducers should normally be used on large negatives; they tend to roughen the surface of the negative somewhat and the resulting marks may be noticeable when big enlargements are made from 35 mm negatives. The paste form is sold by various manufacturers, Abrasive Reducer, Putz Pomade, and others.

PREPARATION OF LINE ILLUSTRATIONS

Although not ordinarily considered under reduction processes, the preparation of certain line illustrations does involve complete reduction of the photographic image. For example, if a map is to be prepared from an existing map which shows far too much detail, the following photographic and mechanical processes may be used to prepare a very satisfactory illustration.

A photograph of the map is made and a print, sufficiently large to work with convenience, is made from the negative. The lines desired over with a waterproof-black ink in the final illustration are gone and the photographic image is then completely removed by the use of a suitable reducer. The most satisfactory reducer for this purpose is iodine cyanide. Although poisonous, it leaves no stain of any kind and completely removes the photographic image, leaving the black ink lines on a white background. Some care must be exercised in the selection of the ink, for some so-called waterproof inks will spread or even flake off in the reducing bath or the washing which follows reduction. Post's extra-waterproof ink has been found quite satisfactory.

REDUCTION OF PRINTS

For increasing the contrast in a print, the iodine-cyanide reducer is excellent. The proportions of Solutions A and B are changed somewhat for print reduction. A suitable formula is:
Solution A (iodine)
402 minims (57.5 cc)
Solution B (cyanide)
70 minims (10 cc)
Water
16 ounces (1 liter)
Remember that this reducer is poisonous. Wash thoroughly after reduction is complete.

To reduce contrast in a print, ammonium persulfate is used. The precautions to be used with this reducer given under negative reduction should be followed with print reduction as well. The formula is:
Ammonium persulfate
560 grains (80 grams)
Sulfuric acid, c.p.
8 minims (1.1 cc)
Sodium chloride, c.p.
6 grains (0.8 gram)
Distilled water
16 ounces (1 liter)
In use, the stock solution is diluted with two parts of distilled water. Wash prints thoroughly after reduction.

Proportional reduction of a print may be secured by the following permanganate reducer:
Potassium permanganate
7 grains (1 gram)
Sulfuric acid (10% solution)
350 minims (50 cc)
Water
16 ounces (1000 cc)
Be sure to observe the precautions on the use of sulfuric acid.

This reducer is useful in removing slight fog. Its action is quite rapid. Prints after reduction in this solution should be bathed in a fresh acid fixing bath, followed, of course, by the usual washing in water.

□

REFLECTORS

There are two kinds of reflectors used in photography. The first is generally small, curved to one of three shapes, and is normally used

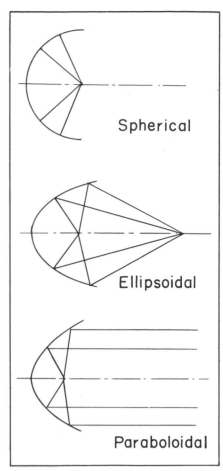

Figure 1. *Diagrams showing the three important curved reflectors and how they control the light. See text for explanation.*

in connection with a lamp of some kind, serving to direct the light from the lamp in a particular manner. The second type of reflector is large, usually flat, and is used outdoors to reflect sunlight for various lighting effects.
Lamp Reflectors

Since the light from an open incandescent or flashlamp proceeds in all directions, a reflector makes it possible to pick up some of the unused light and to redirect it to the desired plane. This usually causes a considerable increase in the amount of usable light. In other cases, it only serves to make the illumination more even, while in still other cases, the reflector is simply doing the work of a lens.

Curved reflectors are made in three shapes, spherical, ellipsoidal, and paraboloidal. Each has its uses, depending on its properties. To understand these, note the diagram (Figure 1) and the following points.

1) A light source, placed at the focus of the spherical reflector, will be imaged in the same place, and at the same size. Thus, the spherical reflector is generally used behind the lamp in a projector; it forms an image of the lamp filament right at the plane of the filament itself. If the lamp is slightly off-center, the image of the filament coils can be placed right between the actual coils of filament. This produces the equivalent of two filaments (the actual coil and the image of the coil) and results in a more uniform and slightly brighter illumination since the gaps in the original source have been filled in by the images of the bright parts.

2) An ellipsoidal reflector has two focal points. A light source placed at one point will be imaged at the other. The main value of ellipsoidal reflectors is in enlargers and projectors where they take the place of condenser lenses. Some new 8 mm projector lamps have an ellipsoidal mirror placed directly inside the lamp. This images the lamp filament at the film in the same way as the condenser lens of the ordinary projector, but with the advantage that the built-in mirror can be focused very accurately. The elimination of condenser lenses also reduces the cost of the projector to some extent.

3) In the paraboloidal reflector a light source placed at the focus produces a parallel beam of light. Its second focus is, in effect, at infinity. The paraboloidal reflector is used in spotlights, searchlights, strobe lamps, and wherever the light is to be limited to a narrow angle.

In practice, the totally parallel beam cannot be attained; it is possible only if the light source is infinitely small. Since all light sources have some size, the beam of light from a paraboloidal reflector will spread; the amount of spreading depends on the size of the light source. Thus variations of source size in similar reflectors produce the well-known reflector floodlamp and reflector spot lamps, as well as the medium-beam types, which have an intermediate amount of beam spread.

Flat Reflectors

Flat reflectors fall into two classes, *hard* and *soft*. The *hard* reflector is a large sheet of plywood or beaverboard, covered with polished tinfoil. Placed in sunlight, it reflects a brilliant beam of light, and is used outdoors in much the same way as a spotlight is used in studios. The *soft* reflector is simply a large sheet of plywood or wallboard painted with white paint. When placed in sunlight, it throws a soft light which can be used to fill-in the shadow side of the face in portraiture, or to completely illuminate the face in a backlighted shot.

The reflectors used by professional movie cameramen are usually about four feet square. They are sometimes made in two pieces, each 2 × 4 feet, fastened together with hinges for folding.

Since in color photography reflected light takes on the color of the reflecting surface, unwanted colored reflections can be a great annoyance. However, for intentional color effects, the use of colored reflectors with color films can produce a variety of very interesting results, limited only by the photographer's imagination.

REFLEX AND DIFFUSION-TRANSFER PHOTOCOPYING

[Reflex copying is a very old process for making negatives of printed or written material without the use of a camera. Its use has been greatly increased in recent years by the development of the diffusion-transfer process which makes it possible to produce the negative and positive copies in a single operation. This article discusses reflex copying, both by direct and diffusion processes, and also special methods such as thermography.]

• *Also see: Microreproduction; Xerography.*

THE REFLEX-COPYING OR REFLECTION-copying process is a photographic method of reproducing documents of all types without the use of a camera. Discovery of the technique is generally attributed to an eminent photographer of the nineteenth century, J. H. Player, and in the older literature reference is frequently made to Playertypes and the Playertype process. In recent years

Verifax Cavalcade Copier has automatic exposure feed, replenishment system with built-in storage cartridge, exposure guide, and automatic copy feed.

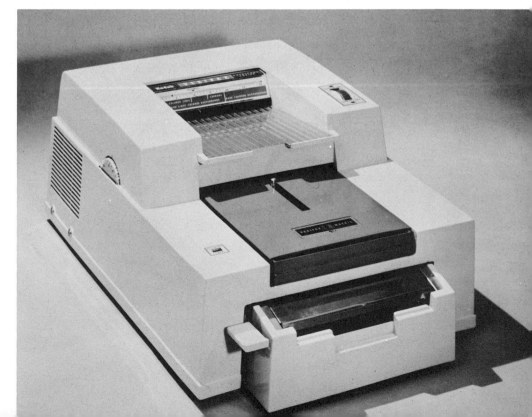

the term reflex copying has been almost universally applied.

The theory of reflex copying is extremely simple. It is known that light passing through the back of a piece of sensitive paper will produce an over-all fog. If, however, the emulsion is closely pressed in contact with written or printed matter, the opaque lines or characters are nonreflective, while the blank or clear-white portions of the document will reflect a high proportion of light back to the emulsion thereby increasing the exposure and consequently the amount of fog over specific portions of the paper. In other words, a negative copy is produced.

The paper receives an over-all exposure and, to keep the parts corresponding to the black letters on the original from becoming fogged over, an exceedingly contrasty emulsion is used. With emulsions of very high contrast, any exposure up to a certain level produces no silver image at all; a very small additional exposure causes the paper to go completely black. On such a paper a very adequate negative can be produced by contact exposure, though of course it is suitable only for copying printed and written matter. It will not produce satisfactory reproductions for continuous-tone material such as photographs.

PAPERS

In general, papers required for this purpose are quite slow, and can be exposed in contact printers with strong light sources. Kodagraph Contact Paper and Ansco Scona Reflex Paper are two emulsions

made especially for reflex copying. Scona Reflex paper requires no darkroom and can be handled in subdued room light.

To make a reflex copy with Scona Reflex paper, any ordinary contact printer may be used. The paper is placed on the glass of the printer, emulsion side up, and the material to be copied is placed over it, printed side down (Figure 1). Exposure is thus made through the base of the sensitive paper, by reflection from the original. The paper is developed in the same way as any contact paper. Exposure should be adjusted for a good black background even if there is some slight fogging of the letters.

The resulting copy will be a negative, reversed left for right. Right-reading positive copies can be made from this negative by simple contact printing. This is done by printing through the negative in the conventional way with the emulsion side of the negative facing the emulsion of the print paper. For the print any contact paper may be used. The result is a positive copy, reading the right way. (See Figure 2.)

With some types of reflex paper contrast is improved by using yellow lamps instead of white. This also produces better copies of colored originals, such as printed matter in blue or green ink.

Any standard paper developer such as Kodak D-72, or Ansco 125 may be used for this work, and fix-

ing and washing is done exactly as in the case of any other photographic paper.

DIFFUSION-TRANSFER OFFICE COPIERS

In recent years many small copying machines based on the reflex principle have been marketed, but with an interesting variation in the processing method. A diffusion-transfer method is used for processing the reflex negative and making the positive copy in a single processing step.

The best known application of diffusion-transfer processing is found in the Polaroid Land Camera, where a light-sensitive negative sheet and an insensitive sheet with a specially prepared receiving layer are used. Between the two sheets, a small breakable pod contains a jelly-like developer composition, which is spread in a thin layer between the two sheets by rollers in the camera. The developer causes the negative image on the sensitive sheet to develop fully. A fraction of a second later, the still-moist negative comes in contact with the positive receiving sheet which causes the remaining silver in the negative to blacken and transfer to this sheet where it produces the positive image.

PAPERS FOR OFFICE COPYING MACHINES

In office copying machines the negative and positive sheets are provided in separate packages. The negative sheet is sensitive to light,

Left: *Figure 1. The principle of reflex copying. Negative paper is placed, emulsion-side-up, and material to be copied, printed sside down, on top of it. Exposure is made through the base of the sensitive paper.* Right: *Figure 2. Making a positive copy from a reflex negative is the same as printing any other kind of negative. The two emulsion surfaces are in contact and light passes through the negative to the sensitive paper producing a right-reading copy.*

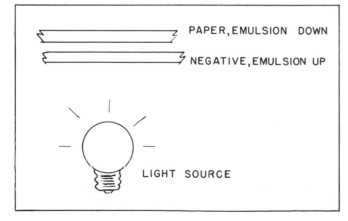

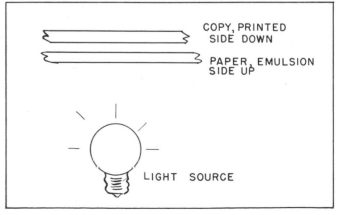

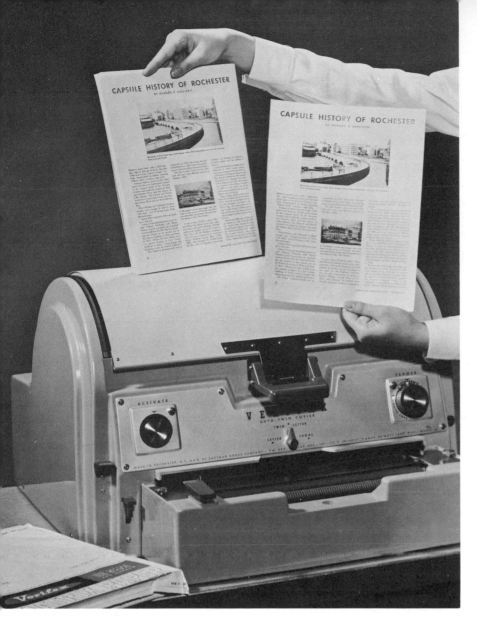

to make it permanent, and is permitted to dry.

The papers used in these machines are specially made and are not ordinarily sold through camera shops, except where the latter also has an agency for a copying machine. The developer is special, and the formulas have not been published.

Some machines use yellow lamps, others a special green fluorescent tube. The latter is mounted in a special rotating socket, and is driven by a rubber-covered friction roller, thus producing a continuous contact printer of very simple construction.

The negative paper itself is orthochromatic, with a strong peak in the green sensitivity. By the use of yellow or green lamps, the entire exposure is restricted to a narrow band of green light. The result is that all other colors appear black; thus these machines can copy writing, printing, or lettering in any color (except for one very rare shade of green) without special adjustment or filtering. A letter typed in black, with a rubber-stamp impression in red and a signature in blue will all reproduce as sharp black on the copy.

KODAK VERIFAX

An interesting variation of the diffusion-transfer process is used in

A. B. Dick Model 120 Photocopier.

but to such a low degree that it may safely be handled for short periods in ordinary room light. The positive receiving sheet is insensitive to light, and contains a special coating to produce a positive image in contact with the wet negative.

The machine is provided with a shallow trough containing the developer solution and usually a pair of motor-driven wringer rollers. The two sheets are fed into the tray, one on each side of a metal separator bar, to keep them from touching until they are fully wet. They are pushed through the solution until their leading edges touch the wringer rollers, which then pick up both sheets, squeegee them together, and eject them from the machine. They remain in contact for about ten seconds and are then separated. The

negative is discarded; since it has not been fixed, it is not permanent and is of no further value. The positive sheet needs no washing

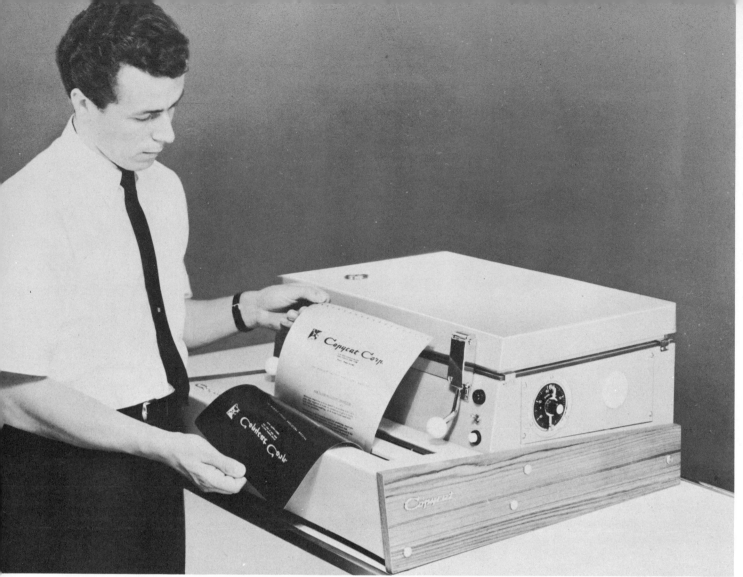

Copycat Offset Platemaker. Produces long-run offset plates in three minutes very inexpensively.

the Kodak Verifax Copiers. Superficially, the process appears the same. However, the negative paper is specially sensitized and has a filter layer built in so that ordinary white incandescent lamps can be used. The machine will copy material of just about any color.

After the exposure is made, the negative sheet is inserted in a tray containing an activator solution. This is not a developer but a special alkali bath, which activates the developing agents which are incorporated in the negative-paper emulsion. The negative paper contains the silver emulsion, the developing agents, and a dye former. The sheet remains in the activator for about 20 seconds, during which time a negative image in silver and a positive image in dye are simultaneously formed. At the end of the activating

period, a receiving sheet is placed in contact with the end of the negative and the two are pulled together from the bath through a squeegee. The receiving sheet is not immersed in the solution at all, and comes out practically dry.

As the two sheets are pulled together in tight contact by the squeegee, the dye image which is a positive is transferred from the negative sheet to the receiving sheet producing a positive copy.

There are several interesting features of this process. One is that the receiving sheet needs no chemical coating of any kind, and is essentially an ordinary bond paper treated to prevent wrinkling when it comes in contact with the wet negative. Various colored receiving sheets, translucent sheets for airmail, and blueprint masters are also available.

Another interesting point is that the negative masters are available

in two types. The original Verifax master, now known as Type CM, produces a very heavy dye layer, from which as many as five successive transfers can be made, producing five separate copies from a single negative. Since the receiving sheet is a simple and inexpensive type of paper, the cost of copies is reduced markedly. The first copy is almost black; succeeding copies are a lighter brown, but still quite legible. Because of the thick coating of the original master, copies are not perfectly sharp but ample for all ordinary office uses.

Where very sharp copies are required, a new master sheet known as Verifax Type CS Matrix Paper is used. This works in exactly the same way as the CM paper, except that the coating is thinner. Only one transfer can be obtained which is jet black and exceedingly sharp. The detail rendition of the CS Matrix is quite remarkable; it will not only reproduce written or printed matter, but it even makes good copies from printed halftone (screened) pictures in magazines or newspapers. However, it cannot be used to copy continuous-tone images.

Activator temperature is quite critical and the activator is designed to work at 81 F. A thermostatically controlled heater is part of the developer unit, so that the correct working temperature is maintained. In hot climates, a special Hi-Temperature Activator is provided and the thermostat adjusted for its use when necessary.

THERMOFAX

Another system of reflex copying, known as Thermofax, is marketed by Minnesota Mining & Manufacturing Company. This, however, is based on a different principle and utilizes infrared or heat radiation instead of light. Since the master sheet is not light-sensitive, it can be handled in any kind of light.

The process depends on the master sheet being coated with a material which changes color when subjected to a given amount of heat. In the copying machine the copy sheet is run in contact with the material to be copied under a source of infrared radiation. The process depends on the ability of the printed matter on the sheet to absorb infrared and become hot enough to cause the necessary change in color on the copy sheet. The unprinted parts are transparent to infrared, do not heat up, and thus do not affect the copy sheet at all. Thus, wherever there is black printing on the original, the copy sheet turns blue, and the result is a positive image directly from the original.

Obviously, this system will only copy material that is infrared-absorbing. Printed matter in black ink, typewriting, and pencil will copy quite well. Inks containing dyes are transparent to infrared and do not copy at all; this includes rubber-stamp impressions, blue fountain-pen ink, and ordinary ball-point pen ink. Special ball-point pens are available with ink that does copy by thermography.

PHOTOSTAT

While not a reflex-copying process, some mention should be made of the so-called Photostat process (also called Rectigraph, etc. depending on the manufacturer of the machine). This process uses a camera, photographing the original directly on bromide paper, thus making a paper negative. The camera is fitted with a prism so that the image is not reversed and where only a reading copy is needed, the negative is adequate. Positives are made as required simply by rephotographing the negative in the same equipment.

Since the introduction of the reflex office copying machine, the use of the Photostat is diminishing, and it is mainly limited to cases where the size of the original must be enlarged or reduced. Commercial artists make considerable use of the Photostat to enlarge or reduce type or drawings to fit a layout, and, since the negative is also right-reading, to reverse a line of type from black to white for display purposes.

XEROX COPIES

The Xerox copier, likewise, does not use the reflex principle, but photographs the material through a lens, onto an electrically charged plate, which is then dusted with a colored powder or toner. The toner is transferred to a blank sheet of bond paper and fused in place with gentle heat to produce a permanent copy. More information will be found in the article, *Xerography*.

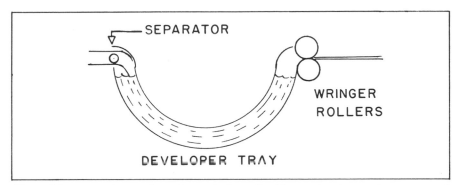

Above: *The processing section of a typical small office copier. Exposed negative and receiving sheet are passed into the tray with the separator bar between them, so that both are evenly wetted by the developer. They are picked up by the powered wringer rollers, squeegeed together, and ejected from the machine.*

Below: *Exposing section of small office copier. A green fluorescent tube is mounted in a special socket so it is free to revolve. It is driven by the rubber-drive roller, and the material to be copied and the negative sheet are driven together in contact with the light tube. Shields are provided to avoid fogging the paper where it is not in contact with the lamp.*

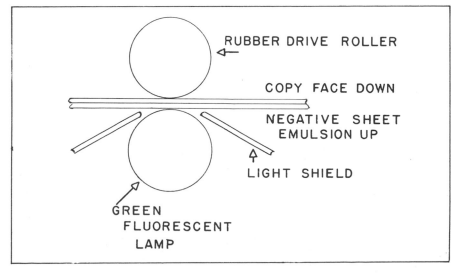

LEGALITY OF PHOTOCOPIES

Many states have made statutory provisions to assure the legality of photocopies and most courts freely admit such copies in evidence. If there is likelihood that a photocopy may be required for court use, it may be certified or notarized. The certificate or notarization should be attached to the photocopy.

In this connection, there are several classifications of material which cannot legally be photocopied. These include obligations or securities of the United States Government, bonds, certificates of indebtedness, currency, or money in any form including fractional notes, certificates of deposit, bills, checks, or drafts for money drawn by or upon authorized officers of the United States. Foreign or domestic postage stamps may be reproduced for certain specified purposes provided that the copies are not exact size. Copies may be half-size, or alternatively not smaller than 1½ times the size of the original. Cancelled revenue stamps appearing on a document may be copied provided the reproduction is performed for lawful purposes.

Adjusted compensation certificates for veterans of the World War I, draft cards, passports, naturalization papers, immigration papers, certificates of citizenship may not be photocopied. The obligations or currency of any foreign government, bank, or corporation likewise may not be reproduced. In certain states legislation prohibits the reproductions of automobile licenses, titles, or drivers' licenses. Care should be exercised in reproducing seals. The Great Seal of the United States, for example, may not be reproduced. One important provision of the copyright law imposes severe penalties for the copying by any method of material of any manner or kind that is protected by copyright. Even though a photocopy operator or firm may be acting as an agent, the copyright laws, if strictly interpreted, make him a party to the violation. If there is any doubt whatever about the legality of photocopying any document or object, an attorney should be consulted.

REFLEX CAMERAS

The reflex camera is distinguished from other cameras by the fact that it has a groundglass screen on top of the camera where the image is reflected for focusing and framing.

The single-lens reflex dates from the turn of the century with early models designed to accept plates and sheet and roll films. Today, the single-lens reflex is available in a variety of makes and models from 35 mm and 2¼ × 2¼ to the larger view-camera formats.

The twin-lens reflex has two separate lenses, one for viewing and focusing, the other for the actual picture taking. Best known in this category is the Rolleiflex although there are many other models in existence. These cameras usually use roll film either in the 120 or 127 sizes, producing square pictures 6 × 6 centimeters or 4 × 4 centimeters (2¼ inches square or 1⅝ inches square) respectively.

SINGLE-LENS REFLEX

In the single-lens reflex the image is reflected upward to a groundglass where it is seen full-image size for focusing and composing. There is no parallax error, since the same lens is used for both viewing and shooting. However, the image seen on the groundglass, while right side up, is reversed right for left by the mirror. This presents some difficulty in photographing moving objects.

Many of the 35 mm single-lens reflexes have prism devices in the viewing head which serve two purposes. First, they make it possible to view the image at eye level instead of having to look down into a hood. Second, they reverse the image again, so that what is seen in the eyepiece is right side up and the right way around.

Shutters

All early reflex cameras had focal-plane shutters, consisting of a curtain with slits of varying sizes which ran directly in front of the film plane. This kept the film covered until released. Then as the slit ran across the film plane, it made the exposure. A simple interlock prevented the curtain from

Revolving-back Auto Graflex with double-extension bellows, available in 3¼ × 4¼ and 4 × 5 sizes, was a favorite for years with amateurs and professionals alike.

The Honeywell Pentax H-3 35 mm reflex with special bellows unit for close-up photography.

being rewound until the mirror had been lowered again to viewing position. In this position it blocks all the light from the film and the curtain can be rewound and the film advanced without fogging.

Some 35 mm reflex cameras work on the same principle, while others have between-the-lens shutters of the Compur type. The Compur shutter must have an additional mechanism when installed in reflex cameras. This mechanism allows the shutter to be cocked and the blades latched open for viewing. When the exposure button is pressed, the shutter blades close, the mirror rises, and the shutter blades open and close again to make the exposure.

Automatic Diaphragm

Modern 35 mm single-lens reflexes are almost all fitted with some sort of automatic diaphragm. In some cases it is semiautomatic with the lens tripped by a separate hand motion before taking the picture. In others, it is automatic and operated directly by the camera button. Very advanced models are arranged so the lens automatically reopens to full aperture immediately after the exposure.

Focusing

One difficulty with the single-lens reflex is that many people find groundglass focusing difficult. As a result almost all recent models are fitted with rangefinders built into the center of the groundglass; these are based on purely optical principles (see *Rangefinders*) and have no moving parts. They produce a split image which joins into a single one when the image is exactly focused. In general, a Fresnel field lens is also fitted so that the image can be seen and framed all the way out to the corners.

INSTANT-RETURN MIRROR

An annoying feature of all reflexes is that the image disappears from the groundglass at the instant of exposure; the photographer often wonders whether something may have shifted at the last moment. The problem is more psychological than real since the exposure is usually made within $1/10$ of a second after the button is pressed.

To overcome this difficulty, many reflexes are fitted with instant-return mirrors which snap upward just long enough to allow for taking the picture and then immediately return to viewing position. In combination with the automatic-reopening lens diaphragm, these make rapid-sequence photography easy. There is merely a momentary blink at the instant of exposure and the camera is immediately reset. The film need only be wound (this usually cocks the shutter at the same time) for making the next exposure.

Lenses

Lenses may be readily interchanged with the single-lens reflex. Since focusing is done visually, no special scaling or mounting is necessary, nor do the lenses need any kind of rangefinder coupling. The lenses of many popular single-lens reflexes are interchangeable on the different cameras either directly or with adapters.

The only problem in fitting lenses to a single-lens reflex is that the mirror requires room for movemnet and short-focus lenses which extend into the camera box may interfere with this movement. Wide-angle lenses for single-lens reflexes are usually of the inverted telephoto construction. These lenses have a sufficiently wide field and at the same time provide ample clearance for proper operation of the camera.

Zoom lenses are available for many of the single-lens reflexes. The Voigtländer Zoomar, for example, can be used with adapters on the Praktina and the Exakta as well as the Bessamatic for which it was originally designed.

TWIN-LENS REFLEX

The twin-lens reflex was the outgrowth of a stereo camera. Frank & Heidecke, manufacturers of the Heidoscope stereo camera for plates

Alpa 35 mm single-lens reflex typifies the present trend in 35 mm camera design for the parallax-free through-the-lens viewing systems.

and sheet films, brought out a roll-film version of the same camera many years ago. The Rolleidoscope, as it was known, was so popular that the manufacturers decided to incorporate the same principle into a single-image camera. This was the original Rolleiflex.

The first Rolleiflex used an obsolete film size (No. 117) which was designed for 12 exposures, 2¼ inches square. The film was wound manually by reference to numbers on the paper backing. An improved version appeared using standard No. 120 roll film which also made 12 exposures of the same size. Since this film did not then carry numbering for square pictures on the paper, a special film-winding and metering mechanism was built into the film-winding knob.

Later a more advanced version was brought out in which the film was wound by a single stroke of a winding lever. Sensing rollers, placed inside the camera, allowed

for winding off the paper leader and positioning the first exposure without reference to the numbers on the paper at all. In addition, the winding lever on this model also cocked the shutter. The new model was named Automatic Rolleiflex. The earlier model was renamed Rolleicord and, as such, remained on the market for many years.

More recent models of the Rolleiflex have built-in exposure meters and other refinements. In addition, there is a smaller model using No. 127 roll film which makes 12 pictures $1^5/_8$ inches square. There are a variety of accessories for the larger models, including close-up attachments and plate and sheet-film backs.

Principles

The twin-lens reflex carries two lenses on a single front panel. The upper lens is the focusing lens and is usually used wide open at all times; the lower is the taking lens and has the shutter and diaphragm. The two lenses are carefully matched so that when the image is accurately focused with the upper lens, the taking lens will likewise be in focus.

Since the two lenses are some distance apart, there is necessarily a parallax error in framing. Various means have been taken to overcome this problem. In some cases, a movable mask is used. In others, the groundglass is made slightly undersize so that the image as seen in the viewer always contains at least as much as the picture which finally lands on the film. For close-

The Hasselblad 500C. This 2¼ x 2¼ single-lens reflex has automatic-diaphragm control and interchangeable lenses.

up work, this method is not adequate and usually a pair of supplementary lenses is supplied. These serve to focus the camera for close-up work. In addition, the upper lens contains a prism which bends its angle of view downward so that it sees the same field as the camera lens at the selected distance.

Most twin-lens reflexes are limited to the lenses built in by the manufacturer. However, the Mamiyaflex has interchangeable front boards with pairs of lenses, matched to each other for taking and viewing. Those who do not mind carrying two cameras can always get a second twin-lens reflex with a tele-photo or wide-angle lens built in.

The great majority of twin-lens reflexes are designed for use with No. 120 or 127 roll film although some professional photographers have devised similar cameras with a larger-negative size. Philippe Halsman had a special twin-lens reflex built to order for use with 5 × 7 sheet film. Peter Gowland likewise had several such cameras built, and the builder now offers the Gowland-flex in several sizes for sale to the general public.

□

REFRACTIVE INDEX

When a ray of light passes from one medium to another of different optical density, the light is bent to a certain degree. This bending is known as refraction.

For purposes of measurement a line is drawn at right angles to the boundary between the two media. This line is called the *normal*. If a ray travels from a medium of lesser density to a medium of greater density it is bent toward the *normal;* if it passes from a medium of greater density to a medium of lesser density it is bent away from the *normal.*

stated in terms of the sine of the angle. The ratio between the entering and transmitted-ray angles is not constant, but the ratio of their sines is. The latter ratio is known as the refractive index for the two substances. In mathematical terms, the refractive index equals the sine of the angle of incidence divided by the

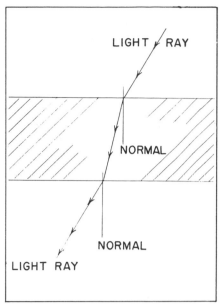

As a ray of light passes from one medium to another it is bent to a certain degree. Such bending is known as refraction.

sine of the angle of refraction.

Since it is necessary to have a fixed reference for single substances the first medium is usually taken to be a vacuum. (A vacuum has the least possible optical density; hence its refractive index is 1.000.) With reference to a vacuum, air has a refractive index of about 1.00029, and different kinds of glass may vary from 1.5 to 1.8. Other transparent media including both solids and liquids also have refractive indexes which are measured and specified in the same way.

The refractive index of a material is constant for any one light color. It varies with the color of the light, being greatest for blue and least for red. For any given material having a certain refractive index, the variation of this index for different colors is known as the *dispersion* or the *Abbe number*.

It is possible to make glasses of high refraction and low dispersion, or of low refraction and high dispersion. The correction of lenses for various aberrations is accomplished by making the lens elements out of these different kinds of glass, choosing the curvatures of the elements in such a way as to bring all colors to focus at substantially the same distance from the lens.

REPAIRING AND MAINTENANCE OF EQUIPMENT

S. L. LOVE
President, National Camera Repair School, Englewood, Colorado
[Proper care in the day-to-day maintenance of your camera may mean avoiding repair bills at a later date. Here an expert in the camera-repair field discusses the operation and maintenance of photographic equipment and gives advice on those repairs the camera owner may safely make at home.]
• *Also see: Dust Elimination; How Your Camera Works; Rangefinders; Reflex Cameras.*

WHEN YOU SEE THE WORD "SHARP" in the same sentence with "photography," your first thoughts may be of a clean-cutting lens, detail that can be felt, and depth-of-field that is compelling and flattering to the technique of the photographer. The word sharp, however, may also be applied to the tools of your trade—your photographic equipment, the camera, the flash equipment, the basic and accessory units you use.

Whenever I think of tools, I remember a carpenter I used to know as a youngster who created useful and lovely works of art from wood. Often, he would caress a plane or a chisel lovingly and say, "This first thing you must learn about good tools, boy, is to keep 'em sharp.'" In photography, certainly, it pays to "keep 'em sharp." I am not for a moment suggesting that you should repair your own equipment but a general knowledge of the technical aspects of the tools you use in photography will be of value in your over-all work.

THE BASIC RULE

While this article deals with many general aids for your photo-equipment maintenance, specifics are at least as important and best obtained through manuals furnished by the manufacturers—an important aid which is often overlooked by photographers. Keep a file of all your manufacturer's instruction manuals Each one deals specifically with the piece of equipment concerned and suggests particular areas and tips for repair and maintenance. Know what each control and adjustment does, and you will then avoid damage through misoperation.

Most instruction manuals offer data covering proper lubrication, minor-adjustment procedures, and replacement of expendable parts (bulbs, batteries, condenser lenses, etc.). Manuals always include important precautions about operating errors. If you own any equipment for which you do not have a manual, see your dealer or camera repairman. They either have such manuals in stock, or will be happy to obtain a replacement for you from the manufacturer.

Extensive additional information has been written specifically for many cameras and other equipment. If there is a text which covers your equipment, add it to your library. You will find further suggestions and ideas for keeping the particular device working well.

GENERAL PROTECTION

Cases, containers, and gadget bags are a worthwhile investment for the safekeeping of your equipment. Since most photo equipment is fragile, physical protection is vital. It is far less costly to replace a scuffed case than a scuffed lens or flash reflector. To gain maximum use, select a case for your camera in which it can remain even during use, making certain that the accessories you normally use can be attached to your camera easily without removing the case.

Be sure that the gadget bag you select is easy to use. If it is so awkward or cumbersome that you are tempted to carry its intended contents in your pocket instead, it is not for you. A fitted case encourages the user to replace individual parts and accessories in specific locations where they may be easily found. Develop the habit of replacing them in their proper locations immediately after use.

When traveling, keep your photo equipment on the floor of your car. Don't place loose cameras and supplies in a glove compartment or on the rear deck of your automobile. The excessive heat which can build up in those locations may be harmful. Moreover, such careless exposure may invite theft as well as damage from heat.

In addition to cases for carrying cameras and other accessories, you will find that covers for projection and darkroom equipment will repay their cost many times. Dirt and dust are the enemies of photography; dust causes wear in equipment and tell-tale spots in photographs. Of course, if you clean a lens every time you notice the need, you can avoid dust problems, but you'll minimize the need for cleaning simply by keeping a lens cap in place most of the time.

REVERSE MAINTENANCE

When you are thinking about protecting and preserving your property, remember that your equipment can *cause* damage as well as suffer it. For example, always select the proper tips for a tripod wherever it may be in use. Most tripods are furnished with sharp tips for general use outdoors and rubber tips for use indoors. You, your camera, and

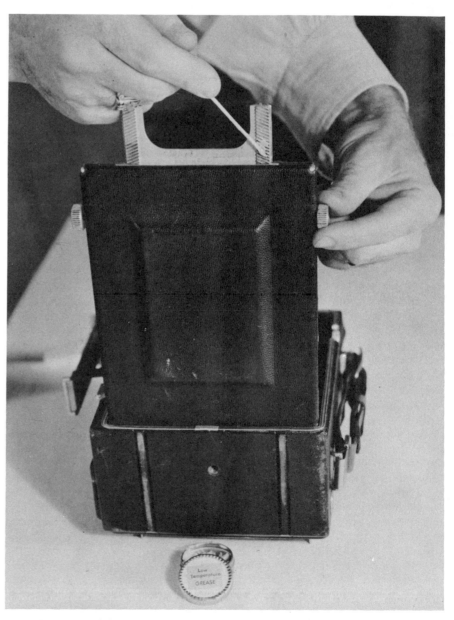

Use lubricants and locations suggested by the manufacturer. Such care will extend the life of equipment but do not over lubricate.

your tripod may all come tumbling down as a result of improper tips or unsure footing, and neither your neighbor nor your wife will appreciate scratches or scuff marks on a polished floor or other evidence that you and your photo equipment have passed by.

While a modern flashbulb rarely explodes, check the signal spot on the bulb for its proper color before firing; it could save embarrassment, a scratched reflector, or even more extensive damage.

Unless you can be sure the borrower has been properly instructed and is capable of avoiding damage, it is better not to lend equipment Anyone who uses your equipment should be as familiar with its maintenance as you are.

IN CASE OF ACCIDENT

Here are pointers which can help you to minimize the effects of some unfortunate unforeseen accidents.

Avoid attempting to move parts that appear damaged following an accident. If your camera opens or folds, be especially careful not to force any part. It is far better to check for misalignment and possible internal injuries than to go on using a camera whose action is stiff or sticking.

If you drop a piece of equipment, careful examination will usually help you see the difference between superficial or critical damage, although some damage which appears to be superficial can be critical. For example, a slightly dented lens mount can be much more serious than it appears.

If you drop a piece of equipment into water, get it to a competent repair shop immediately. If this isn't possible within a matter of a few hours, there are two alternatives. You may force-dry a piece of equipment internally by gently warming in an oven (not over 150 F), or you may immerse the equipment in a bucket of water to prevent air from reaching corrodible surfaces during the trip to the repair shop. Either of these procedures is less harmful than natural air-drying.

If your equipment has been subjected to a severe accident, don't

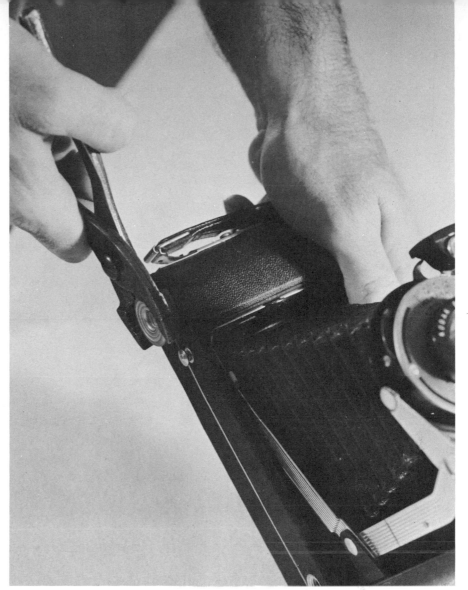

Does this seem exaggerated? It's surprising how many think a "stuck" camera-wind knob can be made to turn easily with a pair of common pliers.

risk additional damage by seeing "if it still works."

Damage from nearly all accidents will be minimized if your camera or meter is enclosed in a case. Some accessories, too, provide double protection. A lens hood not only minimizes flare, but can serve as a shock absorber when you drop your favorite camera nose first. Similarly, if you must subject your camera to salt-water spray, at least protect its lens by using a filter or clear optical-glass disk.

PRE-USE CHECKS

It is well worthwhile to check your equipment each time you plan to use it, or possibly each time you open it for reloading. It takes but a moment to run through the operation, checking for obvious malfunc-

tions as well as some of the more easily overlooked difficulties. At the same time you can dust the equipment internally, check its freedom of movement, and test its need for lubricant by looking and listening. It's the habit that counts; checking takes only a few moments each time and may save many hours— and dollars—later.

To help eliminate variable camera operation, form the habit of regularly setting the shutter or winding still and motion-picture cameras just prior to making any exposure. You'll minimize the danger of spring fatigue and ensure that a fresh piece of film will be in position, ready for the picture, in both types of cameras.

While most routine maintenance is relatively easy and will extend

Equipment is sensitive to the sun and attractive to kleptomaniacs. Protect your investment by careful storage.

the life of your equipment considerably, do not attempt anything but the simplest repairs yourself, such as replacing an external part. If you were to get into trouble and require the services of a trained repairman to right the damage, the job could be extra costly. And if your equipment is still under warrantee, it is not unlikely that the manufacturer's guarantee would be voided under such circumstances.

What about specific parts of cameras and other photo equipment? Here are some suggestions for keeping your equipment in top shape.

SHUTTERS

Modern shutters are marvels of precision, sturdiness, and dependability. However, like many other samples of today's technical achievements, complexity and susceptibility to damage go along with improved performance.

Handle the shutter with loving care. Understand how it is supposed to work (that manual again) before you attempt to use it. If it is accidentally subjected to dust, dirt, oil, or water penetration, remember the warning—do not attempt to "see if it still works." You can do more damage tripping the shutter

release once under those conditions than would normally occur in a lifetime. Familiarize yourself with the sounds made by your shutter when it is operating properly. Shutters which seem to deliver the same speed at all settings (or a group of them) can be checked by holding the setting lever to prevent its too rapid movement while simultaneously tripping the release lever.

Listen for the tell-tale buzz of a geared retard mechanism. If you don't hear it, extensive and expensive repairs may be indicated. On the other hand, a shutter which sticks at slow speeds, and is merely sluggish or satisfactory at higher speeds, may need only a routine cleaning. Look for shutter blades that do not quite close completely for signs of impending serious damage. Shutter blades which remain slightly open can be a frustrating source of light leaks and ghost images.

Sometimes it is difficult to watch the shutter go through its cycle slowly. Nevertheless, it is important to be aware of the proper cycling of a shutter, especially when it is a little unusual. For example, certain between-the-lens shutters on reflex cameras remain open during the focusing operation, only to close

prior to mirror movement and actual exposure.

Focal-plane shutters on still cameras are becoming commonplace. One frequent sort of focal-plane shutter damage is "sunburn." If you carelessly permit such a camera to lie face up in sunshine, the lens may easily focus the heat of the sun on the shutter curtain with sufficient intensity to burn a hole in it. Fortunately, most 35 mm cameras are of the reflex type, and the mirror protects the curtain when the shutter is closed. Nevertheless, a similar accident can occur if the heat from the sun is concentrated on the groundglass or prism, either of which can easily be cracked or damaged by the intense local heat. These possibilities re-emphasize the importance of the protection afforded by a case, a lens cap, and simple care in placing your camera.

One hole resulting from an accident is repairable; many pinholes in a cloth focal-plane curtain are generally the result of age and indicate that the curtain should be replaced. An attempt to repair such a curtain would be uneconomical. Although the repair of a single hole is not difficult, the materials and placement can be critical, and the work should be entrusted to a competent repairman.

Never oil a shutter of any kind unless you have adequate training or experience.

WIND MECHANISM

Most cameras have some provision for moving the film to the next exposure on a roll. Many modern cameras combine this function with the winding of a shutter or the movement of a diaphragm or mirror, as well as other functions. Because so many camera functions may be interrelated and interlocked, damage to one part may easily affect others. Probably the best advice you can follow is to avoid forcing any mechanism. If a part should move and doesn't, force may easily damage assemblies still in good working order. Even in the case of a simple camera with a straightforward film-wind knob, a minor malfunction can turn into a major repair problem as soon as force is applied.

Once again, be certain that you are familiar with the operation of your particular camera. Many cameras have special interlocks which stop the wind mechanism, the shutter-operating mechanism, or some other function as a safety precaution under certain circumstances. That simple rule, *do not force,* will save the day.

Take advantage of your checkout period when reloading, or at the beginning of a picture-taking session, to turn the entire camera through its cycle several times. With some cameras, it is necessary to hand crank a sprocket, or otherwise move a part internally in order

to cause it to function without film. This is desirable, and you should learn how to do it with your particular camera. It not only allows you to check out your camera but also serves to "exercise" the mechanism. It is not unusual for a shutter to fail, for example, if it hasn't been used for quite some time. Simply winding and tripping it a few times is enough exercise to assure its regular operation for the picture-taking session ahead.

Operate all your cameras at least once a month. If you have one or more cameras not regularly used, put them through their paces periodically. Tripping the shutter of a camera which is used only rarely

and expecting it to work the first time is a presumption which is not worth the chance.

If a piece of equipment has been out of use for longer than a month, use exceptional care in first operating it. The "setting-up exercises" are wonderful for revealing stiff joints, but there might be a joint or two so stiff that it will crack or break before working.

LENSES

The optical quality of lenses is obviously subject to deterioration if grease, dirt, or other foreign material is allowed to collect on the surfaces. Less obvious to photographers are the mechanical features of lenses, which are becoming more critical.

Most lenses are hard-coated. This means that they have had a thin layer (only molecules thick) of any of several materials deposited in order to reduce damaging surface reflections. Depending on the age of your lens, such a coating may be natural, very soft, or as hard or harder than the lens itself. This is a clue to the care that is required in cleaning any lens. Regardless of the age of your lens, remember that optical glass is generally softer than the glass from which pop bottles are made.

Lens Tissues

There are a number of prepared materials, chemicals, cloths, and papers which are marketed as lens-cleaning aids. Use caution in selecting any such materials. For example, certain silicone-impregnated lens-cleaning tissues can remove the special coating on the lens. A lens so old that it was not deliberately coated may have acquired an anti-reflective coating (bloom) merely by virtue of its age. Such a coating should be allowed to remain and improve with age. Some optical glass is so soft that anything but the most careful wiping can cause damage. Older coated surfaces are also soft, and excessive wiping will remove the coating.

In general, most preparations marketed for chemical cleaning (liquids) are relatively safe for use on optical glass, although the manufacturer's instructions should be

The obvious in preventive maintenance. Setting your camera up on unfamiliar ground can be disastrous.

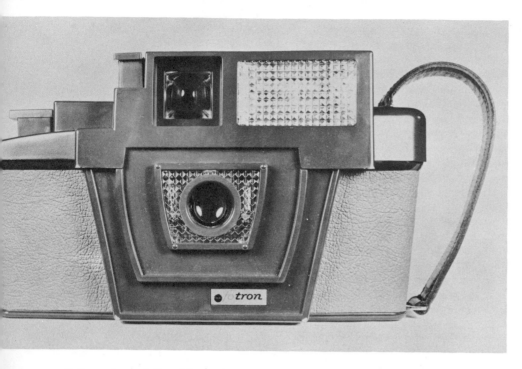

As cameras become more automated, it is very important to keep them free from dirt, dust, and hard knocks. This Fotron camera, which is a complete automatic unit, has built-in exposure meter, electronic flash, automatic winding, and other convenient features. A rugged camera, but like any fine instrument not immune to hard knocks and other abuses.

followed carefully. More dangerous is the possibility of excess liquid seeping around the edges of the lens and into the lens mount where it tends to deteriorate the metal of which the mount is made. If you must use a liquid lens cleaner, use it sparingly. Better still, avoid the use of any liquid whatever: the moisture that will condense on the surface of the lens from your breath is generally adequate for any but the most stubborn stains.

LENS DAMAGE

Lenses today are cemented with resistant cements which are stable at great temperature extremes. However, older lens cements may become soft at relatively lower temperatures—hence the danger of separation of glass elements. It should be clear that subjecting lenses to heat should be avoided.

Some lens cements are natural resins and in certain climates have a tendency to attract fungus growths. If fungus appears either in the cement or on the surface of a piece of optical glass, it should be cleaned from the surface immediately. If you notice a separation or a fungus growth within a lens, prompt action will avoid the damaging effect which extended presence of a fungus would cause. Such fungus can so damage the glass surface that it

will require repolishing.

A cracked or otherwise-damaged lens element is not generally replaceable. Most high-quality lenses, even those having the same name and focal length, are subject to slight variation in design from batch to batch in order to compensate for unavoidable variations, such as composition of the glass of which they are made.

Tiny scratches may appear on the surface of a lens, usually as the result of continued careless cleaning. Sometimes they can be polished out by a professional lens polisher. However, if a scratch is anything more than a mere surface blemish, it cannot be removed since polishing to a great enough depth to remove the scratch would tend to change the shape of the lens. Such deep scratches can be polished out with the use of a properly shaped lap, but the cost and danger to the lens would not be worth the effort.

If a lens is inadvertently scratched, a repair is possible that will affect the lens action little if any, since the only damage a scratch can cause in the function of a lens is the scattering of light which happens to strike the scratch. Such a scratch can be filled by rubbing with an engraver's black-lacquer stick, which will eliminate the reflections. Although there is a loss

of light transmission where one area of the lens is covered with black lacquer, the net result is generally undetectable, since such an area is relatively small. If the scratch is in the center of the lens, the effect will be more noticeable, particularly at a small aperture.

LENS CARE

The major cells of a lens can generally be unscrewed so that the external surfaces can be cleaned. In reassembling the lens, use caution to avoid crossing the fine threads and make certain that all lens cells are replaced "hand tight." The spacing of individual elements, as well as the main cells themselves, determines the accuracy of focus and the quality of the image. It is not unusual, by the way, to discover that a loose rear cell (somewhat hard to detect) is at the root of many poor pictures.

If a lens is accidentally subjected to moisture, fingerprints, oil or other contaminators, clean the surface at once. While they may not damage the lens immediately, a fingerprint that remains on the surface for an extended period of time may remain there forever.

Check your lens mounts regularly for looseness or other signs of potential loss of adjustment. Screws around the lens mountings should be checked occasionally and retightened whenever necessary. Focus adjustment may be disturbed in any lens mount. Make certain that parts like bed-track stops are firmly fastened to avoid inadvertent changes in focus.

It is usually a simple matter to insert a bit of groundglass in a focal plane to check the image of an object at infinity. Do not rely on some other distance in or around home, even if you have measured it, for the focusing scale may not be accurate at any distance but infinity. Make certain that the graduation marks line up at infinity when the lens is turned or racked to its stop.

Whereas few parts in the camera require lubrication, some focusing mechanisms are properly lubricated by following the instructions in the owner's manual. Exposed focusing tracks of the geared variety should be carefully lubricated with tiny amounts of a good instrument grease or oil. Remember that grease attracts dirt. Whenever a part is relubricated, it should be thoroughly cleaned.

AUTOMATIC DIAPHRAGMS

It is essential that the parts of automatic- or semi-automatic-diaphragm lenses move freely. Discover the linkage by which the automatic diaphragm functions on your camera. The connection between camera and lens should be free to operate smoothly. The diaphragm should adjust easily, for most linkage systems are designed to slip if the mechanism within the lens hangs up or jams. Along with the automatic features of the lens, such as diaphragm-actuating and focusing systems, inspect the automatic or quick-return mirror mechanism in single-lens reflexes. Make certain that the quick-return mirror moves fully to both retracted and extended positions. You can best examine this tripping action when there is no film in the camera.

RANGEFINDERS AND VIEWING SYSTEMS

If your camera has an accessory-type rangefinder, freedom of movement of the coupling arms and firm contact with the focusing track or lens mount are critical. Rangefinder as well as viewfinder windows can be cleaned just as you would a lens. Tiny squares of chamois cemented to the ends of old cotton-swab sticks are recommended for the job. By the way, the cotton swabs themselves have obvious value in cleaning intricate parts of your photo equipment.

Although most internal rangefinder or focusing adjustments are beyond the scope of this article, you can be aware of proper adjustment and make quick checks to be sure that the focusing mechanism is working correctly. The only reliable way in which to check any

An exposure meter is the heart of your camera equipment. Dirt, heat, and humidity will quickly affect your meter. A neck strap and case are added precautions against damage.

rangefinder is to examine the actual focus on a groundglass (under magnification) after the best possible adjustment using the rangefinder.

Most rangefinders cannot be adjusted specifically for different distances. This means that once they are set accurately for any distance, such rangefinders are reasonably accurate at all other distances. The best distance at which to check lens focus or rangefinder adjustment is infinity. Be certain that you choose a test subject which is at an adequate distance. Normally, this distance is about 600 to 800 times the focal length of the lens under test. It is wise to select a subject at least one-half mile away. If both lens and rangefinder then agree at infinity, chances are they will agree at other distances as well. A photographic test is a sure technique, but if you can examine a groundglass image with a magnifier, you can save time, naturally.

It is not uncommon for focusing scale calibration to be somewhat inaccurate. You can compare lens image with rangefinder adjustment at shorter distances, noting errors that may exist in the focusing scale

Motion-picture cameras and projectors are subject to all the problems found in still-camera equipment. Dust is one of the common problems to overcome in the projectors. See text for details.

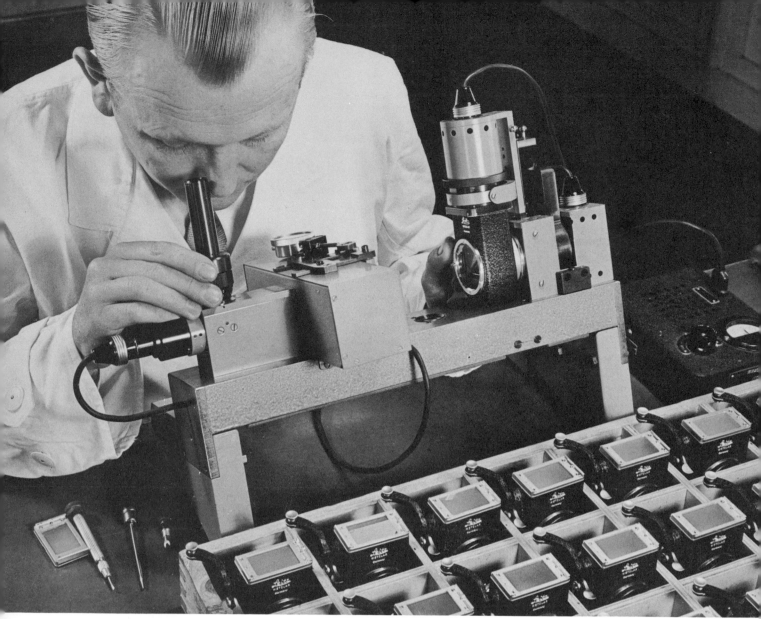

Enormous time and effort is expended by photographic manufacturers to guarantee that equipment is in top working condition. If proper care is taken, there is no reason why your equipment should not remain in this condition for years. Here a Leitz technician is testing Visoflex housings before shipment from the Wetzlar factory in West Germany.

but avoid trying to adjust such errors out. Rangefinders of the press-camera type can be adjusted for such accuracy, and should be checked at several distances. Avoid attempting an adjustment yourself, however.

The reflex viewing system of a twin-lens reflex may be regarded much like the rangefinder, for its focus should agree with the focus of the taking lens. Similarly, the focus on the groundglass of a single-lens reflex should be the same as the focus on the film, but may, through accident, differ from it.

When making any test to determine the focus, question yourself and the camera setting before you attempt or demand an adjustment. This area of camera adjustment is very critical, but the tolerances allowed are such that in normal picture-taking use no errors would be detected.

CAMERA BODIES

Stiff- and soft-bristle brushes in your kit will be valuable for removing film chips, dust, and other contaminants from camera bodies, both still and motion-picture. While many people use reasonable care in cleaning the inside of a camera, darkroom equipment, which is still more susceptible to dust accumulation, is often neglected. Use appropriate brushes to clean various parts of all of your photographic equipment. Bellows are chief offenders in this respect. While only a few cameras now incorporate bellows, most enlargers gather a great deal of dust in the bellows folds. If cleaned periodically, such dust will not find its way to the negative or the film. Try a vacuum cleaner for periodic darkroom and general clean-ups.

Probably one of the most common body problems is light leaks.

There are many places in the average camera where light can leak, but most confusing of all is the leak in the apparently impregnable plastic body. Look for broken light traps around the back. Look for a shutter that isn't quite closed when it should be. Look for hair-line cracks in the case which are hard to detect until the body is strained under pressure.

A bellows will show minute pinholes when it is ready for the scrap pile. Never patch a bellows unless the hole is obviously the result of an accidental puncture. In such cases, a patch can be made which will last as long as the rest of the bellows. Use a minute scrap of focal-plane curtain material, and cement it inside the bellows, using a good grade of flexible cement. Use tweezers to jocky the bit of material into position, rubberized side toward the bellows.

Dull-black lacquer may be used to touch up spots inside the camera that might reflect light undesirably. Any bright spot that develops between the lens and the film is a special hazard of this kind and should be painted. When a camera closure (the back of a folding camera, the side of a movie camera, etc.) is not tight, leaks can easily

occur around the edge. First, examine the locking mechanism; if it is tight or cannot be adjusted, a judiciously glued bit of black light-leak yarn can eliminate many of your problems.

A bellows-test lamp is the easiest way to locate light leaks, without prolonged testing with sensitive materials and darkrooms. It is convenient because it can be poked into any out-of-the-way spot to provide tell-tale sparkles of light through the smallest pinhole.

Bellows are often attacked by various fungi. Often the leather or cements used are attractive to such growths, but alcohol or carbolic acid will destroy almost any fungus. If you use alcohol on a leather bellows, be sure to treat the bellows immediately afterward with a leather dressing of good quality.

Leather, plastic, wood, and metal surfaces of camera bodies will last longer and look better with an occasional surface treatment. This is the sort of repair you can take care of yourself; usually all that is involved is cleaning up and cementing the covering, refinishing leather and metal trim, and checking for light leaks.

Artificial-leather trim is difficult to refinish when it is badly scuffed, and worse when it is torn. Leather coverings are best cemented with tincture of shellac. Plastic coverings may be refastened with a good flexible adhesive. Follow the adhesive manufacturer's directions and avoid lumps of excess cement which will show in the finished job. Don't fret about cement oozing around the edges—it can be cleaned up easily after it has set with a solvent.

Minor defects in real and artificial leather can be camouflaged by cementing loose edges, cleaning, and refinishing. Alcohol will remove most foreign matter, but should not be applied to leather unless a preservative is used immediately afterwards. Scuff marks can be dyed, and the entire surface finished with a fine-leather preservative for long-lasting good appearance.

Stripped screw holes in wooden bodies can be repaired with good results by filling with slivers of wood. Dip each sliver in casein glue before forcing it into the hole. After the glue sets, the excess wood can be trimmed and the screw reinserted. Damaged metal trim can be refinished for better appearance

If you use an electronic flash, such as this Braun F80, remember to exercise the unit. The capacitors, which are the heart of the power unit, need this exercise in order to hold a full charge of ellectrical power for the flash.

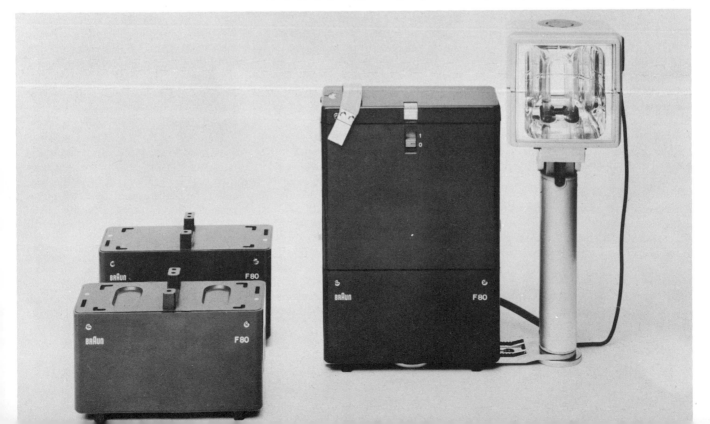

with moderate care. Satin-chrome finishes having minute defects can be touched up quickly and neatly with ordinary silver model-airplane dope. Black-enamel surfaces can be repaired with automobile touch-up enamel. Beware of large chips; they can be handled also, but only if you carefully sand the edges smooth so that the finished job will not reveal your handiwork.

If your camera has a film-number inspection window, check it occasionally for fading. Such a faded inspection window can be the cause of frustrating light leaks. It is quickly and inexpensively replaced by your repairman.

Certain hinges, folding mechanisms, film rollers, and similar moving parts may be lubricated as described in your owner's manual.

Pressure pads in both motion-picture cameras and still cameras are generally spring-mounted and must move freely for proper action. Occasionally a burr will develop on some portion of a camera in contact with moving film, which tends to scratch the film. Such burrs can be removed, but unless you have experience with polishing, the work should be entrusted to a competent repairman.

Polaroid cameras and some motion-picture cameras easily accumulate bits of emulsion or other chemicals from the constant passage of the film. Often a wet cloth or cotton swab is the best material to remove such deposits. (Here is another opportunity to examine all screws and tighten if necessary.)

If your camera has an accessible groundglass viewer, you may want to brighten the image by rubbing the ground side with a tiny amount of good grease or vaseline. While such treatment brightens the image, it also provides a place for loose dust to settle. For this reason clean such groundglass regularly.

If you use film holders, cleaning and brushing regularly will minimize dust. Store empty holders covered but with dark slides removed to extend the life of light-trap material.

EXPOSURE METERS

While most cameras are delicate, precision instruments, your exposure meter is probably the most fragile of all of your equipment. All of the precautions that have been mentioned above apply to exposure meters. A neck strap on an exposure meter is probably the greatest single insurance item you can use with that unit. Whereas any camera may be damaged if dropped, an exposure meter may be rendered useless with what appears to be a minor bump. Anything that will help keep it off the ground will be worthwhile. Dirt, heat, and humidity will quickly affect the meter.

If the meter is installed in a camera either as an accessory or as part of an automatic exposure-setting system, the entire camera becomes as delicate as a meter alone would be. If the automatic diaphragm in your camera is meter-controlled and battery-boosted, be sure that the battery is changed regularly to avoid damage. Dirt and dust that would not ordinarily affect camera operation can put an exposure meter-camera combination completely out of operation.

FLASH

More and more photographic equipment is electrical, either by nature or by design. A few hints, regularly applied, will eliminate most of the problems common in electrical or flash equipment. Be particularly concerned with the cleanliness of electrical contacts. Also, cables and connecting wires are subjected to a great deal of abuse and should be inspected often. Finally, many photographers seem to think that batteries and other power supplies should last forever with no attention; inadequate power is probably at the root of half of all flash difficulties.

If your shutter has an accessory synchronizer, keep it clean for free movement and dependable operation. If your shutter has a built-in synchronizer, be knowledgeable about its type and possible adjustment. No amount of maintenance will permit the satisfactory use of a No. 5 bulb with a shutter synchronized for electronic flash at $1/_{200}$ second.

Make certain that connectors and mountings on shutter and flash guns are mechanically secure. While some electrical couplings have a mechanical device to lock them in place, most rely on friction of one part against another. Sometimes judicious reshaping of a thin metal connector will increase the friction so that flash cords will remain mechanically and electrically assembled. Such re-forming should be restricted to the connecting cable, not the camera or flash gun.

Today's connecting cords are very small in diameter, quite flexible, but still subject to occasional flexing breaks or, worse yet, semi-breaks. A defect like this in a cable which appears normal can be frustrating. Rather than worry about finding such a break, which can sometimes be next to impossible, a spare cord is a desirable addition to your maintenance kit.

There was a time when many photographers developed the habit of wetting flashbulb bases for better contact. Initially, the moisture served to improve the electrical connection. However, over a period of time, corrosion developed in the bulb socket, with trouble ever after. It is better to use the modern trick and cement to your flash gun or camera a bit of sandpaper on which the tip of the bulb can be quickly scraped before inserting it into the socket.

All cords and connectors are subject to corrosion. Cords used for high voltage (house current, for example) often develop corrosion. If you attempt to use the same cords for low-voltage, battery-fired flash equipment, you may run into resistance difficulties. Be sure that the cords used for lighting or extensions are large enough to carry the required power.

Remember that the greatest source of trouble in all flash work is power supply. If your equipment uses dry cells, make certain that the cells are fresh and deliver adequate power. Low-voltage cells (the 1½-

This photo was taken with a 30-year old camera and lens and is proof that good equipment, properly cared for, can provide service for many years. Leica Model G and 50mm Hektor f/2.5 lens. Plus-X film exposed 1/100 of a second at f/6.3. (Photo: Michael L. Edelson)

volt round cells of various sizes) should simply be replaced regularly, depending on how often you use the equipment. For example, never keep a set of cells in a battery case or flash unit longer than four months, even if you use your unit only occasionally. Naturally, if you use the equipment more strenuously, you will actually wear batteries out and should replace them as often as every 50 to 100 exposures.

If you use an electronic-flash unit, remember to "exercise" your flash unit as you would your shutter. The capacitors, which are the heart of the power unit of an electronic-flash gun, need this exercise in order to hold a full charge of electrical power for the flash. You must give them a chance to breathe deeply of such power occasionally, or they won't be able to hold a charge when the need arises. By the way, if your flash unit is capable of operating on either a-c or d-c, perform the exercise cycle (called *forming* of capacitors) using a-c power.

If your flash unit uses rechargeable batteries, make sure that these are always recharged after each use and each exercise period if you don't use your flash unit regularly. Since electronic-flash units generally operate on rather high voltages, use caution in handling, and avoid making repairs unless you are familiar with this type of circuitry.

PROJECTORS

Although photo equipment has been described as instruments, projectors of various kinds are machines as well. Generally they include electrical and mechanical accessories like motors, switches, and lamps. The mechanical parts of still and motion-picture projectors (including automatic and sound equipment) are extensive, including gearing, belts, pulleys, etc. Lubrication and cleanliness are critical on all such equipment. Follow the manufacturers' instructions for oiling and cleaning, and keep your equipment under dust covers.

Watch for potential damage through misalignment of a hot lamp with its reflector and optical system.

Alignment can be checked in several ways. Carefully remove the bulb and examine its filament construction. Make a note as to the number of coils, their direction and arrangement.

If you can remove all the optics of the projector, it's possible to look into the projector, through the lens opening, to check the filaments and their reflection as produced by the reflector. Reflection effectively doubles the filaments. If the reflector is properly positioned, it concentrates the light of the bulb by doubling the number of coils in the bulb.

In the event that it is impossible to remove all the optics, you may be able to make a similar observation simply by looking into the lens, although dark glasses may be desirable. Another alternative is to project onto a screen without film and adjust the lens focus until the filaments themselves are imaged on the screen. Because of heat, alignment can change over a period of time. Adjustment is best left to a competent repairman, but regular checking is desirable.

Automatic slide projectors should be checked regularly for freedom of movement. The instruction manual is your best bet for learning how the equipment should work normally. Malfunctions detected early are your best protection against expensive damage.

The sound drum of sound projectors has a peculiar movement with which you should become familiar. Basically, this consists of a flywheel system to keep the movement of the film smooth and even, and free from flutter and wow as the film passes the sound-reading head. All sprockets, pulleys, and belts can be checked regularly for signs of damage.

The same maintenance techniques used on projectors may be applied to enlargers, although heat is not generally so great a problem in the latter.

MOTION-PICTURE CAMERAS

Movie cameras are subject to all the problems found in still cameras and in motion-picture projectors taken together.

One common cleaning problem is often overlooked and deserves your attention. The very small lenses found in movie equipment, especially 8mm, can be virtually obliterated by a few dust particles. Use the tiny chamois for reaching and cleaning the small surfaces involved. Look for film and emulsion buildups inside the camera, especially on the pressure pad. Lubricate only when your instruction manual indicates.

OTHER ACCESSORIES

Tripods and certain darkroom equipment require special care. Tripods can often be improved with wax or other dry lubricants for smoother function and protection. Film holders should be cleaned and checked regularly for light leaks and be identified or numbered to facilitate detection of leaks.

Electrical darkroom equipment should be used where it is not subject to the dangers of moisture; keep such equipment dry and clean. Regularly examine electrical cords for frayed or damaged areas where bare wires may be exposed, and reinforce such areas before the damage is critical, using plastic electrical tape.

Sinks, trays, and similar darkroom equipment can be repaired with standard commercial preparations if, for example, an enamelled surface becomes chipped. However, such repairs must be initiated promptly before any rusting begins.

Safelights should be checked and filters replaced if any of the normal tests reveal possible fading. Generally, the greatest danger to safelights is the use of lamps of excessive wattage. Use bright-colored walls to increase visibility and small lamps to reduce the possibility of fog.

TESTING

Probably the greatest aid to keeping your equipment in shape is regular testing. For example, a safelight test simply requires fully handling and processing a piece of the sensitive material to be used under that light. Compare with another sample of the material that has merely been fixed. Fog is quickly evident. Many tests can be made quickly and easily on your own or as part of your use of the equipment.

There are makeshift tests for virtually any technical phase of equipment operation. For example, you can use flashbulbs in a mirror to determine synchronization. You can take pictures of objects moving at a known velocity and measure the blur in order to judge exposure at various shutter speeds. Most such tests are costly, in terms of time and material, and of minimum accuracy. If you're far from professional repair facilities, such testing may be of little value anyway.

Many photographers enjoy making tests to prove or determine the quality of lenses. If you're interested in measuring resolving power, standard test objects and instructions are available from a number of sources, including the National Camera Repair School and the National Bureau of Standards. For average use, simply taking somewhat controlled pictures of a brick wall, newspaper or other easily available subjects will give enough of an idea of quality to satisfy most photographers.

For thorough testing at both minimum cost and time, make use of the services and facilities of a professional camera repairman, or a photodealer equipped with a service department. Look for National Camera ServiShops personnel to provide you with the kind of expert advice and facilities you need. While no one can guarantee that your camera will always work perfectly, your repairman's help, inspection, and care is the best insurance you can have.

Without wasting a bit of film or a single flashbulb, your camera can be put through its paces to find out exactly how it will behave when you are taking pictures. Your well-equipped dealer or repairman has precision instruments which can show you the facts about all of your equipment, regardless of its age or kind. You can see for yourself how your still or moving-picture camera is working. Whatever kind of flash equipment you may have, it can be tested and adjusted easily.

The ServiShops Motion Analyzer is a precision test instrument which shows, on a television-like screen, how your still-camera shutter works; or how smoothly your motion-picture camera operates; or how accurately and dependably your photoflash equipment functions. The tests will quickly determine if your equipment is working properly, and you can see for yourself when cleaning or repairs are necessary.

METER TESTING

One piece of equipment that should be checked regularly is your exposure meter. Unfortunately, meters vary considerably, especially from brand to brand and type to type. Do not expect a large and relatively rugged hand meter to read exactly the same as the automatic unit in a movie camera. It's not at all unusual for meters to vary a full stop at certain light levels. Two particular meters may agree at one light level and vary a stop and a half at some other light level. It's much better to recognize the differences that can occur and live with the situation.

MAINTENANCE KIT

The following items are suggested as logical components of a maintenance kit which you can keep in your gadget bag. It is not complete, nor does every item need to be included. However, it will give you a good idea of the sort of small tools and materials which can serve you well.

Jeweler's screwdrivers, 2 (.050" and .100" blades)

3" pocket screwdriver

4" straight-blade screwdriver

4" Phillips screwdriver

Small chain-nose pliers

Cotton-tip application sticks

Chamois lens-cleaning tools

Pair of tweezers of good quality

Bellows-test lamp

Several brushes of varying stiffness, from a soft lens brush through an old toothbrush

Cleaning solvent

Extra cords, botteries, projection lamps and similar ordinary replacements

The very small lenses found in movie equipment, such as the 8mm Leitz Leicina, can be virtually obliterated by a few dust particles. Use the cleaning techniques described in the text. Also, look for film and emulsion buildups inside the camera, especially on the pressure pad.

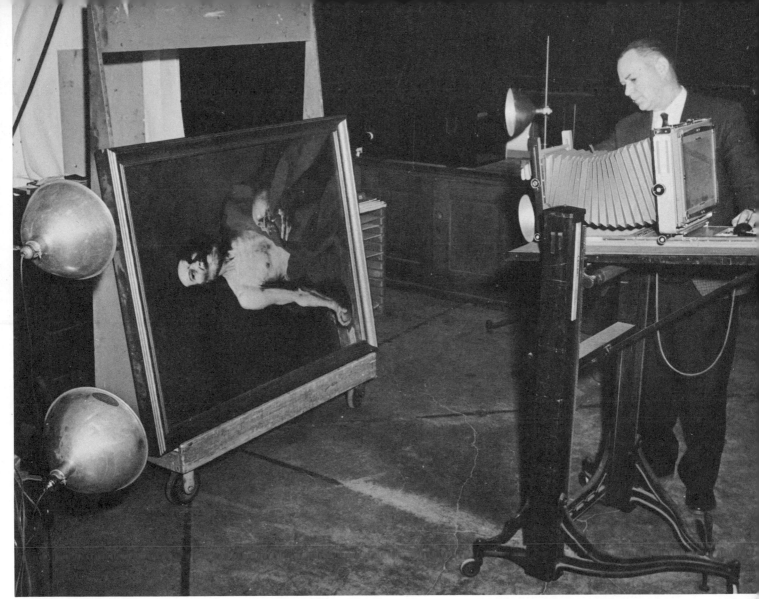

The author makes final adjustments for copying a painting. Note position of the lights and the tilting of the camera to line up with the painting.

Lens tissue
Small container of instrument oil
Leather dressing
Toothpicks
Bottle of casein glue
Tube of household cement
Bottle of Pliobond
Single-edge razor blades
Light-leak yarn
Ear syringe
Bottle of black lacquer
Tincture of orange shellac
Denatured alcohol
Small square of focal-plane shutter material

Your kit may be expanded with the addition of such things as an adjustable MultiSpan wrench with replaceable tips, soldering iron, etc. Most of the tools and materials are available by searching various stores; all or part of them may be purchased from National Camera Supply, Englewood, Colorado.

REPRODUCING AND INVESTIGATING PAINTINGS

JAMES K. UFFORD
Head of Photographic Department, Fogg Art Museum, Harvard University, Cambridge, Mass.

[There are several special techniques involved in the copying of paintings by photography. These techniques are discussed with particular reference to equipment, lighting, and exposure. The author also discusses the special field of detecting repaintings and frauds through use of X-rays, ultraviolet, and infrared light.]

• *Also see: Copying and Close-up Photography; Infrared Photography; Investigating Documents with Photography.*

A REASONABLE KNOWLEDGE OF light and photography will enable the amateur to get acceptable results in copying paintings. But even the finest print will only be "acceptable" because a perfect rendition in this field is virtually impossible.

The major problem in photographing a painting lies in the difficulty of transposing a colored work of art into a black-and-white print with its many shades of gray. Since deviation from the original tones is rarely desired, the photographer should simplify his procedures and confine himself to the production of the best possible monochromatic rendition of the painting.

Rendition of the painting is further complicated by the fact that

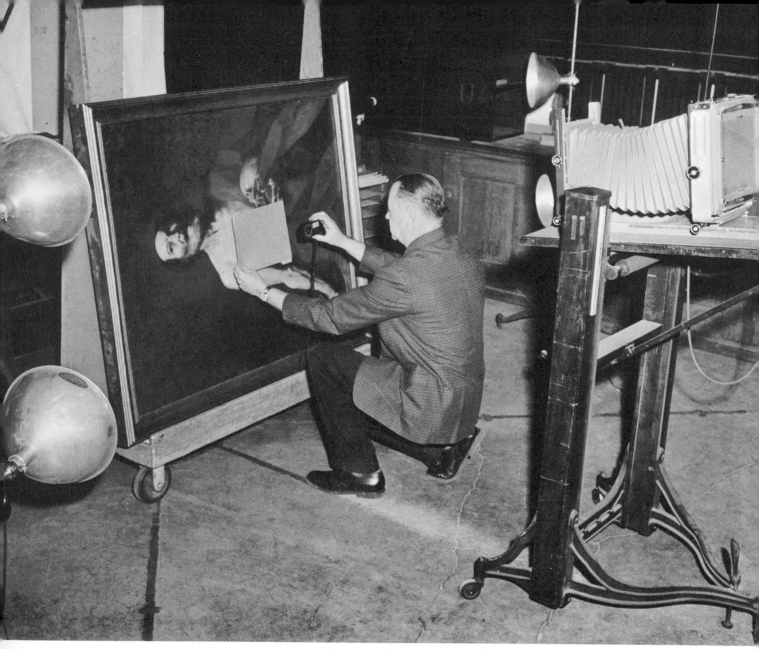

A plain gray card is used for checking the meter reading. Accurate exposure control is very important when copying paintings.

no two people see colors exactly alike, nor does the sensitivity of the film exactly correspond to that of the eye. Also the emulsions of various panchromatic films will vary according to different manufacturers.

For all these reasons, when I say the work of copying paintings can only be acceptable, I mean that even the finest photographic rendering is at best a compromise.

EQUIPMENT

For this kind of work the best equipment is a view camera with a double-bellows extension, a rising front, and any other features that overcome distortion. Such equipment will meet all situations for photographing a painting, whether

the painting is hanging on a wall, set on an easel, or in some inaccessible place. An 8×10 negative size is recommended for clear, sharp contact prints; a contact print always seems sharper than an 8×10 enlargement from a smaller size. Also, details from an 8×10 negative can be enlarged without any loss of definition.

Generally, anything less than groundglass focusing is inadequate. In this type of work a focusing cloth and magnifying lens for critical focusing is a must. A big advantage of the 8×10 format is the larger image size making it easier to detect nonparallel sides and ends.

Photographing from the exact center of a painting is the best method. Otherwise swings and tilts will be needed. The center can be determined by using a string to measure from each corner of the painting to the lens. Tilts can then be used if it is impossible to work dead center.

If the painting can be removed from a frame the possibility of shadow is eliminated and the problem of reflection is lessened. However, a painting conservator should first be consulted since improper removal can be injurious to the canvas and surface texture of the painting.

A good anastigmat lens of normal or longer focal length for the size film to be covered is satisfactory. Under some conditions, such as a large painting and short space, a wide-angle lens must be used. Above all, be sure the image is square.

LIGHTING

Even light is essential in copying paintings. Photofloods, tungsten-reflector floods, etc, all will do, provided the same type is used on both sides. I prefer two adjustable lights on each side. Next, take a meter reading from a white or gray card from each corner and the center of the painting. Moving the lights away will help balance illumination.

A polarizing screen is almost always a necessity in the copying of paintings since it is almost impossible to place the lights in such a way that there are no reflections on any part of the painting. If a polarizer is used, it is possible to eliminate most of these reflections by turning the axis of the polarizer toward the source of light causing the reflection.

Many old paintings on which the varnish has crystallized and started to oxidize show a general haze when illuminated by strong light. This haze is caused by each crystal reflecting a minute beam of light toward the camera lens. Here again a polarizer will absorb the reflected light and remove the haze which would otherwise obscure fine detail.

It is possible to use a polarizing screen over the light source as well as on the lens. With this technique the lights may be placed in any position which will produce uniform illumination. There are drawbacks to this procedure however. Polarizers used in front of the lights become very hot and tend to discolor, thus upsetting the color sensitivity of the film. Also, a double polarizer absorbs an appreciable quantity of light and causes inconveniently long exposures.

Placing the Lights

The most difficult procedure in the copying of paintings comes in the proper placing of the copy lights. The surface of most paintings, when examined closely, is far from the perfectly smooth plane it appears to be from a distance. The artist usually applies his pigments in a thick viscous state causing every brush mark to stand out. Thus the surfaces of paintings are a series of hills and valleys running in all directions. If a beam of light at 45 degrees falls on such a surface, it may reflect back into the camera lens while a beam making a more acute angle with the surface of the painting has less chance of being reflected to the camera. It is therefore customary to make the angle between the copy lights and the painting as small as possible with even illumination.

Figure 1 illustrates this lighting technique. Too small an angle between light L and L', and P (the painting) will result in uneven illumination. It is good practice to make this angle as large as possible without obtaining direct reflection. If the photographer sights the camera at C, he can watch for reflections and adjust the lights to make the angle LPA just small enough to prevent serious reflections at A and A'. Increasing the distances PL and PL' will aid in obtaining uniform illumination.

The polarizer may then be held before the eye and turned until any remaining reflection is removed, the polarizer is then placed on the front of the lens. This procedure makes it possible to do all the focusing with strong front illumination on the painting and then to adjust the lights for best illumination without watching the faint image on the groundglass.

Most paintings can be lighted according to the procedure outlined above. Special cases will tax the ingenuity of the photographer. The painting does not necessarily have to be lighted from both sides. If the working space on one side is limited, it is perfectly feasible to use two reflectors on the same side, one illuminating the near side of the painting and the other turned so that the brightest portion of its beam is thrown to the far side. This general arrangement may also be used if the painting is hung on a narrow wall so that the lights have to be placed on the floor and pointed upward. Sometimes just a little light from the floor will serve to even up the gallery illumination, permitting a satisfactory photograph.

In all these arrangements the main object is to obtain an even flood of light over the entire surface being photographed. Rarely will any other type of light be required. Occasionally, the photographer will be required to illuminate the surface with a strong raking or crosslight in order to bring out the surface texture of the painting or to emphasize the individual brushstrokes. A spotlight may be used for such lighting, but if a spotlight is not available, it is possible to mask off all but the center portion of the reflector or to turn a reflector so that only the light which spills out at the edge is used to illuminate the painting. A panchromatic film is recommended. It need not have a fast emulsion.

CAMERA ANGLE

Fully as important as proper lighting is the proper placement of the camera in front of the painting. Any distortion introduced by the photographer can be easily detected by the resulting out-of-square image.

In order to achieve an undistorted negative, a camera with no movements must be placed exactly on a perpendicular to the center of the painting. In this way the image may

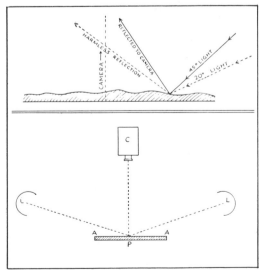

Figure 1. *Diagrams illustrating the lighting technique for photographing paintings. See text for explanation.*

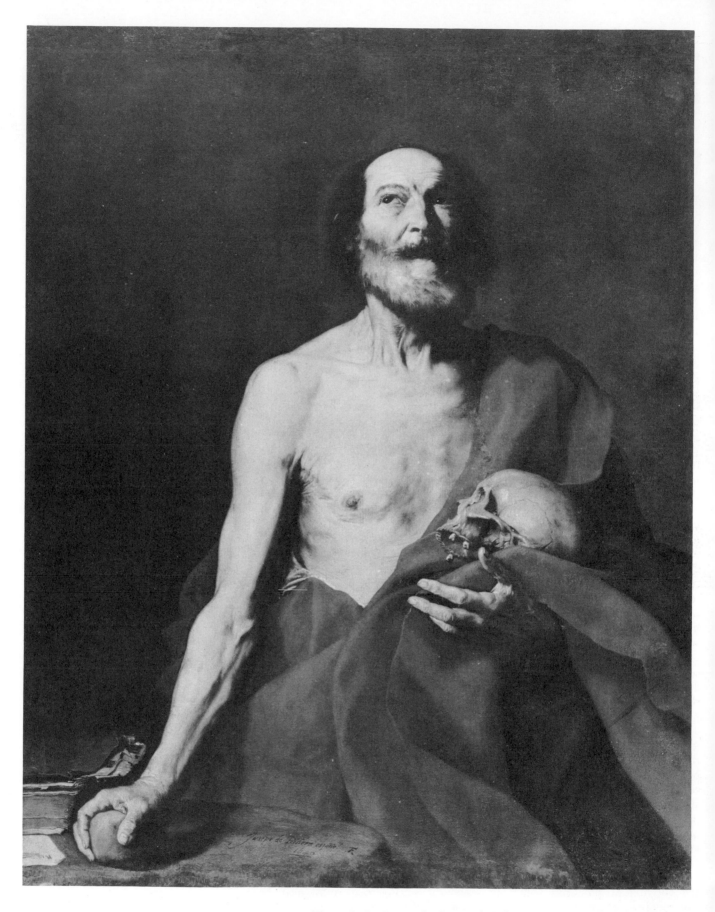

Figure 2. *St. Jerome by Jusepe de Ribera, as it appeared before cleaning.*

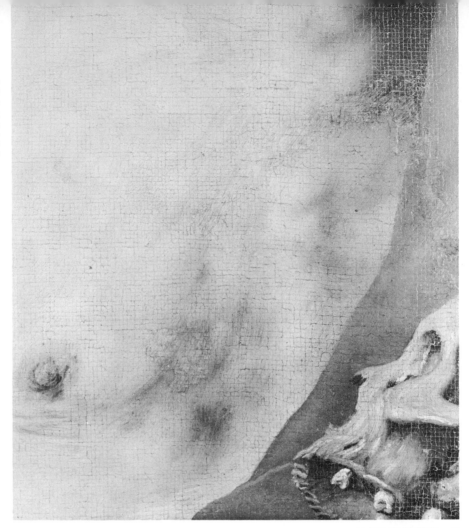

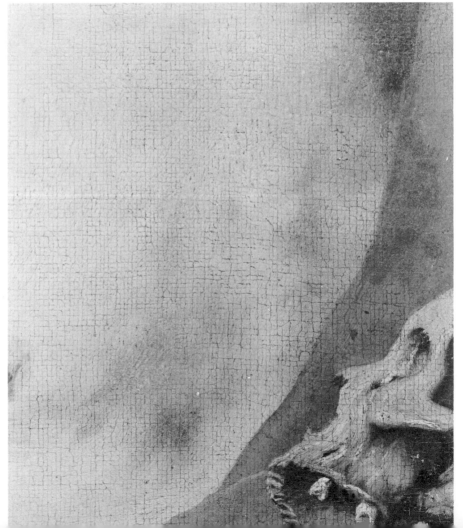

be centered on the groundglass and then the back may be swung until the edges of the painting are parallel to the edges of the groundglass. This procedure will automatically place the back of the camera parallel to the painting, a necessary alignment if the negative is to show no distortion.

If the camera is a little off center, the image on the groundglass should be watched carefully while the lens is stopped down to insure sharpness over the entire field. An adjustable level could be used in this case to get the camera back at the same angle at which the painting is placed. One length of string from the lens to each corner of the painting will aid in centering it on the groundglass, and the tilting feature will eliminate distortion. If your camera does not have tilts or swings, you will find that a tripod with a pan held is helpful in overcoming this deficiency.

EXPOSURE

Any reasonably accurate method of determining exposure will be satisfactory in copy work, but taking a reading of the illumination of a white or gray card held against the painting is most often used. The scale of tones which can be obtained with pigments and dyes is well within the scale of any ordinary film, and therefore an exposure determined by the amount of light reaching the painted surface will be correct.

One method of determining exposure is to take a series of test exposures at approximate settings. The film which shows the best detail in the darkest areas of the painting is then adjudged to have the best exposure. All the pertinent facts—light intensity, bellows extension, stop, shutter speed, type of film, and filter are then recorded, and any other painting photographed under similar conditions may then

Figure 5. *St. Jerome, detail. Taken before cleaning, with raking light. Notice that the repainted area is smoother than the original surface.*

veloping normally. Even then, three or four varying exposures on color stock are recommended. Be sure to include a gray scale and color chart, plus register marks, if your color work is to be published. Also, remember a dark painting will require more exposure than a light one, regardless of meter reading.

None of these cautions regarding color film should discourage anyone with proper equipment and a fair knowledge of photography from attempting color transparencies, for they offer a method of reproduction which can never be equalled by black-and-white. Duplicates with but a slight loss of quality may be made from transparencies and the transparencies themselves may be used as the basis for color prints.

Double check your bulbs to be sure they are right for the film used, check your meter periodically, and watch for line-voltage changes.

DETECTING REPAINTING

Photography today is an invaluable aid in determining restoration. The camera becomes a valuable tool of the restorer by revealing details not visible to the naked eye.

Many people may be surprised and even shocked to learn that a number of paintings by old masters have been damaged sufficiently to make restorations and repairs necessary. But when the age of these paintings is considered in addition to hazards to which they have been subjected, such as fire, vermin, and neglect, we may consider ourselves fortunate that so many works of art have survived. These damages are usually of a nature which mars the paint film, such as abrasion, cracking, tearing or deterioration of the support, chipping, and blistering.

It is now considered proper to make restorations and repairs so that from normal viewing distance the repair is scarcely visible, although the extent of the repairs may be readily seen upon close examination. Formerly, however, an attempt was made to repair in a way which would be invisible to the eye.

For example, an abraded section of paint film might be filled with a new ground material which would then be painted to blend exactly

be photographed with the same exposure. Any change from standard conditions will require a corresponding change in exposure to produce a negative of similar density.

It is better, if possible, to actually photograph a gray scale and have the results read on a densitometer; or to expose on a standard gray card and pull the slide out by seconds as you expose, much as a test strip is used during printing.

Some people standardize on their light; say, 65 at a given stop. From this standard they can then calculate for any variables.

COLOR

With color film there is a wide variety of types available plus conversion filters for almost every type of light source. Basically, the procedure is the same as that used for black-and-white. Read the directions that come with the film and proceed accordingly. Some photographers prefer to work with a color-negative film since this can produce transparencies, color prints, and black-and-white from one negative.

Exposure can be determined by exposing a black-and-white film of the same emulsion speed, and de-with the surrounding paint surface. Often this repaint would be carried over the original for some distance in order to obtain a better match. There are even cases in which the entire surface was repainted to hide a poorly preserved original surface. This method was used by unscrupulous restorers as a means of disguising an obviously old but seriously damaged painting as a valued old master.

In the hands of an experienced technical man the camera becomes useful in the detection of repainting, but perhaps more important, it often makes it possible to determine the exact nature and extent of the damage under the repaint. The beginner in work of this sort is often disappointed if the results obtained are not startling or clear, but he should remember that as in many other scientific studies the record is only clear to experienced eyes and that the value of some of the results may be controversial. It is possible for the relatively inexperienced photographer to make photographs which may be invaluable to the technical man. If called upon to do this type of work, the utmost care should be exercised to follow directions exactly.

SPECIAL METHODS

X-ray shadowgraphs and photographs by ultraviolet and infrared light are the methods commonly used in the study of paintings and the results of work with these mediums receive considerable publicity, but the lack of equipment for X-ray and ultraviolet photography does not preclude this use of photography as an aid in the study of paintings. A photographer who handles his lights and camera competently can make photographs which show valuable detail and which some experts feel may be as revealing as those produced with the more specialized apparatus.

The accompanying photographs show not only the results which may be obtained with X-rays, and ultraviolet and infrared light but also the suprising and interesting fact that

equally revealing photographs may be made by using a view camera and ordinary lighting.

A SPECIFIC EXAMPLE

A painting of St. Jerome by Ribera, 1588-1656, was chosen because it showed definite but not too clearly defined traces of repaint. Figure 2 shows the painting of St. Jerome as it appeared after removing the repaint. We may safely assume that this is also a good representation of its appearance before some forgotten restorer made extensive repairs. Figure 3 is a detail study of the tear which appears on the shoulder of Saint Jerome. It should be noted that this photograph outlines the damage

much more clearly than the photograph of the whole painting and therefore it may be said that the ability to make good detail photographs is requisite to all work of this type. The only difference from the arrangement for taking the whole painting was moving the camera closer to the painting.

Figure 4 illustrates the same section of the painting in its repainted state. Note that in this detail the damage is all but invisible. This photograph was made in exactly the same manner as Figure 3. Slow panchromatic film was used for the first four details in order that the photographic rendering should correspond as nearly as possible to that of the eye.

Figure 6. *St. Jerome, detail. Taken before cleaning, with strong and close-frontlight.*

Raking Light

Figure 5 is the same detail taken by raking light. In this case a single strong light was placed at one side of the detail close to the painting in order to bring out the surface texture of the paint film. This type of lighting is often the best way of showing surface texture, but here the results are not entirely satisfactory, although there is a clear indication of the repair.

The raking light casts shadows into the surface indentations giving the effect of high relief even though there may actually be a difference of only a few thousandths of an inch between the high and low spots. Notice that the filled in and repainted area is much smoother than the original surface where the grain of the canvas is clearly discernible.

Strong Front Light

Figure 6 shows the tear illuminated by strong frontlight furnished by a light source as close to the camera as possible. This type of light serves to show irregularities as well as the raking light when the surface illumination is only slightly irregular. In this case it is more satisfactory than the raking light, for it not only shows the area repainted but also shows clearly the size of the holes in the canvas.

Ultraviolet Light

Figure 7 is what is commonly referred to as an ultraviolet photograph. What is photographed is actually visible fluorescence caused by ultraviolet light. A light-yellow filter over the lens prevents any ultraviolet rays from reaching the film.

For work of this type a special ultraviolet-light source is required. This light source should be so filtered that all visible light is absorbed and only ultraviolet rays which cause fluorescence reach the painting.

The position of this light is relatively unimportant as long as even illumination is secured, because any direct reflection of the rays is absorbed by the filter on the lens. In this photograph we see a distinct difference in fluorescence between the old and new paint. This may usually be attributed to a difference in paint medium rather than to a difference in pigments. Although it is true that many pigments will glow in ultraviolet light, the fluorescence from the medium in which the pigment is suspended is usually strong enough to overshadow any fluorescence from the pigment itself.

Infrared

Figure 8 illustrates the same detail photographed by infrared rays. Ordinary 1000-watt bulbs were used and placed in the same manner as for Figures 3 and 4. A Wratten A filter was used in conjunction with infrared film. Although the repainted area is clearly visible in this photograph, the results are not outstanding. This may be attributed to a chemical similarity between the old- and new-paint pigments. Two pigments of the same color but differing chemically will often absorb infrared in quite different degrees, thus making a division between the two pigments distinguishable in an infrared photograph.

X-ray

A radiograph of the same section of torn canvas showed very clearly the damage to the ground coating beneath the paint, but it gave no indication whatsoever of the amount of repaint. X-ray photographs alone furnish valuable evidence and, in

Figure 7. *St. Jerome detail. Taken before cleaning by ultraviolet light, with the different fluorescing powers of the old and new paints shown.*

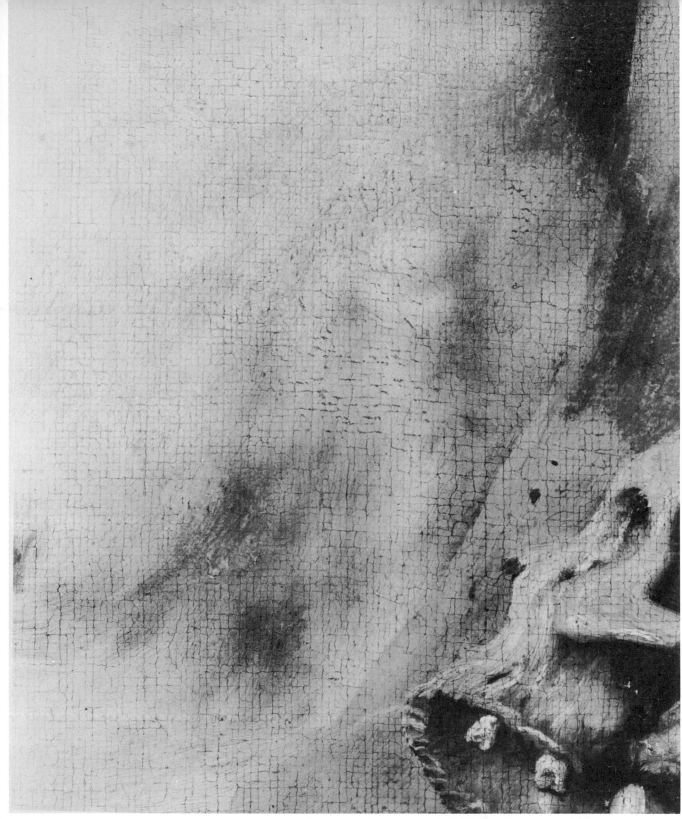

Figure 8. *St. Jerome, detail. Taken before cleaning, with infrared light and film.*

combination with photographs made by simpler means within the reach of the average photographer, they round out the evidence gathered concerning any questionable area.

CONCLUSION

A painting may be thought of as consisting of three layers; the surface layer which the eye sees, the layer of pigment which gives body and depth to the color, and the ground or support layer which serves as a foundation for the other two. Evidence concerning the first layer is furnished by the ultraviolet light. Information concerning the second layer is obtained from the infrared photograph, and the X-ray gives the condition of the base layer.

Much information concerning all three layers may be obtained, however, by a judicious use of ordinary equipment, if the photographer is able to bring out differences in surface texture by skillful handling of his lights and camera.

Left: **WHAT IS IT?** National air-raid alert brought these expressions on Monkey Island in Cleveland Zoo. Mamiya C-2 with 180mm lens. Tri-X film exposed at f/11 for 1/125 of a second. (Photo: Ray Matjasic)

Top Center: **THRILLING SPILL.** Six-day bike racer hit top rail breaking both bike and one leg. Speed Graphic 4X5 and Super Panchro film exposed at f/11 for 1/400 of a second with strobe. (Photo: Ray Matjasic)

Top Right: **TUMBLING DOWN.** Fire causes wall to collapse atop stores below. Speed Graphic 4X5 and Super Panchro film exposed at f/8 for 1/125 of a second. (Photo: Ray Matjasic)

Right: **RAGING RELATIVES.** Leaving courthouse for workhouse, woman's husband and brother attack photographers and newsmen. Speed Graphic 4X5 with Type B film exposed at f/11 for 1/400 of a second with fill-in strobe. (Photo: Marvin M. Greene)

REPTILE PHOTOGRAPHY

A. PIERCE ARTRAN
Former Curator, California Serpentarium

[An almost untouched, yet fascinating, field of nature study is the photography of reptiles —particularly of snakes and lizards. An authority who has taken pictures of reptiles both for pictorial and scientific purposes tells in detail about the techniques involved. He covers the methods of handling snakes, the precautions involved, how to photograph them in cages and in the field, and how to get action shots.]

• *Also see: Animal Photography; Nature Photography; Zoo Photography.*

REPTILES ARE FASCINATING SUBJECTS for photography. Their unusual forms and rhythmic poses permit dramatic compositions and a wide variety of pictorial treatments. Seekers after the S curve can find it in profusion among the snakes and the sinuous lizards. Others will be challenged by the proper rendering of the texture of scales or plates.

A few reptiles are dangerous. The ability to distinguish the poisonous from the nonpoisonous reptiles of the United States can be learned easily from any authoritative book on the subject. It is also worthwhile for those interested in reptiles to see the dangerous species in the flesh. The keeper of the reptile house in any zoo will be glad to point out the venomous species which may be encountered in the area. Anyone who plans to work with venomous reptiles should first observe their handling by some zoologist in the vicinity who is trained in this field.

WHERE TO PHOTOGRAPH THEM

Reptiles are usually found in such a tangle of grass, brush, or rocks that the jumbled background would hide or obscure the center of interest in a picture. Reptiles have many enemies and they shun the open places where they are more easily seen. A majority of these animals have protective coloration

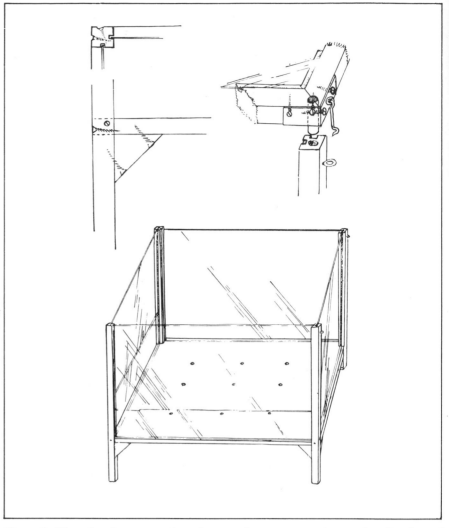

Figure 1. *Plans for the construction of a cage for average snakes, turtles, lizards, and alligators. The complete glass-sided cage is shown; below and above are details of corner construction and the attachment of the removable glass roof. Recommended dimensions are 30×40×24 inches, with ten-inch legs. The corner posts are of hardwood and the grooves to fit the glass may be cut by the lumber yard. The dowel pins for the cage top are 3/8-inch across, and the top may be of window glass. The sides should be of flawless glass.*

which blends into most backgrounds. It is therefore difficult to get satisfactory pictures of many species in their native habitats.

Successful pictorial or illustrative pictures of reptiles are therefore rarely obtained in the field. It is far better to capture the specimens and pose them in a cage with models, lighting, and background under control. Very natural effects can be secured in this way, and many beautiful compositions obtained.

THE CAGE

The accompanying drawings (Figure 1) show a cage which makes the photographing of reptiles a simple matter. It is inexpensive and may be made in any size, but it should be at least three feet wide. A cage this size will be adequate for all native reptiles except the largest snakes, the larger turtles, and adult alligators.

The floor of the cage may be covered with various colors of sand, gravel, or soil, and a wide variety of other props may be introduced to simulate the natural habitat of the reptile. Rocks, branches of trees, or bushes are the most common additions to raise the reptile off the ground and bring his profile against the sky which is the back of the cage.

For pictorial and illustrative pictures the rocks chosen should have a light-reflection value distinctly different from the specimens, unless its protective coloration is to be emphasized. In the latter case, typical rocks which closely resemble his coloration should be taken from his habitat.

Many snakes and quite a few lizards climb in bushes and trees. These species can often be most satisfactorily posed on a branch in the cage; they are more likely to remain still when given this support.

The branch used should be simple, without small twigs to clutter the picture (Figure 2). Even with simple branches, watch that part of the branch does not photograph to look like part of the reptile.

The specimen should be posed as far from the back of the cage as is practical so that the texture of this background is out of focus. If a rock is to be used to support the specimen, build up the soil or sand between the rock and the back of the cage so that the reptile will have no place to hide.

TWO APPROACHES

In a pictorial photograph of a reptile I see no reason why a simplified set such as a single rock or branch should not be used. This need not be exactly the kind of rock or branch on which such a species is found in nature but however simplified it may be, the set should suggest the habitat of the animal. Do not, for example, place a desert reptile on a branch with verdant leaves, or an aquatic specimen which lives among water-rounded rocks on a piece of rough rock.

For scientific pictures of reptiles

Figure 2. *Arizona vine snake. A simple branch with few projections was selected for this natural pose.* (Photo: G. M. Bradt)

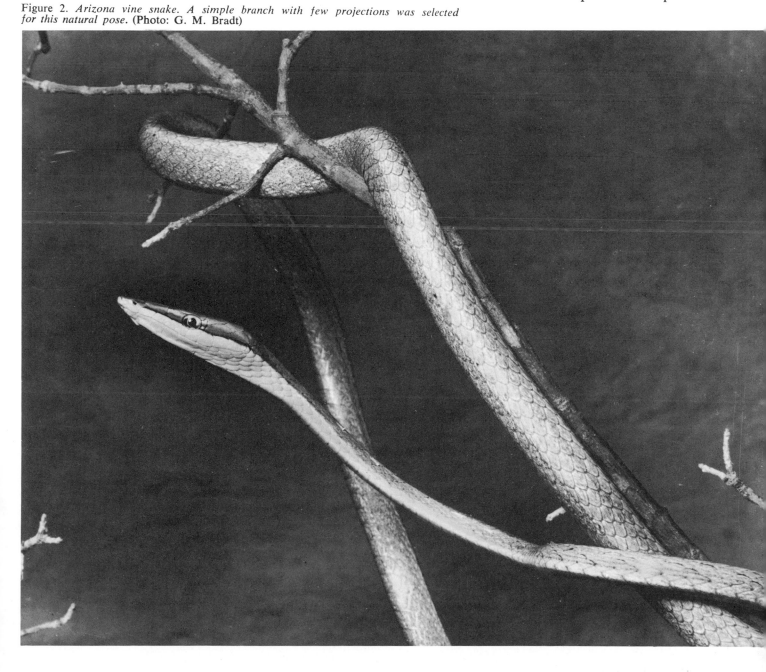

in their habitats, those made with the cage are usually superior to actual location shots. Very realistic habitat sets may be built up in the cage. The materials to make up these sets should be collected from a typical habitat location. Small growing plants may be uprooted, brought home, and placed in shallow tin cans of soil (the soil in the cage will hide the cans). By a careful observance of the natural habitat and the proper choice of materials a set can be constructed which will be more typical of a given species' preference than most locations found in nature. This constructed environment will have the added advantages of confining the reptile to this particular scene under controlled-lighting conditions.

The set should be as honest a representation of the habitat as can be made. Faithful reconstruction of the surroundings and natural pose of the specimen are primary considerations in a scientific habitat photograph; composition must be secondary. Regardless of its purpose, any picture should tell its story clearly and be pleasing to the eye—all of which points to the superiority of the cage-made picture.

POSING REPTILES

Some reptiles will pose themselves remarkably well. In fact, some will hold so still that time exposures may be used. Others are much less tractable and require patience and finesse on the part of the photographer. Some specimens can be picked up and placed where wanted. Others are frightened by handling and should be gently coaxed into position by a light touch with a small switch. Most reptiles have ticklish tails and a light touch there will make them move. A light touch on the nose is somewhat effective in stopping them.

Frequently a reptile can be frozen into a pose by suddenly bringing the flat of the hand, or an object of

Texas Alligator Lizard. Posing these active creatures can be a lively chore, especially in warm weather. See text for a method of refrigeration that helps in the posing. (Photo: G. M. Bradt)

Portrait of a rattlesnake, Crotalus ruber. *Here I have attempted to depict the rattler in the sinister aspect in which he is held by most people. This feeling is heightened by the black background above the head, and by the rattler looking the viewer right in the eye. This shot was made by holding the snake at a pre-arranged spot before the lens as described in the text. It should be noted that this is an almost straight profile. What appears to be another nostril set between and below the nostril and the eye is the distinctive pit found in all pit vipers.* (Photo: A. Pierce Artran)

similar size, a few inches in front of his face. Too much coaxing will merely frighten the average speci- men. If he becomes jittery, it is best to leave him alone for a while until he calms down. Quick moves frighten captive wild animals and many domestic ones as well. If you will adopt slow motion and forego gestures and pointing you will make faster progress.

Some of the most successful poses can be secured by focusing the camera and sitting down beside it. The reptile, in moving about its cage, will soon come into a satis- factory pose. If a specimen happens to be in the mood to lie still, a slight jarring of the cage will usually start it moving.

Temperature

It is not strictly accurate to say that reptiles are cold-blooded. The scientific term describing their tem- perature is *poikilothermic,* which simply means that the body heat is variable and is approximately that of their surroundings—a reptile is cold on a cold day and warm on a warm day. The temperatures at

which reptiles function best are about 98 F for the diurnal species, 90 F for the nocturnal forms, and perhaps 80 F for those living in water.

Reptiles have a considerable temperature tolerance below these optimums, but very little tolerance above them. At five degrees (body heat) above these temperatures the various forms of reptiles become very restless; if the body temper- ature reaches 10 to 15 degrees above the first figure they will die. Closed cages placed in the sun often result in death of the reptiles, and prolonged exposure to close photo- flood lamps also may kill them.

When a specimen proves too active, it should be put into a glass jar or closed can and placed in the refrigerator for twenty or thirty

minutes. There need be no holes in the lid as there is sufficient air in the jar for the reptile's needs at a low temperature. After cooling, the reptile should be carried from the refrigerator in the jar and then lifted gently and placed in the desired pose. If the specimen can be gently slid from the jar into a pose, this is even better because it may be frightened by handling and the heat of your hands.

All lights should be controlled by one switch. When the subject comes into a pleasing pose, one hand can turn on the lights and the other operate the shutter. This sudden snapping on of the lights is very helpful in causing the reptile to hold the pose, at least momentarily, be- cause for a moment he is light- struck or dazzled.

Sidewinder, Crotalus cerastes. *This type of background is too similar to the speckled pattern of the reptile for a clear photograph.*

Shutter Speeds

The shutter speed must be gauged by the activity of the specimen. I have shot some posed specimens at one-half second, but such long exposures are rarely satisfactory. The reptile's scales create a multiplicity of sharp lines and the slightest movement will cause blurring. One twenty-fifth of a second is a safe speed when the reptile is still. (At this speed movement caused by breathing will be stopped.) Reptiles usually pause in their breathing at the end of both inhalation and exhalation; watching the breathing will show you when to click the shutter. One fiftieth of a second will stop most head movements; $1/_{100}$ of a second is a safe speed for fast or jerky specimens. For action shots the fastest speed

on your shutter is the best, with $1/_{250}$ of a second as a minimum.

Snakes extend their tongues to taste the air, much as mammals sniff it. This tongue movement usually consists of rapid dartings in and out. This movement can be caught at $1/_{100}$ of a second but few photographers are quick enough to trip the shutter in time. It is more satisfactory to shoot just after the tongue is drawn in than to take a chance on it causing a blur. Some snakes, notably the pit vipers (rattlesnakes, copperheads, water moccasins), will extend the tongue and slowly wave it up and down. One twenty-fifth to $1/_{50}$ of a second will stop this motion if the tongue is caught at the top or bottom of the

swing. *Caution:* this slow movement of the tongue is evidence that the snake is aroused and angry.

Because of the amount of heat involved, it usually is impractical to produce sufficient artificial light to shoot at shutter speeds faster than $1/_{100}$ of a second. Placing the cage in strong sunlight provides a better source of light for such speeds and a light-reflecting floor is particularly effective.

When using flash it is best to make a thin white-silk diffusing disk to fit in front of the flashbulb in order to tone down hot highlights from a shiny specimen. The silk will absorb about half the light, so exposures should be doubled.

Some action shots are quite satisfactory with the flat lighting produced by one flashbulb mounted alongside the camera; better modeling is obtained with two flashbulbs, one being set two to four feet to one side.

LARGE REPTILES

For the larger native reptiles anything except a very large cage is likely to have an inhibiting effect on the reptile. Such shots are best done by turning the specimen loose in an open area of light-colored soil or sand. With the more agile species it is wise to have an assistant "surround" your subject to keep him in range of your camera. Such shots will be better lit if done with the sun over your shoulder during the first half of the morning or the last half of the afternoon.

For action shots of venomous species it is much safer to work through a shield. A shield can easily be made of a piece of cardboard about 2 × 3 feet. The cardboard should be fastened so that one of the long sides can be held against the ground. The lens should be eight to ten inches from the bottom of the shield for low-angle shots. Turning the shield over will raise the lens to a higher angle.

A shield will work better with a reflex camera and permit a kneeling or crouching posture. With other types of cameras, a good angle for most action shots will require the photographer to lie on the ground. Such action shots should not be attempted by those who are unaccustomed to working with venomous reptiles, or by those whose reaction time or muscular coordination is below normal.

CONTRAST

Some reptiles are black and white, or cream and dark olive, or of similar contrasting colors. This excessive contrast, combined with a seemingly polished surface, creates a challenge to any photographer's skill. Injudicious lighting, exposure, or development under such conditions can tax an emulsion beyond its limits. Lighting should be softened by diffusion and be no stronger than necessary for the desired shutter speed and aperture.

The two main lights should be set so as to strike the subject at oblique angles from each side in order to create textural highlights in the darker areas, with a third light above and slightly in front to fill-in the shadows. Daylight is sometimes superior to artificial light for such contrasty specimens. Set the cage up in the shade of a building so that it gets the even light from a bright sky.

It is not a good policy to put the full amount of artificial light on the specimen before you are ready to take the picture. I use a medium-gray card placed in the spot where the subject is wanted for the average tone subjects. For the high-contrast patterns it is always best to use both a black and a white card to get the minimum and

Banded Geckho. The weathered-tree background gives a good base for photographing this colorful specimen.

maximum readings.

A perfect exposure over such a wide range is, of course, impossible and the question must be what sort of compromise is best. If the specimen is dark with light spots, the exposure must be sufficient to get the detail in the dark areas, which will mean losing it in the light spots. Conversely, an exposure that is not too much for the highlights of a light-colored reptile with dark spots cannot pick up detail in the spots.

SHADOWLESS WORK

Another type of reptile photograph is seen in pictures illustrating scientific articles—a shadowless picture without any background. This effect is obtained by photographing the specimen on a large piece of groundglass evenly lighted above and below. Place the ground side up. The frame holding the glass can then be supported by two boxes or any other supports.

It is better to have about a half-dozen small lights under the glass than two or three large ones, as this will provide more even illumination. These lights need not be in reflectors; they may be rigged by mounting a half-dozen sockets on a piece of plywood the size of the glass. The top surface of this board should be coated with aluminum paint.

Toplighting consists of two lights in reflectors on either side of the camera and at approximately the same height as the camera. These lights should strike at about 45 degrees to the axis of the lens, but each should be focused on the far side of the specimen so that the rays cross each other. This crossing of the lights will give more even illumination.

A third light must be used to fill in the shadows. This may be set directly above the subject, or it may be held in one hand so that it can be quickly shifted to follow the movements of the specimen. Both bottom and toplights should be controlled by one switch.

Since the bottom lights heat the glass, the specimen if cold will (with most species) lie more or less still and gratefully absorb the heat. But after a minute or two the glass will become too warm for comfort and posing will then be difficult. Have everything ready before putting the reptile on the glass.

FIELD PHOTOS

The most interesting area for the photonaturalist is that of reptile behavior in the field (Figure 3). Photographs of reptiles taken in nature should be accompanied by complete information. All too often such pictures lose much of their value because they lack accompanying data. This data should include location, date, time of day, state of weather, temperature, and a factual description of what was observed.

Some behavior patterns that are of particular interest and value are courtship and mating, capture and eating of prey, reptiles being attacked or eaten by other animals, unseasonal appearance, unusual location, or any other instance or action which seems unusual. A sequence of shots showing each detail of the behavior should be obtained. The picture story should be complete.

Courtship and mating behaviors have been observed in only a few species, and these were largely of specimens in captivity. The interpretation of photographs of courting behavior is very difficult unless the sex of each specimen concerned is known. Rivalry between two males, for instance, might be misinterpreted as courtship. Those who are able to secure such pictures should then attempt to capture the reptiles so that a zoologist can make a definite determination as to their sex.

The food of most reptiles is fairly well known from examinations of stomach contents, but very little is known of some of these animals' methods of capturing their prey. A fascinating series of pictures can be made along this line alone. I have seen a lizard leap out from a rock and catch a flying insect on the wing. Such an action shot could make the front page of any picture magazine or Sunday newspaper.

Unseasonal appearances are always of interest since there are, for instance, recurrent tales of various reptiles being found upon snow or ice. Of much greater interest would be a recorded investigation of the reason the reptile was in this predicament. Can its track be traced to where it came from? Was the hibernating den flooded? Digging into the den from which the tracks lead, or into likely looking dens in the immediate vicinity might establish the reason. The air temperature at the time together with the maximum and minimum temperatures for the day and the preceding day should be learned from the local weather bureau. A flooded condition of the area or heavy rain would also be relevant.

One of the least known phases of reptilian life is that of the reptiles' enemies. Nonpoisonous reptiles are eaten by quite a number of mammals, birds, other reptiles, and fish. Photographs of these attacks will add to our knowledge of these animals' relationships to each other. A subject of even greater interest (and mystery) is that of the enemies of the poisonous snakes and the gila monster. I know of no recorded enemy of the gila monster (which is our only poisonous lizard) but it is reasonable to suppose that they have enemies besides man. Information on an animal which eats this species would be of extreme interest.

Among the listed enemies of juvenile and/or adult poisonous snakes are eagles, hawks, owls, badgers, skunks, weasels, deer, hogs, roadrunner turkeys, chickens, herons, cranes, crows, king snakes, indigo snakes, and racer snakes. How do these various animals attack venomous serpents without being bitten? The manners of attack by some, especially eagles, hawks, and owls, are a genuine mystery. Any photographer coming upon an animal attacking or eating a reptile should try to get as many pictures of the act as possible, and at the last (or at least) frighten the attacker away and get a close-up photograph of the remaining portion of the reptile so that positive identification of the species can be made. It would also be helpful to take the uneaten remains to a zoologist for identification.

A telephoto lens is a valuable

Figure 3. *This black-headed snake has just shed its skin and poses with all its fresh sleekness in a natural environment.* (Photo: G. M. Bradt)

accessory for one who photographs reptiles in the field. This type of lens enables the photographer to obtain photos that would be impossible with a normal lens. The vision of many reptiles is adjusted to close range; many see in only are not able to recognize objects a blurred manner at distances of 20 or 30 feet. This means that they are not able to recognize objects at this distance, but can only detect movement. If the photographer is a good woodsman, stalks his quarry with care, and keeps his own movements to a minimum, he may get pictures of a reptile unaware of his presence. To keep his odor from the quarry he should

consider the wind as much as possible. Another tip is to tread softly. Snakes have little or no hearing, but they are quite sensitive to the vibrations of footsteps transmitted through the ground. Telephoto shots of reptiles are frequently better when shot against the light as this makes the subject stand out from the background.

THE SNAKE STICK AND NOOSE

For those who have occasion to photograph venomous reptiles a few words of advice may be in order. Such reptiles may be handled by pinning down the head and grasp-

ing the neck. Pinning the head should be done with the standard snake stick (Figure 4). If the pressure on the snake's head is too much, the delicate bones in the snake's skull are broken; if the pressure is not enough the snake may jerk loose and bite the operator; if the snake is improperly grasped by the neck he may easily get one fang into the hand holding him. If any slip occurs a serious case of snake poisoning will probably result.

In spite of the care and experience of the operator, manual handling of venomous snakes is bound to

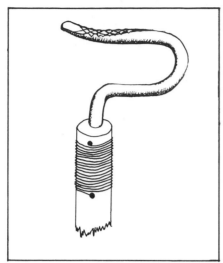

Figure 4. *The standard hooked snake stick made of 3/8-inch steel and a hardwood handle. This is for moving venomous snakes short distances. When placed under a spot about one-third of the distance from the head to the tail, the snake can be lifted and will usually not slide off the hook.*

result in an accident every so often. Therefore, manual handling is not worth the risk. For photographic purposes all handling, except quick shifting of the snake within its cage or to a cage immediately adjoining, should be done with the noose (Figure 5).

In use the noose is slipped over the head of the snake and worked down to a point about one third of the length from the head. With snakes that are reluctant to be noosed a little strategy is necessary. If the open noose is held perfectly still in front of the snake's head and its tail touched with another stick, it will usually crawl into the noose. When one third of the snake's length has passed through the noose it is pulled just taut enough to keep the snake from sliding or crawling further. With this hold on the snake he can be safely lifted, carried, or held as long as the hands are kept farther from the bottom end of the stick than the one-third length of the snake which is free to strike at that distance.

Never place the noose around the snake's neck. This is terrifying to the snake causing it to thrash around so that it cannot be posed or even handled safely. This violent thrashing may break the snake's neck or result in other injuries causing death.

Never use a noose made of cord or wire. A narrow noose is bound to break some of the snake's ribs, and cause so much pain that the snake will fight violently.

Never use a tighter noose than is necessary to keep the snake from slipping. Always lift and move a snake gently and slowly. If it becomes badly frightened and violently fights the noose, put it down on the floor (to return it to its accustomed support) for a minute or two and see that your noose is not too tight. If the snake tries to twist itself out of the noose, return it to the floor and slacken the noose for an instant so that the painfully twisted skin under the noose can straighten out. Remember that to frighten or anger a venomous snake not only increases the risk, but makes posing it extremely difficult, thereby adding to the photographic problems.

OTHER PRECAUTIONS

Shifting of a venomous snake from one cage to another, or otherwise removing it from its cage is most safely done in a closed room without furniture. It is no easy matter to remove a poisonous snake from the coiled springs in upholstered furniture. Workers should always wear high leather boots or leggings. Gloves are inadequate protection from a poisonous-snake's fangs, but an old pair of leather dress gloves offer good protection against the bites of harmless snakes.

The first requirements of anyone working with poisonous snakes are a thorough understanding of these various snakes' characteristics, dangers, and limitations; the proper treatment of the various types of venomous bites; and a good kit for the first-aid treatment of snakebite on the spot.

Figure 5. *Three views of a noose used for handling poisonous snakes. The stick, made of hard wood, is about $\frac{1}{2} \times 1\frac{1}{2}$ inches and almost five feet long. The leather strap is 24 inches in length, with the grain side next to the stick and with a 24-inch control rod at the end. The end of the stick is padded with heavy felt.*

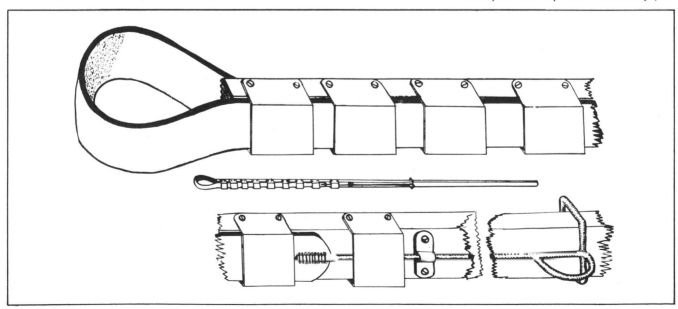

RESEARCH AND BACKGROUND MATERIAL FOR THE PHOTOGRAPHER

ALBERT BONI
Author, "Photographic Literature"
[There is such a vast amount of photographic information in print that it is now a problem to find the book or reference that pertains to your immediate problem or interest. The following summary will be of special value to all photographers.]
• *Also see: Museums and Collections of Photography.*

THERE IS NO OTHER FIELD OF popular activity which receives the bounteous published aid that is given to the photographer. Handbooks and manuals for his camera, film, paper, and other apparatus pour out in a continuous stream from the manufacturers. Data books, photographic primers, professional guides, instructions, and aids to highly specialized techniques are issued by numerous book and magazine publishers. The photographer is offered every possible assistance in technical fields from radiography, photomicrography, photogrammetry, and high-speed photography, to space technology, motion pictures, and television. Hundreds, even thousands of new books are issued every year.

BASIC REFERENCE WORKS

The basic aids for finding books in general are the annual publications, *Books in Print* and *Subject Guide to Books in Print* (R.R. Bowker Company, New York). Neither of these titles need be purchased since they are available in every library and practically every bookstore. *Books in Print,* as its title indicates, is a listing of books which publishers have in stock, listed by author and title. It should be consulted when you know author or title of the book and want to find the publisher and availability. *Subject Guide to Books in Print* has the reverse information. In this volume you look up the subject in

ADAMS & CO.'S 'A1' VENTILATED PORTABLE TENT.

This is, without exception, the most perfect changing tent ever manufactured, and is extremely portable, the size when folded being only $18\frac{1}{2} \times 13 \times 1$, and the weight 5 lbs. When open, the working space from right to left is 33 inches, the rigid portion being 18 inches long × 12 broad × 12 high, and the remainder made flexible.

A greatly improved and efficient ventilator is now fitted.

Price 21/- net ; postage -/9.

Fig. 212c.

ADAMS & CO.'S 'CHALLENGE' DARK TENT.

This tent is specially recommended for travellers, as it is substantially made, 'and will stand much rough usage. It is made in the form of a neat case, the sides of which form the rigid sides of the tent. It is fitted with a window on runners, so that white light may be obtained if desired. It is suitable for developing any size plates up to $8\frac{1}{2} \times 6\frac{1}{2}$.

Size, $24 \times 17 \times 5$.

Weight 12 lbs.

Price £2 2s.

Tripod for same, 18/6.

Fig. 213c.

Since the development of photography can be traced through advertisements, these are collected for future reference and research. This ad appeared in the 1884 British Journal Almanac. (George Eastman House Collection)

which you are interested and you will find the titles listed under subject classifications with cross references.

PHOTOGRAPHIC REFERENCES

A finding aid devoted completely to photography and related subjects is *Photographic Literature,* edited by Albert Boni and an editorial board of specialists, New York, Morgan & Morgan Inc., 1962. *Photographic Literature* lists over 12,000 basic books, professional journals, magazines, articles, technical papers, patents, etc.

References are arranged in more than 1200 subject headings from

Abady's Photometer to Zoopraxiscope. References cover inventors, scientists, industrialists, photographers, writers and historians, as well as products, processes, techniques, theory, portraiture, nature, cameras, optics, television, etc.

For the person seeking highly technical information, we recommend *The Theory of the Photographic Process,* revised edition, by C.E. Kenneth Mees, New York, Macmillan, 1954. In addition to being the magnum opus on the subject, it includes more than 2500 references to other literature.

A briefer and more recent work covering the same subject is *Fundamentals of Photographic Theory,* 2nd edition, revised, by T.H. James

This aeronaut is shown with a special camera used for photographing aerial views from a balloon and appeared in the February, 1912 issue of Scientific American. *Extensive collections of these historical photographs are housed in a number of museums throughout the world for both the amateur photographer and the researcher.* (George Eastman House Collection)

Many museums contain photographic collections for researchers since considerable information can be obtained from historical photographs. This is the First Pennsylvania Light Artillery ready for action before Petersburg on June 21, 1864. (National Archives)

and George C. Higgins, New York, Morgan & Morgan, Inc., 1960. Also of value is *Photography, Its Materials and Processes,* 6th ed., by C.B. Neblette, New York, Van Nostrand, 1962.

The outstanding histories are:

The History of Photography, by Josef Maria Eder, translated by Edward Epstean, New York, Columbia University Press, 1945; *The History of Photography from 1839 to the Present Day,* by Beaumont Newhall, New York, Museum of Modern Art, 1949; and *The History of Photography from the Earliest Use of the Camera Obscura in the Eleventh Century up to 1914,* by Helmut and Alison Gernsheim, New York, Oxford University Press,

1955.

The best dictionary of photographic terms and processes is the *Dictionary of Photography,* edited by A.L.M. Sowerby, New York, Philosophical Library, 1956.

The best one-volume encyclopedia is the *Focal Encyclopedia of Photography,* available in a desk edition as well as in a larger format, New York, Macmillan, 1956; London, Focal Press, 1960.

A basic reference work for every photographer, studio, laboratory and camera shop is the *Photo-Lab Index,* edited by J.S. Carroll, New

York, Morgan & Morgan, Inc., annual. It contains over 1400 loose-leaf pages gathered into 24 sections, giving formulas, processes, and data about photographic products from Kodak, Ansco, DuPont, Ilford, Agfa, Polaroid, Gevaert, General Electric, Westinghouse and others, as well as information on general subjects such as optics, chemicals, cine, color, photomechanical, etc. Annual supplements keep the book constantly up-to-date.

Imperative for all who would keep up with the new developments, the ever widening horizons, and the most recent applications of photography, are the many general magazines, such as *U.S. Camera, Popular Photography, Modern Photography,* and specialized journals and annuals, such as *Journal of the Society of Motion Picture and Television Engineers, Photographic Science and Engineering, Journal of the Society of Photographic Instrumentation Engineers,* and the *Journal of the Optical Society of America.*

We also draw special attention to the periodical *Aperture,* edited and published quarterly by Minor White, 72 Union Street North, Rochester, New York. This magazine is notable both for the elegant quality of its reproduction as well as for the experimental artistic nature of its work.

LIBRARIES AND MUSEUMS

For all who are searching to extend their knowledge and interests, please bear in mind that every community has one or more libraries containing collections of books on every subject. These are at your disposal and you will be served by librarians anxious to help. In addition to the books and files of periodicals, many of these libraries have separate collections of photographic material. The outstanding collection is, of course, The Library of Congress in Washington, D.C., which has in its Print and Photographic Division millions of photographs and more than 70-million feet of motion-picture film.

The New York Public Library has one of the finest collections of photographic literature of any library in the country and, in addition, maintains an excellent pictorial collection. Also in New York, the famous Epstean collection of photographic literature now forms a part of the special collections at the Columbia University Library. The superb collection in the Photographic Division of the Museum of Modern Art in New York is limited to modern photography.

The greatest special collection of photographs and photographic literature in one institution is the George Eastman House at Rochester, N.Y. Eastman House is well worth a special visit or a vacation trip by everyone interested in photography.

RESOLVING POWER

JOHN S. CARROLL
Editor, "Photo-Lab-Index"
[Resolving power still has considerable meaning in the measurement of image quality as produced by lenses, films, and other parts of the photographic system. Here the author covers the subject in depth.]
• *Also see: Acutance.*

RESOLVING POWER IS THE MEASURE of the ability of a photographic system to distinguish two closely spaced objects. The measurement of resolution is expressed in terms of the spacing of two objects that can be separated on the film, or in the visual image in the case of instruments such as microscopes and telescopes.

Measurement of resolving power is always made in the image plane and is given as a number of *lines per millimeter.* To determine resolving power, therefore, the test object must have varying numbers of lines and spaces, equal in width. Thus, the width in millimeters of a single line or space is one half the rated numerical value. For instance, a test pattern showing 25 lines per millimeter has line spaces which are each $1/50$ of a millimeter wide.

MEASURING RESOLVING POWER

Usually, measurements are made by photographing or viewing the image of a large chart whose final image size is reduced by a known amount. This is because it is easier to make a large chart accurate; as the image size is reduced, possible errors are also reduced. The Bureau of Standards chart is actually 25 times as large as its image is intended to be. When photographed at the proper distance (26 times the focal length of the lens and not 25 times as might be imagined) the image on the film will have the spacings as indicated by the numbers on the chart—that is, the spacings will be from 3.5 to 56 lines per millimeter. All sets of lines are in pairs, each pair consisting of a vertical and a horizontal set of lines. The reason for having both is to check for astigmatism, in addition to resolution.

Strictly speaking, to test a lens

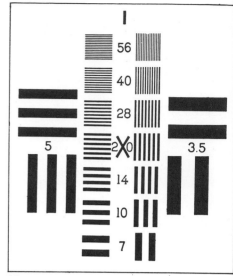

Measurements are usually made by photographing or viewing the image of a large chart, such as this one from the Bureau of Standards. It is easier to make a large chart accurate; possible errors are reduced when image size is reduced. All sets of lines are in pairs, each pair consisting of a vertical and horizontal set of lines, in order to check for astigmatism as well as resolution.

with such a chart the lens, without camera, should be focused on the chart and the aerial image it produces then examined with a microscope. Only in this way can we be sure we are testing the lens and only the lens. In practice, however, the charts are usually photographed on film, and the measurements to determine how many lines are actually resolved are made by examining the film. This is obviously not a test of the lens alone, but of lens, film, camera focusing errors, etc. Such tests will often, therefore, give disappointing values for what are purported to be fine lenses. If this occurs, it pays to see where the flaw in the system really lies.

A SIMPLE TWO-ELEMENT SYSTEM TEST

To begin with, the resolution of a system cannot be better than the resolution of its poorest component. Also, each element tends to destroy some resolution; thus, in a simple two-element system (a lens and a film), it is probable that the combined resolution of both will be something like:

$$\frac{1}{R} = \frac{1}{r_f} + \frac{1}{r_l}$$

where R is the combined resolution, r_l is the resolution of the lens, and

r_f is the resolution of the film.

Take for example, an ordinary lens which can resolve about 50 lines per millimeter. Suppose we make the test on our usual fast pan film, which can also resolve about 50 lines per millimeter. Then:

$$\frac{1}{R} = \frac{1}{50} + \frac{1}{50} = \frac{2}{50} = \frac{1}{25}$$

Hence $R = 25$ lines per millimeter.

Do you now see the fallacy of the common belief that lens resolving power need be no better than that of the film?

Suppose now that, in place of our ordinary lens, we test one lens reputed to resolve 200 lines per millimeter. Such a lens, four times better than the other, will naturally cost a great deal more. We should, therefore, expect much better performance from it. So we photograph our test chart, again using the same 50-lines-per-millimeter film. What have we now?

$$\frac{1}{R} = \frac{1}{200} + \frac{1}{50} = \frac{5}{200} = \frac{1}{40}$$

So, our fine, expensive lens has improved the resolution of the system from 25 to 40 lines per millimeter. But this is still far short of the 200-line resolution which we have been promised for the lens.

A definite improvement results from the better lens. But, the resolution of the system can never be better than that of its poorest element and photographing a test chart will not as a general rule give an accurate measure of the performance of the lens alone.

We could, of course, get a better result by using a film of higher resolution. But this would prove very little unless the same film were also to be used regularly with the lens. Even then, we would still be measuring only the performance of the system and not of the lens or film alone.

FILM RESOLUTION

We have been discussing lenses, but the same principles apply to films. Attempts to verify manufacturer's claims for resolving power of various films usually fail because we are measuring not only the film but also the lens. Manufacturer's tests are usually made with special lenses having resolving powers far greater than ordinary camera lenses. This results in resolution ratings higher than can obtained with an ordinary camera lens.

Lenses used for testing purposes are usually specially made microscope objectives. They can, if necessary, be used with filters which limit the light to one color and eliminate chromatic errors. For maximum resolution, we need the largest possible aperture, and since the lens will be used to focus on a single plane, it can be made to the theoretical maximum of $f/0.5$, or even larger if the space between lens and object can be filled with liquid. We have a very different situation than when using a regular camera lens and the resulting resolution figures for the film may be very close to those of the film itself.

A camera lens, on the other hand, is necessarily a compromise of a great many factors. It must cover a fairly large field on a flat plane; it must have minimal astigmatism; it must be corrected for color and chromatic difference of magnification, and also for coma and distortion. Since all these corrections interact to some extent, it is not possible to satisfy them all. And, in practical photography objects are normally at varying distances, and good depth of field is required, so we can not ordinarily aim for the theoretical maximum speed.

MEASURING TESTS

For measuring tests several charts are used. The charts are located in both the center and edges of the field for tests of lens resolution. If we are testing the film alone, only the center of the field need be used. After the film has been exposed and developed, the image is examined with a magnifier. The finest line pattern which is still clearly resolved is taken as the resolution.

Some care is necessary in this testing to avoid spurious resolution. Due to diffraction, double or triple images will at times be formed, and these, falling on top of each other but displaced by one line, can give the appearance of resolution to a pattern which is actually not resolved. Sometimes we may even find a pattern resolved, the next smaller pattern not resolved, and a still smaller one resolved again.

This is obviously spurious resolution, and it can usually be identified by counting lines. In a case of spurious resolution, we will usually find too many or too few lines.

MODULATION TRANSFER

A more modern way to test is to use a special type of test object which is not simply black lines on white, but which has lines graduated in tone from white through all possible grays to black, and black to white again in the same manner. The chart is a continual repetition of this pattern, except that the spacing of the lines decreases continually. They start widely spaced and become closer and closer until they cannot be resolved even by the best system.

The resulting image is then scanned in a special densitometer which can read very tiny areas and simultaneously draw a curve plotting the densities as it travels. The result is a wavy line, going up and down in accordance with the densities on the film. The height of each pulse in this line represents the density, and the trough between pulses shows the minimum in the spaces between lines. Thus, the differences between the high and low points represents the response at each spacing.

From this information a simple curve can be drawn showing the entire response of a film from the coarsest to the finest line spacing. And by establishing a criterion for cut-off we can easily determine the resolution figure for the film. In addition, we can tell from the shape

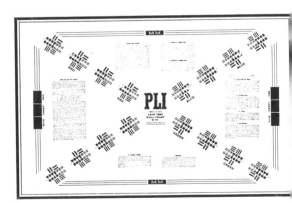

The Morgan & Morgan lens-test wall chart is a 20×30-inch chart printed in four colors. All instructions are printed in the chart enabling the photographer to test his own lens, film, and camera performance.

of the curve whether the film was high or low acutance and how it will respond to high contrast or low-contrast subject matter.

This system can be used directly with lenses, and then with lens and film combinations. By mathematical methods, it is then possible to determine the exact contribution of each component to the final result.

Modulation-transfer figures will, we expect, gradually take the place of resolving-power data as photographers become accustomed to the new system and realize the amount of useful information it conveys.

RESOLVING POWER AND FOCAL LENGTH

The resolving power of a lens is usually given by the so-called *Rayleigh criterion*. This states that, for any given lens stop, the resolution will be:

$$R = \frac{2000}{f/\text{stop}}$$

This, of course, is theoretical, in the sense that is presupposes a lens without aberrations. Such lenses have been made for specialized scientific uses, but are not available for general photography.

For example, a perfect lens at $f/4$, would resolve 2000/4 or 500 lines per millimeter in the image plane. At $f/2$, the lens could resolve 1000 lines per millimeter, while at $f/8$ its resolution would be only 250 lines per millimeter.

The importance of this figure lies in the simple fact that there is nothing in the formula concerning focal length. That is, any perfect lens at $f/4$, regardless of its focal length, will resolve 500 lines per millimeter.

This resolution, to repeat, is in the image plane. But in the subject plane, resolution will increase with the focal length of the lens.

To make this clearer, imagine a brick wall, with bricks two-inches thick, photographed at 100 feet with a six-inch lens. The image of each brick on the film will be $1/200$ of two-inches or $1/100$ inch. With a 12-inch lens, the image of the same brick at the same distance will, of course, be twice as big, or $1/50$ inch. But, both lenses, if perfect, would have the same resolution at the same aperture. And, since the 12-inch lens makes an image twice

as big, it could resolve the same bricks twice as far away with the same aperture.

Thus in aerial reconnaissance there is no substitute for focal length. The high-altitude pictures made from the U-2 reconnaissance planes probably were made with lenses of at least 24-inches focal length, although the exact figures have not yet been released.

Putting it another way, no matter how fine the film and no matter how well corrected the lens, under the same conditions an 8 mm movie camera can never produce the image detail of a 16 mm camera. And the 16 mm camera can never produce the detail of a 35 mm. Likewise, for enormous movie screens, the use of 70 mm film is clearly necessary if the huge image is to contain as much detail as the smaller picture usually shown in a theater.

Similarly, a first-class 8 × 10 negative will always contain more detail than a 4 × 5, assuming the 8 × 10 was made with its normal 12-inch lens and the 4 × 5 with a six-inch lens. And, the 35 mm camera with a two-inch lens will have even less detail, and a subminiature with a 25 mm lens will have still less.

□

RESTRAINER

A photographic developer is a special form of reducing agent that has the ability to reduce exposed silver-halide grains to metallic silver while leaving unexposed grains unaffected. Developing agents vary in their ability to distinguish unexposed from exposed grains and nearly all developers have a tendency to work on both. This produces a veil of silver in unexposed areas which is known as developer fog. To prevent this fogging, a chemical known as a *restrainer* is usually added to most developer formulas.

POTASSIUM BROMIDE

The most common restrainer is potassium bromide. Its effectiveness varies depending on the quantity used and the developing agent involved. With metol, for example, only a small amount of bromide is used, because excessive bromide reduces the developing power of

metol even on exposed grains. With hydroquinone, however, considerable bromide can be used without effecting its developing power. High-contrast developers are often heavily bromided to keep unexposed areas clear while permitting the growth of heavy densities in exposed areas.

OTHER BROMIDES

Sodium bromide can be used in place of potassium bromide. The effect is about the same, but since sodium is lighter than potassium, only six parts of sodium bromide are needed to replace seven of potassium bromide. Other bromides, such as lithium bromide, work equally well, but have no particular advantage while costing much more. Ammonium bromide should be avoided as the carbonate present in most developers will release ammonia from such salts. Ammonia has an unfortunate effect in many developers; it may even cause dichroic fog.

RESTRAINERS FOR PAPER DEVELOPERS

For paper developers some synthetic-organic restrainers are used where blue-black tones are desired. Such restrainers include benzotriazole and 6-nitrobenzimidazole nitrate. These are powerful antifoggants, but do not have as much tendency to slow down the normal action of the developers as do the bromides. These restrainers are particularly valuable when used with overage papers and films to avoid fog due to deterioration of the emulsion. They also extend the life of the developer by reducing its tendency to fog as it oxidizes.

Potassium bromide, when used as a restrainer for paper developer, may cause the image to become brown or greenish.

□

RETICULATION

Reticulation is an over-all, leathery wrinkled effect produced in the gelatin emulsion of a film by excessive temperature change during processing. The effect is not confined to the gelatin; it can also cause a break-up of the silver image.

Reticulation is not purely a temperature effect; it is possible to process films at fairly high temperatures without reticulation if proper

An example of severe reticulation.

on the temperature—at higher temperatures gelatin absorbs more water.

THE SALT EFFECT

One other phenomenon is of importance—the *salt effect*. In general, gelatin absorbs less water from solutions containing dissolved salts than it does from pure water. The nature of the salt itself is not important although neutral salts cause less swelling than alkaline salts such as the carbonates.

A developer with a salt content of ten percent can be used up to 90 F without excessive swelling of the emulsion. However, in such cases there is great danger of sudden swelling and reticulation when the film is transferred to the rinse. The rinse which contains no salt will be absorbed with almost explosive rapidity at 90 F, and reticulation will probably result.

PREVENTING RETICULATION

Instead of a plain-water rinse the film is usually treated in a stop bath containing a small amount (about three percent) of acetic acid to neutralize the developer, and 100 grams per liter of either sodium sulfate or sodium sulfite. This high salt content prevents undue swelling of the film and consequent reticulation during the rinse. The film may then be transferred to the fixing bath which should be at the same temperature as the developer and stop bath. Since the usual fixing bath contains up to 25 percent of hypo, plus sodium sulfite and other ingredients there is little danger of excessive swelling while the film is in this bath.

In spite of the hardening the film may reticulate if it is transferred at this stage from the warm hypo to cold wash water. Therefore washing should be carried out in stages. The first rinse should be at the same temperature as the hypo bath, and the rinse water may be loaded with sodium sulfate. This is followed by successive rinses, each in slightly cooler water and each containing

less salt. The final wash is given in pure water at 68-75 F, after which the film may be safely dried.

SUPERHARDENED FILMS

A number of modern films are superhardened in manufacture. These films are intended for high-temperature processing and some can be handled in baths of 125 F without special precautions. But, unless the film is known to be pre-hardened, it should be handled with all possible precautions and never at temperatures higher than 90 F.

Prehardening baths are recommended where films must be processed at high temperatures. These baths always contain formaldehyde (which is notably unpleasant to use) and has an adverse effect on the developer as it usually causes fogging. These baths sometimes contain an organic antifoggant to avoid this problem but this, unfortunately, tends to lower the emulsion speed of the film.

DELIBERATE RETICULATION

Reticulation is sometimes deliberately used for artistic effects. Generally, it is easy enough to produce reticulation when desired, but in some cases it requires using a developer at temperatures as high as 125 F.

To avoid accidental loss of the picture in case the reticulation is not as desired, the negative is processed normally and dried. It is then treated in a ten-percent sodium-carbonate solution at 120-125 F, after which it is transferred to cold water, washed, and dried.

Some control of the fineness or coarseness of the reticulation pattern can be exercised depending on the temperature, time of treatment, and how well hardened the negative was in the initial processing.

It is best to make a normal negative of the subject desired and then to make the copy negatives by any regular method. The copy negatives are then used to experiment with reticulation. In this way various effects can be tried on the same subject. Printing a normal negative through a texture screen will often produce equally satisfactory results with considerably less difficulty.

precautions are taken. For instance, reticulation is unlikely to occur even at 80 or 85 F if the developer, fixing bath, and wash are all at the same temperature. At higher temperatures, reticulation will take place even if all temperatures are kept equal.

The cause of high-temperature reticulation is believed to be a sudden change in the swelling of the gelatin layer occurring as the film is changed from one processing bath to another. It will often be found that a film will not reticulate in the developer but that a reticulation pattern will appear as the film is being rinsed before the hypo bath. In other cases, the film can be carried all the way through the developing process and will suddenly reticulate in the wash water.

GELATIN STRUCTURE

Gelatin is a sponge-like material with many tiny pores. It has the property of swelling as it absorbs water but does not dissolve in water. The amount of swelling depends on the amount of water absorbed by the gelatin which, in turn, depends

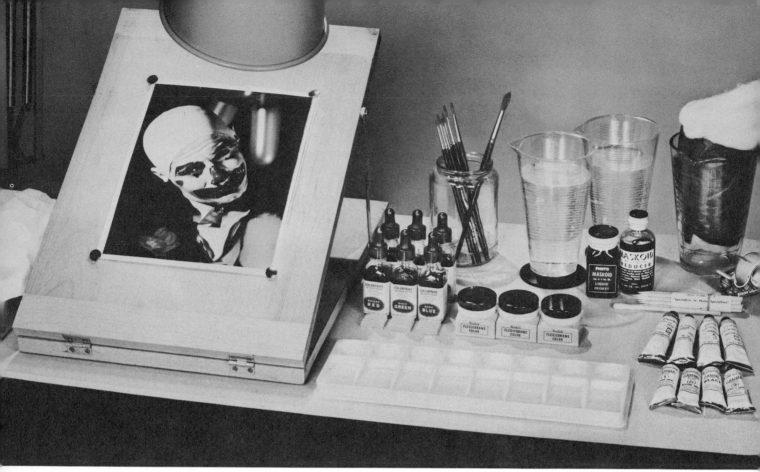

View of table with materials for retouching. Arrange materials on right-hand side if right handed, on left-hand side if left handed. Overhead is light for good visibility. Large prints require a drawing table which tilts. For smaller work, as shown, two boards may be hinged at one end, with opening hinges at the other end to provide a comfortable tilt to the work. Not shown are the alcohol solvent for flexichrome and the bleaches referred to in the text.

RETOUCHING COLOR FILMS AND PRINTS

FRANK P. TARTARO
Director of Color Department,
Germain School of Photography,
New York

[A certain amount of spotting or retouching can be done right on the color print. Unwanted lines, facial blemishes, wrinkles, or shadows can be removed or modified and the print greatly improved. In this article the author gives his easily learned technique for color retouching.]
• *Also see: Retouching Color Transparencies.*

PRINT FINISHING, THE FINAL OPERA-tion in preparing the completed color print, marks the truly conscientious and knowledgeable amateur or professional. Even when care is taken in earlier steps, the final product often exhibits a need for some finishing touches.

Blemishes on the original subject must be removed, marks of various sizes and shapes caused by lint or dust during printing need correcting, and deficiencies in tone and color-correcting masks may be objectionable and need adjustment. Time and economics permitting, the job may have to be redone from the stage where the error first occurred. If too much hand work has to be done to the final print, it loses its photographic quality and takes on a hand-drawn look.

FIRST PRINCIPLES OF COLOR-PRINT RETOUCHING

Good retouching should be invisible to the average informed viewer. To aid in achieving this objective, always work under a level and quality of light equal to, or brighter than, the final conditions under which the print will be viewed.

Tack, tape, or otherwise secure the print to prevent it from slipping around during retouching. A slightly inclined table top will be comfortable for most work except for very wet operations when the print should lie flat.

Whether removing unwanted density or adding density to light areas, the work should progress gradually and blend naturally into the surrounding area. Avoid overcorrection, which is usually more noticeable and objectionable than undercorrection.

Keep these thoughts in mind: 1) work slowly, 2) blend gradually, 3) *stop before you're finished*—stand back, review the work, redo areas needing more attention.

TEST ON REJECT PRINTS FIRST

A most important and useful habit in retouching is to practice the desired correction on a reject print of the same type. Some of the colorants used in adding density are difficult to remove if overdone. Some of the bleaches are very easily overdone, compounding the retouching problem. A careless error at this stage could necessitate a complete remake of the print.

We shall describe in particular the retouching techniques used with the dye-transfer process and Ektacolor prints, the two processes which have gained widest acceptance among such critical clients as national advertisers. However, similar techniques can be tried where other processes are used, particularly those processes concerned with the addition of density to the print.

THE TREATMENT OF DARK SPOTS AND AREAS IN DYE TRANSFER PRINTS

Small spots of white (missing color) may be caused by dirt, lint, or dust in the making of the separation negatives, or by a defect in the original subject. Large-area errors are usually caused by a deficiency in the colorants used, or a miscalculation in the use of earlier tone or color-correcting masks. For example, the masking procedure employed may not have removed enough cyan from red areas, resulting in a greyness of the red and other warm-colored areas. Improvement could be effected by the local removal of cyan. Similarly, greenish areas would be brightened by a local removal of magenta, and bluish areas by removing yellow. Bear in mind that the colors we see in our modern-print materials are formed by some combination of the three colorants: cyan, magenta, and yellow.

The Basic Colorants

The amount of cyan (blue-green) dye deposited determines how much we see of its complement, red, that is, how much red is reflected or transmitted; the amount of magenta (red-blue) dye deposited controls green light; and the amount of yellow (red-green transmitting) dye deposited controls blue.

The colorants may also be thought of in terms of the complements they absorb: cyan is minus-red; magenta is minus-green; yellow is minus-blue.

The addition of complements forms a neutral or black, the specific density of the neutral depending on how much of each is added. Cyan plus red equals a neutral, as do magenta plus green and yellow plus blue.

Bleaches

In determining bleaches required, the following is helpful: removing cyan from the print makes the working area redder; removing magenta makes the print greener; and removing yellow shifts the print toward blue. In addition to the color change effected, the entire working area becomes brighter. A selective bleach for the cyan image in the Dye Transfer Process can be prepared by mixing a solution of potassium permanganate. First attempts should be tried with a very weak solution, made by dissolving approximately one-fourth gram per liter of water (a pinch in a quart). With experience, the solution may be made stronger. Too strong a permanganate solution leaves behind a brown stain which is difficult to remove. Always try it first on a reject print.

A clearing bath to eliminate the permanganate stain is prepared by mixing a one-percent or slightly stronger solution of sodium bisulfite (about ten grams in one liter of water). The bisulfite solution is itself a mild bleach for the cyan, so care should be taken to avoid spilling it onto areas of the print other than the one being corrected.

Handle concentrated chemicals carefully. Keep them away from

Step 1 in good brush work. After mixing required color, pick up small amount with bristles of brush. Press against side of well as you remove brush to leave behind the bulk of color, retaining only a small amount in the brush.

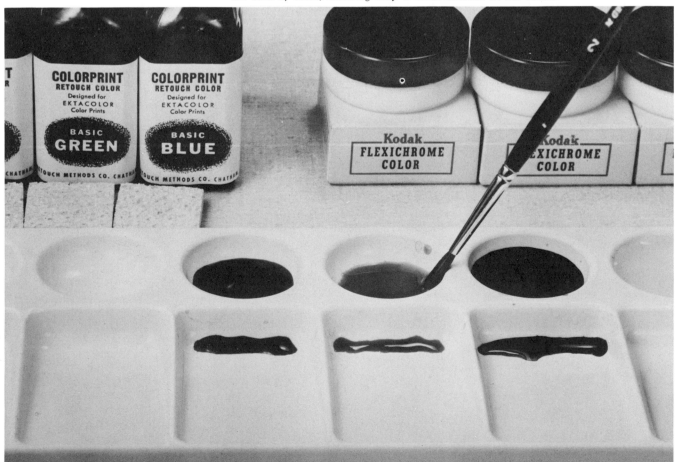

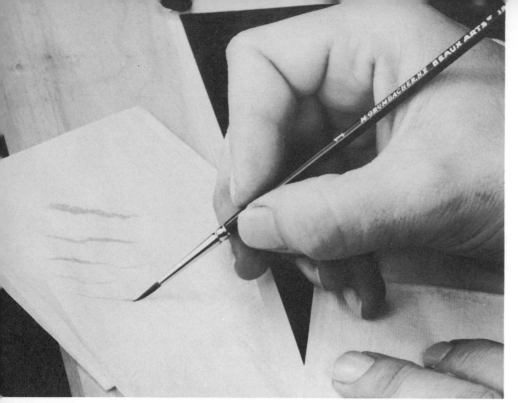

and finally the bisulfite. Blot between and after applications.

In addition to removing cyan, this bleach will also attack the other colors, particularly when using a strong solution. First the yellow goes, followed somewhat later by the magenta. This new fault can be corrected by removing the now excessive magenta or adding some yellow.

For areas about the size of a half dollar, or larger, use swabs of cotton on skewers or held in the hand. The larger the working area, the more the bleach should be diluted to allow time for uniform wetting and bleaching. Use a separate cotton swab for each bath. Instead of blotting, wipe the area with a piece of clean cotton dipped in clear water and wrung damp-dry.

Step 2. Work out excess color by drawing brush against an absorbent material. Draw the brush along with a twirling motion to help form point. In bringing the brush from the palette to the absorbent material, do not pass over the print.

open wounds. If such wounds become contaminated, flush the skin area thoroughly with clear water.

CORRECTING CYAN

For small spots, use brushes reserved for use with the cyan bleach exclusively. Keep the permanganate solution and the one-percent sodium bisulfite in separate containers. Use a separate brush for each or keep a third container filled with clear water for cleaning the brush between applications.

For spots up to the size of a quarter, choose brushes according to the size of the spot to be worked on. Touch or swab the area being corrected with a brush which has been dipped into the potassium permanganate. Blot with lintless blotter or paper hand towel. Next, touch or swab area with a brush which has been dipped into the cleaning bath and blot. Repeat until desired

reduction of cyan is obtained.

With practice, the needed correction may be achieved on the first few tries, thus minimizing the danger of spilling over good areas of print. After the initial applications, the print has some saturation of sodium bisulfite, which restrains further action by the permanganate.

When the minimum removal of cyan is desired, first apply the bisulfite, secondly the permanganate,

USE OF FRISKETS

The use of a liquid frisket, such as Photo Maskoid, is helpful where large areas are to be bleached as well as for areas enclosed by sharp edges, within which a very uniform reduction is needed. The Maskoid is applied to all areas to be protected with a brush used only for this purpose. The brush should be cleaned in Maskoid Thinner.

The Maskoid dries to a rubbery plastic finish which seals against moisture. The controls can then be safely used in the uncovered portions of the print. After partially

Step 3. Carefully work the color out of the tip of the brush by several short strokes on a piece of reject-print paper. Repeat until about 15 strokes are required to show density being added. The brush is now ready to be applied to the print in highlight areas. When density shows after about ten strokes, apply to medium values; and after about five strokes for shadow areas.

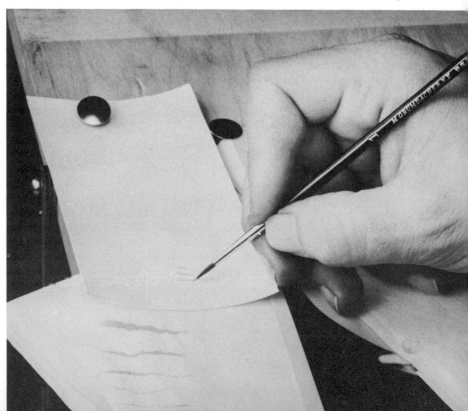

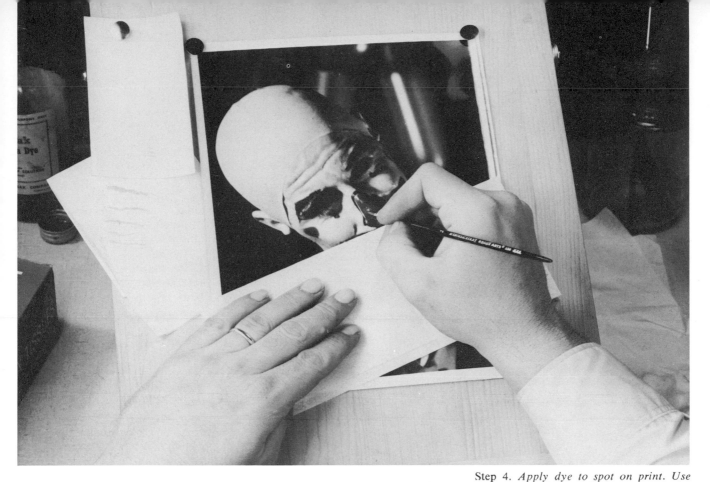

Step 4. *Apply dye to spot on print. Use a protective sheet of lintless paper under the hands. Work slowly. Blend. Stop before you're finished. Check and re-apply as needed.*

blotting and drying, remove the Maskoid film by lifting it with a piece of tape.

A selective bleach for the magenta in dye-transfer prints is readily available in the form of Kodak Photo-Flo, widely employed as a wetting agent in the final wash of black-and-white negative materials. Used in its concentrated, undiluted form, Photo-Flo removes magenta.

In small spots, apply Photo-Flo with brush, blot dry, and repeat until desired reduction is obtained. For areas about the size of a dime or larger, cotton swabs saturated with Photo-Flo should be used. Rub area with Photo-Flo until you see traces of magenta appearing on the cotton. At this point, take a fresh, clean piece of cotton and wipe off the excess.

A frequent mistake at this stage is the use of the same pieces of cotton again and again. Magenta retained in the cotton tends to transfer back to the paper, and could result in staining highlights and other areas with unwanted magenta.

Keep manipulating the cotton swabs to place fresh portions against the print, or use more cotton. As soon as you feel you have removed the desired amount of magenta, swab the area with cotton dipped in clear water or one-percent acetic acid to remove traces of bleach.

This control appears to work best on freshly made prints. Tremendous amounts of magenta can be removed while the print is still damp-dry. Immediately after making the print, if you are using a flat dryer, lift the blanket on the dryer when the print is partially dry, apply control, close dryer, and complete the drying.

When using a rotary dryer, work on the print as soon as it comes out. The heat speeds the action of the Photo-Flo. In cases of prints several years old, preheating the print from the back with a lamp will intensify the action of Photo-Flo. For maximum effect, leave the Photo-Flo undisturbed on the print for up to 20 minutes. Try this on a reject print first, or you may suddenly find yourself with too much magenta removed.

A selective bleach for the dye-transfer yellow is prepared from five-percent sodium hypochlorite (available commercially as Clorox). As described above, the bleach may be applied full strength using a brush or cotton swab. However, it is very potent, and continues to act until the print is dry. Therefore, especially with the yellow bleach, it is necessary to work slowly, blend carefully, and *stop before you're finished.*

Dry, and review your work; you can always go back and take out more. It is suggested that three dilutions be prepared from the Clorox, 1:20 parts of water, 1:10 and 1:5. In removing yellow, start with the weakest bleach; apply bleach, blot, swab with cotton dipped in clear water and wrung damp-dry. Let print sit awhile or dry it. Repeat operation as needed.

In each of the bleaches mentioned above, keep in mind the shape and form of the subject. You may remove too much from the light areas before enough has been taken out of the darks. Apply controls in the darker areas first

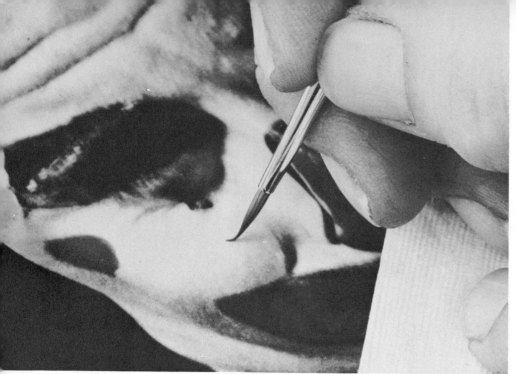

DON'T *press so hard with brush that the bristles spread out. Do not use a wall-painting maneuver to fill in the spot as the color will spread over the edges of the spot, resulting in a dark ring or donut shape.*

and then work your way toward lighter areas.

REMOVING DARK SPOTS

If a more potent bleach is needed for the removal of dark spots, Kodak recommends the use of its reducing formula R-2. This is a two-bath solution containing potassium permanganate and sulfuric acid. The two stock solutions, labelled A and B, are mixed together in equal proportions for use. A brush used for this bleach only is dipped in the mixture, touched to the dark spot, and the area blotted. The resulting stain is cleared with one-percent sodium-bisulfite solution, as for cyan bleach. After the spot has been sufficiently lightened, it should be retouched back to blend into the surrounding area.

Most commercial workers prefer to take care of dark spots by retouching the separation negatives or etching the matrix images before the final print is transferred. The spots then transfer blended or lighter and are spotted back.

Another procedure for dark spots is to hide them by retouching around the spot with an intermediate value and then blending into the surrounding area. In applying dye in such cases, use a stroke which is either nondirectional, such as circles or stippled dots, or one which follows the texture of the area.

OPAQUE COLORS

An alternative treatment for dark spots is to cover them with opaque colors such as Grumbacher's Airbrush Water Colors. Mix the available colors to match the area surrounding the dark spot, diluting to a very thin paste. Pick up a little with a fine brush, and draw the brush across blotting paper to remove excess. Twirl the brush to shape and hold point. The brush should be damp-dry. First try the spotting on a reject print, then touch several times to spot.

One advantage of opaque colors is that they are not absorbed and can be easily removed with dampened cotton. A disadvantage is that the dried water colors are somewhat duller in surface finish than the print. This can be hidden to some extent by touching the spot with a brush dipped in diluted gum arabic; or the adhesive used on flaps of envelopes, picked up with a moist brush.

Very large areas, of course, may also be covered with opaque colors. However, this requires considerable practice and skill in the use of an artist's airbrush. Moreover, since the opaque obliterates the detail under it, it may be necessary to draw in the detail by hand. For this reason, if a large area needs extensive lightening, use bleaches or reprint the job with appropriate dodging.

Small bright highlights, such as sometimes appear on metallic objects, may be emphasized with the use of an etching knife. Commercially, where the print is to be copied for reproduction, the change in surface characteristics of these highlights may be acceptable. However, in prints for display it is often necessary to reprint the job with a corrective mask or negative retouching.

If the final print is to be sprayed with a matte or glossy lacquer finish, uniformity of surface quality will be restored, and greater liberties can be taken with etching and the use of opaque colors to hide dark spots.

If considerable local wet work is done before mounting, the print may not lay flat due to uneven retention of moisture. Large raised areas could fold over and crease during mounting. To avoid this, rewet and redry the entire print. For moderate correction, soak in plain water for not more than one minute to prevent bleeding of the dyes. In extreme cases, first soak the print for about 30 seconds in clear water to help remove residues of bleaches used, and then transfer it to a tray containing one- to two-percent acetic acid, in which the print may stay for several minutes without increased danger of bleeding. Squeegee or blot off excess moisture and dry.

DYE TRANSFER, TREATMENT OF LIGHT SPOTS AND AREAS

Possible causes of light areas are as follows: defects in the original subject; dust, dirt, or lint on films and glasses used in making final exposures during printing; over-retouching of separations; etching of matrix images; or errors in tone and color-correcting masks used. Any of these results in spots or patches lighter than the surrounding area. While opaques can be used, the preferred technique is to apply dye which is absorbed and leaves the surface unchanged.

The first choice of dyes are the colorants of the Dye Transfer process itself, since these are readily available wherever the prints are made. Use the concentrated dyes and dilute for use as indicated below. The cyan, magenta, and yellow dyes when properly mixed should match any color existing in the print. An hour or so spent in practicing color mixtures will pay dividends in later work. Prepare a reference chart by applying known mixtures to a piece of clean dye transfer paper. Mix by counting out drops of color from an eye-dropper: for example, mix varying proportions of cyan and magenta to make a range of blues, different amounts of magenta and yellow to make a range of reds, and different amounts of cyan and yellow for a range of greens.

Very few colors appearing in our prints are as pure as the basic colorants. That is, most colors contain some amount of gray or neutral. One or two of the colorants establishes the hue. The amount deposited determines the saturation of pure color as compared to pure white. The remaining colorant(s) added determines the formation of black, lending shape and form and controlling the brightness of the color. Most areas contain some neutral; in fact, many light spots in dark fabric, foilage, muted colors, and similar areas can be successfully hidden by spotting with gray. Therefore, prepare a neutral by mixing cyan, magenta, and yellow dye, or obtain some black dye, such as Spotone's or the black in Webster's Photocolors. After mixing a particular hue, you will find it much easier to control its brightness by adding gray instead of the complement of the hue.

DO use a stipple stroke as often as possible, particularly with small spots. This is a straight up-and-down motion with just the very tip of the brush touching the spot. The density is built up with a multitude of tiny dots. Larger spots, tiny commas, elongated zeros, or figure eights may be executed, but always with care...so that the stroke used matches the direction of the pattern or texture in which the spot appears.

RETOUCHING LIGHT SPOTS

Light spots are of two types. In one case, the dust, dirt, or lint repeats itself on each of the exposures making the cyan, magenta, and yellow images, and the spot shows up as white. In the second case, the spot is on one image only, or it has moved around during exposures, and varied colored spots appear. For the white spot, mix the colors to match the surrounding area; for the others, replace the missing color. If the spot is reddish, cyan is missing; if greenish, magenta is missing; and if bluish or purplish, yellow is missing. The reverse is also true: to a cyan spot, add red prepared by mixing magenta and yellow; to magenta, add green (cyan plus yellow); to yellow, add blue (cyan plus magenta).

Aside from the new problem of color mixing to match specific areas, the application of color to dye-transfer prints is the same as applying the neutral and warm-tone dyes to black-and-white prints.

To dilute the dyes, use water to which a little Photo-Flo has been added. Although used as a magenta bleach, Photo-Flo in greatly diluted form does not have this effect, but helps to avoid droplets forming at the end of brushstrokes. Do not dilute more than recommended for the final wash of black-and-white negatives.

Pour into sections of a palette some cyan, magenta, yellow, and neutral. Mix colors as needed and dilute. Use any good brush from No. 0 to No. 2, provided it will come to a good point. Pick up some color with the brush and holding the brush at an acute angle to the blotting paper, draw it along with a slight twirling action to remove excess color and form a point. The brush must never be sopping wet when applied to the print.

If the Kodak dyes and the Webster Photocolors are used, they are quickly absorbed and difficult to remove. Working on a reject piece of paper, gently stroke the surface with the point of the brush until you see color formed. If you are spotting in a dark area, perhaps four or five strokes should be necessary to see color formed; then the brush is applied to the print. For middle values, work out the color until about ten strokes are needed to form color. For extremely light pastel areas, work out the excess until perhaps 15 strokes are required to deposit noticeable dye.

It may require half a dozen to a dozen touches of the brush to hide a spot. The more strokes required, the better the blend, and the less likely the spot is to be noticed later. Remember: 1) work slowly, 2) blend gradually, and 3) *stop before you're finished.* Stand back and review your work; redo where necessary. Do not lean directly on the work; keep a piece of clean paper

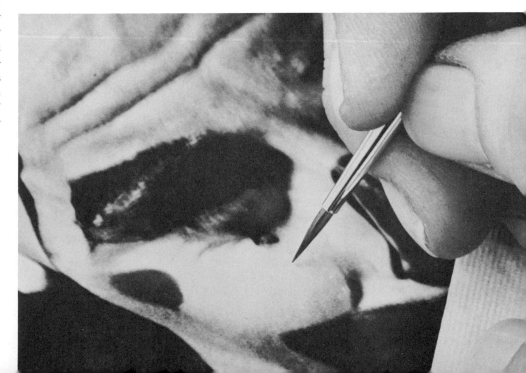

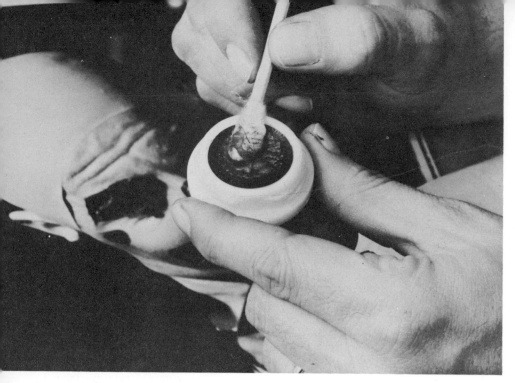

To apply Flexichrome to a larger area, pick up some dye with a cotton-wrapped skewer or a small wad of cotton. The dye in the small jar may be diluted by adding just a drop or two of alcohol to it. Do not use water in the method illustrated.

The spraying of transparent dyes over large light areas permits darkening or intensifying without obliterating photographic detail. Care must be taken throughout to maintain gradation. Spray more into the shadows, less into highlights. Dilute the dyes for use in the airbrush with one-percent acetic acid. A more uniform absorption of dyes is effected by first swabbing the area to be sprayed with cotton damp-dried with one-percent acetic acid.

OTHER METHODS

In addition to the dyes of the Kodak Dye Transfer Process, Webster's Photocolors, Dr. Martin's, Spotone, and Flexichrome may be used.

Dyes of the obsolete Flexichrome process apparently will be sold indefinitely because of their wide use in retouching. An advantage to beginners using Flexichrome dyes is that they are not as readily absorbed by the emulsion of dye transfer or Ektacolor paper as the other dyes mentioned. Working on a thoroughly dry print, the colors tend to set on the surface. In case of error, they can be wiped away with Photo-Flo or a moist piece of cotton. However, the more moisture present in the emulsion, the more easily the Flexichrome is absorbed.

To some extent, they can also be used like transparent oils. With dry cotton, the Flexichrome color is picked up and rubbed onto the print

under your hand.

Keep close by, or in your free hand, a piece of clean, damp-dry cotton when working with dyes that are absorbed into the emulsion. In case of accidentally overdoing a spot, if you immediately swab the area with the damp-dry cotton, some of the excess will be removed, perhaps just enough to save the print. When working on dye transfers, the cotton is dampened with water or one-percent acetic acid. For Ektacolor prints, it is preferable to use buffer solution to dampen.

RETOUCHING LARGE AREAS

For areas too large for a hand brush, cotton swabs may be used. Dilute the dye greatly with one-percent acetic acid. Dip cotton wrapped on a skewer or held in the hand into the dye. Squeeze out excess and gently rub into print. Start in the heavy areas, and work towards light areas. A uniform wash of color over an area without gradation will look false because the shadows do not have enough color and the highlights are stained.

The action of dye addition or bleaching must sometimes be sharply

restricted to a particular area. In this case, use a liquid frisket such as Photo Maskoid, applying it to the portions of the print to be protected; it dries to a rubbery plastic film.

As was mentioned earlier, reserve a brush for use exclusively with Maskoid and clean the brush in Maskoid Thinner after each use. After the control has been applied to the print, the Maskoid is removed by lifting it with a piece of tape.

For very large areas, add needed density with an artist's airbrush.

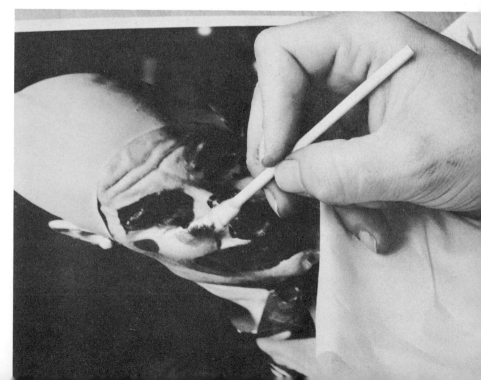

Gently rub the dye onto the area of the print requiring added color. The print must be thoroughly dry or the dye will be immediately absorbed.

with light pressure, and then rubbed down with clean cotton to the density desired. The color is then locked into the emulsion by steaming the print or breathing moisture on it. For matching colors other than those appearing in the Flexichrome set, dilute the dyes with denatured alcohol, such as that used in thinning shellac, mix for color, let the alcohol evaporate, and then proceed with the application.

Although not used to any extent commercially, Marshall Oil Colors can be employed to effect changes over large areas, such as flesh tones in portraits. A considerable advantage to the beginner is that, in case of error, the oils can be removed from the print with turpentine and small applications can be applied directly to the print. However, in working over large areas, it may be desirable to increase the "tooth" of the print with an application of Marshall's Pre-Color Spray or some other dull-finish lacquer coating.

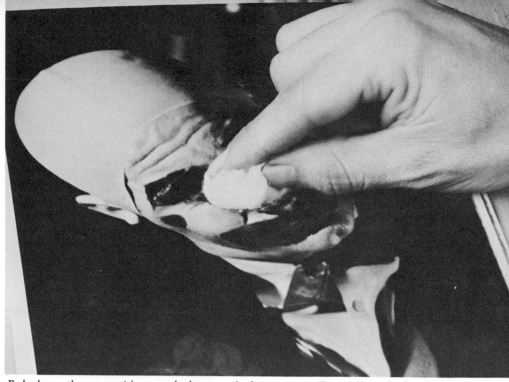

Rub down the area with several changes of clean cotton. Especially rub down the edges for a smoothly-blended effect. When the desired smoothness and density have been obtained, the retouching may be set by breathing moisture onto the print or permitting moisture from a vaporizer to reach the print.

EKTACOLOR, TREATMENT OF LIGHT AREAS

Practically all of the statements concerning the application of transparent dyes, opaque colors, Flexichrome, and oils to Dye Transfer prints apply almost identically to Ektacolor prints. Let us concern ourselves only with the points of difference.

Ektacolor paper and similar print materials are multilayer emulsions. Whereas the Dye Transfer paper is fairly tough, multilayer materials such as Ektacolor are considerably softer. The emulsion bruises easily, picks up fingerprints, is easily scratched, and tends to absorb dyes more readily. Excess wiping must be avoided, so the work must proceed more carefully.

Do not lean directly on the print; keep a piece of lintless paper or blotter under the hand holding the brush. When much handling has to be done, particularly with Ektacolor, the use of white-cotton gloves or their equivalent is recommended. It is comfortable to work with the brush hand ungloved for a natural feel, and the other hand, which is usually against the print, gloved.

If Maskoid is used to protect areas of an Ektacolor print during retouching, great care must be taken

in removing it. The Ektacolor emulsion, particularly when wet, is easily lifted away, that is, separated from the paper base. Let the print dry, with moderate heat and a fan if desired. Peel back the Maskoid by lifting with tape and pulling at an acute angle to the surface, rather than straight up or perpendicular to the surface.

Dyes may be diluted with water and applied as previously discussed. If too much color has been used, most of the Flexichrome, some of the Webster, and a little of the Dye Transfer colors can be removed by wiping with cotton and Photo-Flo.

Ektacolor paper, when wet, holds the moisture in such a way as to become somewhat opalescent. The result is that most of the incident light is reflected from the uppermost surfaces, giving the print a bluish cast and making the color almost impossible to evaluate.

To minimize this effect to a greater or lesser degree, some workers prefer to dilute the dyes with alcohol. The more alcohol used, the more rapidly the applied color dries. For routine spotting, use very little alcohol, since the brush will dry out before the spotting is done. When applying color to larger areas, the print must be thoroughly dry to avoid

streaking, even if straight alcohol is used to dilute.

Most processors are probably using some proportion of print flattener added to the final step in the process. The flattener holds moisture in the emulsion. Try this technique on a reject print, of the same type and processing as the final print to which the Flexichrome is to be applied. Some commercially available alcohols recommended for diluting the dyes are sold under the trade names Tecsol, Solox, and Quixol.

If any final swabbing of the Ektacolor print is necessary, buffer solution should be used. However, careful handling of the print to avoid dirt and scuff marks should preclude the need for this swabbing, which could remove some of the dye applied and streak or remove the opaque colors.

If both transparent absorbed dyes and opaque water colors are used in retouching, the transparents are applied first, the opaques last.

EKTACOLOR, TREATMENT OF DARK SPOTS AND AREAS

In correcting dark spots on Ektacolor prints, we are more limited at present than in Dye Transfer. Etching is usually not recommended because of the multilayer structure of the paper, except occasionally for accenting specular highlights in prints intended for reproduction.

Formulas for experimental bleaches for Ektacolor are not publicly available. However, one bleach usually on hand is the Clorox solution mentioned earlier as a bleach for yellow in dye-transfer prints. On Ektacolor and other multilayer materials it acts as a physical reducer, etching away gelatin from the top and removing dye. Since the cyan is uppermost in Ektacolor, this bleach will be useful in brightening reds and other warm colors through the removal of excess cyan. Excessive use or rubbing can result in an undesirable difference in surface characteristics between the working area and others.

The most highly recommended procedure for attacking dark spots and areas in Ektacolor and similar processes is to retouch the negative; dodge in printing to lighten over-all; or dodge with a filter to lighten a particular color. Much can be done with ordinary black-and-white techniques in spotting and retouching thin areas of an Ektacolor negative to avoid difficult problems in the print. (See *Enlarging Photographs*.)

Another alternative is to cover dark spots with opaque water colors, as described for Dye Transfer prints.

Some spots can be hidden—by mixing an intermediate value and retouching around the defect we can blend it into the surrounding area. Retouch with dyes and apply with a nondirectional stipple or circular stroke. If the area contains texture, use a stroke matching the direction of the texture.

The objective of all the retouching methods discussed has been to achieve retouching which is invisible and which does not change the original-paper surface. Where acceptable, surface variations can be made uniform after all retouching is complete by an application of Kodak Print Lacquer, Marshall's Pre-Color Spray, Krylon Clear Lacquer, or equivalent products. If the directions for each product are followed, the use of Kodak Print Lacquer can yeld a glossy or semi-gloss finish; Marshall's a matte finish; and Krylon a glossy finish.

Kodak Transparency Illuminator is used when applying dyes and for all types of retouching on transparencies.

RETOUCHING COLOR TRANSPARENCIES

RUTH SCHOTTLAND
Professional Retoucher and Instructor, Germain School of Photography, New York
[A working knowledge of color retouching is useful for improving transparencies that may have blemishes or color areas that need correcting. Here an experienced instructor explains the techniques involved in handling the dyes, bleaches, and tools of the retoucher.]
• *Also see: Retouching Color Films and Prints.*

THE FIRST STEP IN RETOUCHING color transparencies is to become acquainted with the nature of the transparency material itself. It should be realized that we are dealing here with a transparent-positive film and that the image can be viewed from either side.

The notches along the edge of the film will help to find the correct viewing side. With the notches in the upper left-hand corner, the film is right side up and the image is viewed properly. This side of the film has a thin coating of gelatin which permits an easy application of dye. The inner layer is an acetate base which makes it possible to cut and merge films together. When the film is turned over (with notches in upper right-hand corner), the image is reversed and the emulsion faces the retoucher. The emulsion is actually three layers (cyan, magenta, yellow) which are chemically reduced individually if film or any part of film is underexposed.

CHANGING PART OF THE IMAGE

Where part of the image has to be changed, for example, removing a textured background and replacing it with a clear-blue background, first mask the area to be retained with Photo Maskoid on the emulsion side. Thus only the area to be changed is left exposed. The part of the film masked should be very carefully checked for pin holes and covered. Place film on a piece of glass or vinyl and tape very carefully so that the bleach cannot reach the gelatin surface next to the glass.

The film is now ready to be Cloroxed. Put a sufficient amount of Clorox in a pan to cover the film completely and then place film in the pan with the emulsion exposed to the Clorox so the emulsion dissolves. The procedure takes a few minutes. After the emulsion is dissolved, remove the film and its backing from the pan of Clorox, and place the assembly in a pan of running water (68 F) for a few minutes until all traces of Clorox are removed.

Now remove the glass or vinyl and then with a piece of Scotch tape remove the Maskoid. By sticking the tape to one part of the masked area and lightly pulling, the Maskoid will lift off very easily. Soak the film again for two to three minutes in running water and then place in a pan containing a capful of Kodak Photo-Flo Solution and 1000 cubic centimeters of water for one minute. The film can now be dried.

When the film is absolutely dry, if the shape of the image that remains does not seem perfect, etch away parts of the outline with an etching knife thus correcting and reshaping areas. Using the edge of the knife, gently scratch the emulsion away until you reach the acetate base. All objects and shapes can be silhouetted in this manner. Etching knives can be purchased at most art-supply stores.

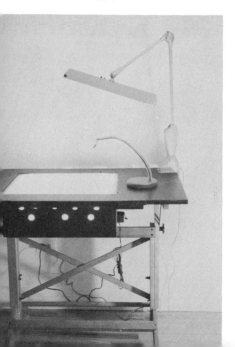

APPLYING DYES

We now have cleared the area and are ready to apply the dyes. Turning to the gelatin side of the film (notches in upper left-hand corner), mask with Maskoid the objects not to be dyed, leaving exposed only the working area. Again, place the film carefully on a piece of glass or vinyl by taping.

Now we are ready to use the dyes. With a piece of cotton, wet the exposed film thoroughly so that the dyes will be absorbed easily and evenly. Using a white-porcelain pallet, mix the dyes to the desired color and apply. (Dr. Martin Transparent Water Color dyes are recommended.) Build color slowly and wipe excess dye off with a large piece of moist cotton. Keep applying the dye until the desired density is reached. If the dye mixed is not right, it can be corrected as the color is built. Always keep in mind that the medium is transparent.

If you desire to gray a color, the use of the opposite color on the color wheel will give the proper effect. If the background is a blue, and you decide the color is too bright and wish to gray or tone it down, the use of orange will give the correct result. This is an important principle and will be used frequently.

Blemishes and wrinkles can be retouched on film by use of color. Actually, color is applied to either side of the wrinkle or blemish and softened. The area becomes less obvious and in many cases seems to disappear. To reduce dye, apply a piece of damp cotton to the area. A 28-percent ammonia solution has a faster effect and can be used by applying on a piece of cotton and gently rubbing the dyed area.

UNDEREXPOSED OR HEAVY TRANSPARENCIES

Underexposed or heavy transparencies in one or any series of the

Right: Way's standard viewer. This vertical viewer is used when applying dyes and for all types of retouching on transparencies.

Left: Horizontal viewer built into standard drafting table. This is used when etching, stripping films together, and masking.

three layers (cyan, magenta, yellow) can be reduced by the use of chemical bleaches. The film is prepared in the same manner as for Cloroxing. If a limited area needs reducing, the rest of the emulsion is protected by the use of the Maskoid. The film is again placed on a piece of glass or vinyl, emulsion side up, and taped carefully. Should the film need an over-all bleach, place on glass or vinyl with emulsion completely exposed (notches in upper right-hand corner).

The film is then placed under running water (68 F) for ten minutes. Prepare a pan of Kodak Photo-Flo Solution (one capful to 1000 cc of water), and after ten minutes in running water place in Photo-Flo Solution for one minute. This preparation is standard for all types of bleach. Following is a list of some of the bleaches to be used on Ektachrome (Kodak E-3) and Ansco films:

Ektachrome (Kodak E-3) Bleaches
Yellow Bleach

Clorox	7 cc
Acetic acid 28 percent	11 cc
Water 68 F	1000 cc

Wash the film for ten minutes in running water.

Cyan Bleach

Sodium hydrosulfite	½ to 1 gram
Sodium acetate, desiccated	20 grams
Water 68 F	1000 cc

Wash the film for ten minutes in running water.

Magenta Bleach

Stannous chloride	12 grams
Water 68 F	1000 cc

Wash the film for ten minutes in

running water.

It is suggested that the bleaches be used in the following order: yellow, cyan, magenta. Should only two bleaches be necessary, they should also be done in the order indicated. After the last ten-minute wash in running water, soak film in Photo-Flo Solution for one minute. The film should then be wiped carefully with a chamois or soft viscose sponge and then dried.

Anscochrome Bleaches

Before using any of the reducers, the film should be prehardened for three minutes at 68 F and then washed for three minutes.

Prehardener

Calgon	1 gram
Formalin (40 percent)	10 ml
Sodium carbonate, mono.	6 grams
Water	1 liter

Yellow Bleach

Stock Solution A

Clorox	30 ml
Water	1 liter

Stock Solution B

Acetic acid glacial	10 ml
Water	1 liter

Stock Solution C*

Sodium sulfate, anhyd.	100 grams
Water	1 liter

* For use if lacquer resist is used. Otherwise use ordinary tap water.

Yellow-Bleach Working Solution

4 parts A
1 part B
25 to 45 parts C

Wash in running water for five minutes.

A more rapid reduction will be obtained by reducing the amount of Solution C to 25 parts. Store stock solutions in stoppered bottles. Mix Solution A each week. Solutions B and C are stable indefinitely. Working-solution life is four hours.

Cyan Bleach

Stock Solution A

3-percent hydrogen peroxide

Stock Solution B

Calgon	1 gram
Sodium carb. mono.	37.5 grams
Sodium sulfate*	100 grams
Sodium hydroxide	0.5 gram
Water	1 liter

* Sodium sulfate not required if lacquer resist is not used.

Working Solution

Add 25 to 50 milliliters of Solution A to one liter of Solution B.

Wash in running water for five minutes.

A more rapid reduction will be obtained by using up to 50 milliliters of Solution A. Stock solutions are stable indefinitely. Life of the working solution is four hours.

Magenta Bleach

This consists of two working solutions used separately:

Working Solution A

Hydrochloric acid, conc.	
	15 to 30 ml
Sodium sulfate*	100 grams
Water	1 liter

* Sodium sulfate not required if lacquer resist is not used.

Working Solution B

Calgon	1 gram
Sodium carb. mono.	37.5 grams
Sodium sulfate	100 grams

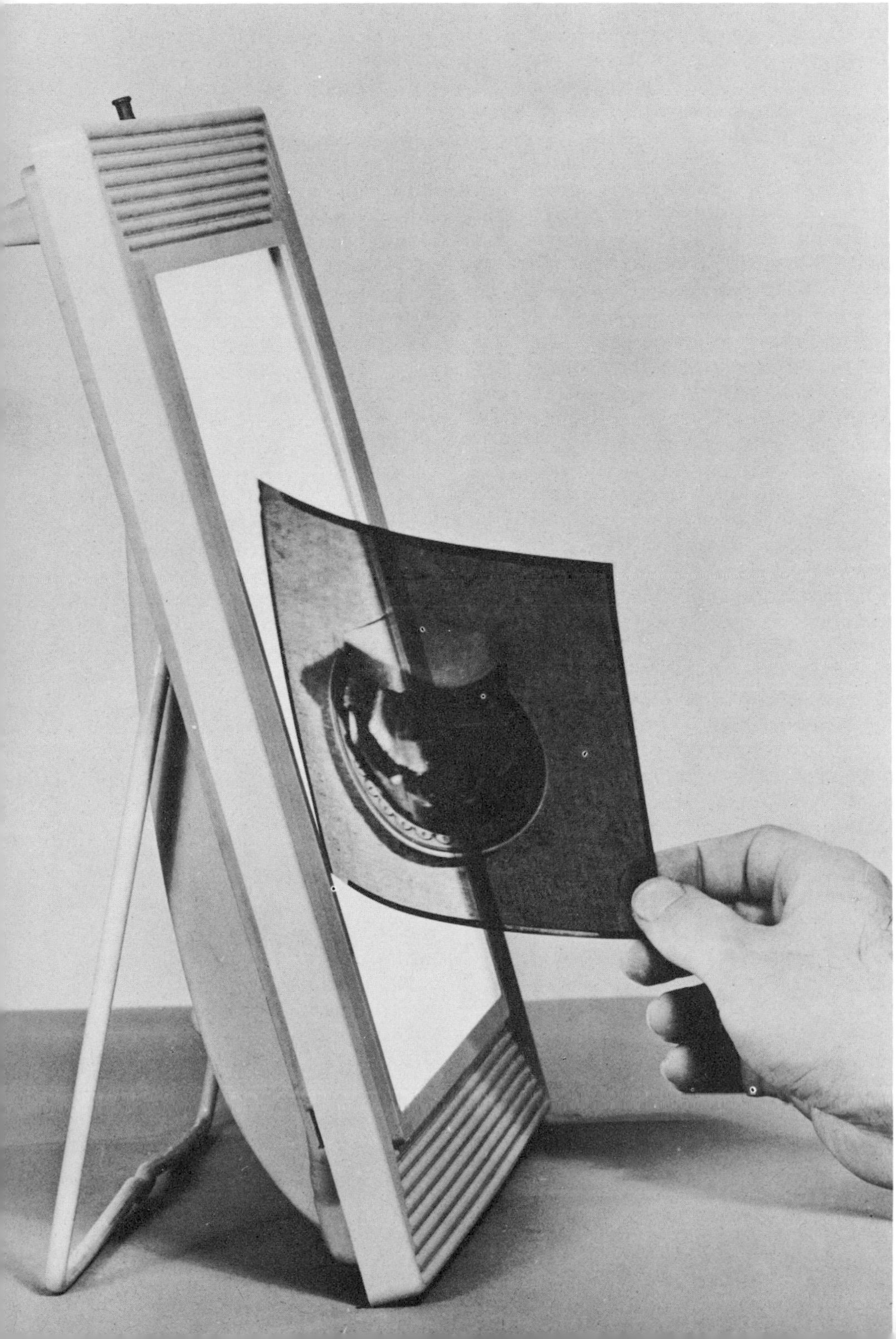

Idealite Model 010 transparency illuminator. This illuminator is only two inches thick and has various operating positions. (Photo: Ideax Corporation)

Sodium hydroxide   0.5 grams
Water   1 liter
* Sodium sulfate not required if lacquer resist is not used.

To use, immerse the transparency in working Solution A. A more rapid reduction will be obtained by using 30 milliliters of hydrochloric acid in Solution A. Treatment in Solution A causes the image to disappear almost completely. Treatment in Solution B results in regeneration of the image, with the exception of the magenta dye which has been reduced. Following working Solution A, the transparency is neutralized in working Solution B for one minute. Working solutions are stable indefinitely but should be discarded if they become cloudy or show sedimentation. Wash film in running water for five minutes.

It is suggested that the bleaches be used in the following order: yellow, cyan, magenta. Should only two bleaches be necessary, they should also be used in the order given. After the last five-minute wash, soak film in Photo-Flo Solution for one minute. The film should be wiped carefully with a chamois or soft viscose sponge and then dried. In order to become acquainted with the proper timing for given effects, it is advisable to test bleaches on discarded film.

STRIPPING TRANSPARENCIES

The artist who has a working knowledge of mechanicals on black-and-white has an advantage in learning stripping (color assemblies) of transparencies. With a very accurate tracing of the exact positions and shapes, the artist is ready to begin his assembly. In this example we will use two films, A and B. Film A is a champagne glass that will be stripped into a colorful background. The two films will be merged and appear to be one transparency.

Using a very sharp razor blade, carefully cut film A on emulsion side. Take film B (gelatin side up, notches in upper left-hand corner) and place over tracing, taping in position. Now take film A (champagne glass), turn to the gelatin side and tape to film B in exact position

according to the layout. With a very sharp razor, start scoring along the edge of film A, being very careful to keep razor straight. When you have removed film A after scoring, there will be an exact image scored on your background. Cut through with a sharp razor, being careful not to deviate from original score line. The two films placed in position can now be merged using either Craig Cement Formula 7 or acetone. Wet a tissue with some acetone and gently rub both sides of film, thus removing cement and acetone stains.

PENCIL

Pencil retouching is used as a finishing touch by the transparency retoucher. It can be used on either side of the transparency. In order for the film to take pencil, Kodak or Ansco Retouching Fluid should be rubbed gently onto the surface. The pencil should have a long sharp point and be used only where and when dye cannot be used successfully. Small details and uneven areas are easily corrected in this manner. Eagle Turquoise Prismacolor Pencils and Eagle Turquoise Drawing Leads (2B) are suitable. Carbon tetrachloride, which is used as a cleaning agent on films, may also be used to remove pencil marks.

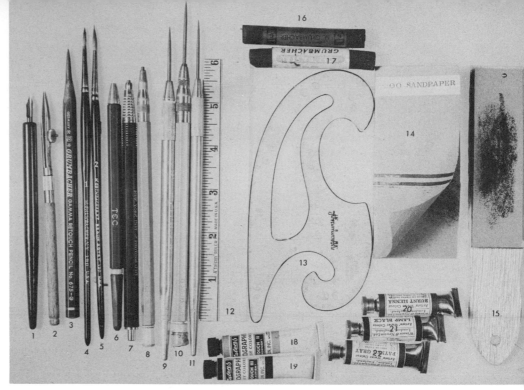

Figure 1. *1) Gillot's fine-drawing pen. 2) Ruling pen. 3) Grumbacher black gamma pencil. 4&5) No. 1 and No. 2 spotting brushes. 6, 7, & 8) Soft retouching pencils, 1B, 2B, and 3B. 9, 10, & 11) Three retouching pencils, 1-HB, 1-2H, 1-4H. 12) Six-inch ruler with brass edge. 13) French curve. 14) 00 Sandpaper. 15) Sandpaper block. 16 & 17) Sepia and black crayon sauce. 18 & 19) Talens blackish and brownish water colors. 20, 21 & 22) Winsor-Newton water colors, Payne's gray, burnt sienna, and lampblack.*

RETOUCHING NEGATIVES AND PRINTS

MORRIS GERMAIN, ARPS
Director, Germain School of Photography

[Retouching techniques are explained in detail in this article written by a photographer with over fifty years of experience. For advanced amateurs and professionals alike, Mr. Germain's discussion of the materials and methods of this type of work will prove invaluable. Hand-sketched backgrounds stripped and blocked backgrounds, lettering on negatives and prints, spotting—these and many additional subjects are included in this comprehensive study which covers all phases of retouching.]

Illustrations by the author except when otherwise credited.

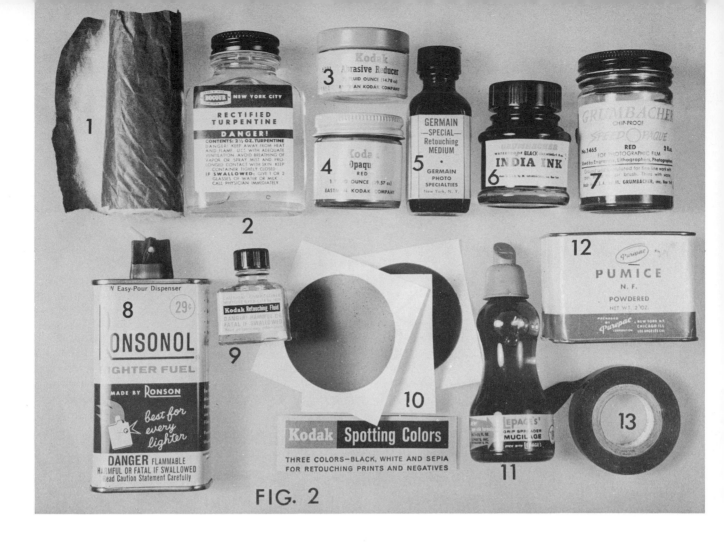

FIG. 2

THE ART OF RETOUCHING NEGATIVES and prints may be divided into three general classifications: portrait-negative retouching; negative retouching in commercial photography, which includes all types of negatives of a nonportrait character; print retouching, commonly referred to as print finishing or print spotting.

The professional retoucher may be involved in one or all of these branches. The advanced-amateur photographer may delve into these various branches and select what he needs for the retouching he requires. Any photographer can learn to do some pencil work on a portrait negative, to opaque a commercial negative to exclude extraneous portions and produce a clear-white ground in the final print, and to spot out unavoidable and ever-present white specks and similar defects in prints.

To assist the beginner the following materials and equipment are suggested: (see Figures 1, 2, and 3).

FOR PORTRAIT-NEGATIVE RETOUCHING

Retouching stand
3 retouching pencils, 1-HB, 1-2H, 1-4H
Bottle of retouching medium
Small quantity of good-quality absorbent cotton
1 sheet of 00 sandpaper
3 spotting brushes, No. 00, No. 1, No. 2
Pad of spotting colors, Eastman
Etching knife
2 sharpening stones

FOR COMMERCIAL AND OTHER NONPORTRAIT NEGATIVES

1 small jar of opaque, Kodak or Grumbacher
3 soft retouching pencils, 1-1B, 1-2B, 1-3B
1 small bottle of spirits of turpentine
1 can of lighter fluid
1 ruling pen
1 Gillott fine-drawing pen
1 bottle of liquid black-waterproof-drawing ink
1 straight-edge ruler, preferably with brass edge
1 French curve
1 roll of black masking tape
1 jar of Kodak abrasive paste
1 Grumbacher black-gamma pencil
1 bottle each of Maskoid and Maskoid thinner

FOR RETOUCHING AND SPOTTING PRINTS

3 hard retouching pencils, 1-4H, 1-6H, 1-8H
Quantity of ordinary small white blotters
1 each of Winsor - Newton water colors in porcelain dish
Payne's gray, burnt sienna, lamp-black
1 tube each of Talen's photographic water colors, blackish, brownish
1 small white palette
1 stick each of sepia and black crayon sauce
Small amount— pumice-stone powder
An ounce or two of gum arabic or gum acacia

Some of the materials in each of the three listings are used for more than one type of retouching.

Figure 2. *1) Absorbent cotton. 2) Rectified turpentine. 3) Kodak abrasive reducer. 4) Kodak opaque. 5) Germain special-retouching medium. 6) Black drawing ink. 7) Grumbacher opaque. 8) Lighter fluid. 9) Kodak retouching medium. 10) Kodak spotting water colors. 11) LePage's mucilage. 12) Pumice powder. 13) Black masking tape.*

MATERIALS FOR PORTRAIT-NEGATIVE RETOUCHING

The retouching stand, homemade or purchased, must be of rigid and sturdy construction (Figures 4 and 5). The table upon which the retouching stand rests must be sturdy as good retouching is virtually impossible with a flimsy stand or shaky table. Adjust a 40- or 60-watt frosted bulb in a suitable fixture (a gooseneck lamp is best) behind the retouching stand for illumination (Figure 6). A blue daylight bulb is recommended but not essential. However, the blue bulb will be found to be less tiring if prolonged time is spent at the retouching stand.

Retouching pencils may be ordinary drawing pencils sharpened with a knife or razor blade and pointed on sandpaper. Even better are the adjustable lead-refill holders made by Venus or Hardmuth. The refill holders are of sturdy wood construction. A lightweight-aluminum refill holder, designed by the author, may be purchased at photo-supply stores. There are three types of lead: HB is medium soft, 2H is hard, and 4H is extra hard. Any one of the three leads or all three may be necessary to retouch one negative although the 2H is most commonly used. The different leads are chosen depending upon the hardness or softness of the negative emulsion.

Retouching medium, sometimes called retouching dope, is applied to make the pencil take. If retouching is attempted without doping the negative, the pencil strokes go on in a spotty and irregular manner.

Figure 3. *Can of light oil. 2) Etching knife made from a hacksaw blade. 3) Stencil cutter. 4) Germain Photo Specialties etching knife. 5) X-acto etching knife with No. 11 blade. 6) Norton Pike Arkansas HB-13 sharpening stone. 7) Kodak etching knife. 8) Norton India combination sharpening stone No. 1B-134.*

A small drop of retouching medium from the end of the glass applicator that is fixed in the bottle cap is applied to the center of the area on the emulsion side of the negative where the retouching is to be done. The drop of medium is spread and rubbed on smoothly with a firm tuft of absorbent cotton about the size of a powder puff. If properly applied the doped area will be smooth and free from streaks and cotton threads.

The 00 sandpaper is used to put a needle-sharp point on the retouching pencils. The pencil points must be from an inch to an inch and a half in length and must always be kept sharp while retouching. Pencil sharpeners may be purchased. They are made of a number of $1\frac{1}{4} \times 4$-inch strips of 00 sandpaper glued together in a pad on a wooden handle. Many retouchers prefer to make pencil sharpeners from a sheet of 00 or 000 sandpaper.

The spotting brushes are used with the *spotting colors* to plug up or spot out pinholes that occur in negatives that otherwise show as black specks in the prints. The 00 brush is used for tiny pinholes and the No. 1 and 2 brushes are used for larger pinholes. The pad of Eastman spotting colors have a leaf each of white, black, light-brown, and dark-brown water colors. The black is used for spotting negatives.

The other colors, including the black, are used with the same brushes for spotting prints.

The etching knife is used in retouching negatives or prints. The emulsion (negative or positive image) whether on film, glass, or paper base is scraped off to accomplish the necessary knife correction. The sharpening stones keep the etching knife honed.

MATERIALS FOR COMMERCIAL AND OTHER NONPORTRAIT NEGATIVE RETOUCHING

Opaque is used to block out objectionable portions of a negative. It is often used to produce solid white backgrounds in prints.

The soft B pencils are used in all phases of retouching where heavy or obvious strokes are necessary.

Spirits of turpentine is used to thin retouching medium that becomes too thick and sticky due to evaporation after long use. Add a few drops at a time with an eye-dropper until the consistency is brought to normal. If the medium is thinned out too much, the application of the retouching lead will not take sufficiently. Half an ounce of powdered resin dissolved in two ounces of turpentine also makes a good retouching medium for negatives.

Turpentine is frequently used as a print cleaner before spotting.

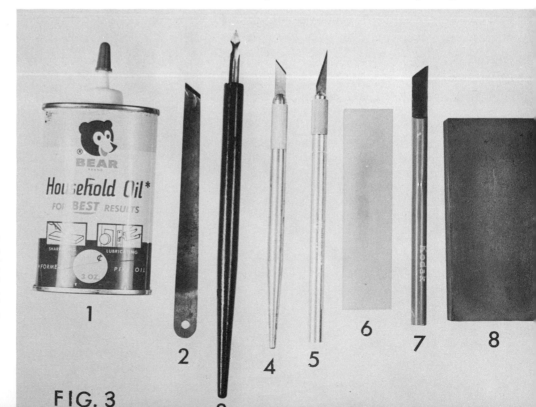

FIG. 3

Figure 4. *Homemade retouching stand. This was made from two 12×16-inch oil-canvas stretcher frames, two Masonite ¼-inch boards (two ¼-inch plywood boards can be used), two small hinges, two adjustable stay brackets, and 5×7-inch flashed-opal glass. A 4½×6-inch opening was cut in the top board and the glass fastened underneath. A strip of wood below the opening holds the negative and a piece of cardboard or opaque-black paper between the negative and glass, cut to fit the working area.*

Apply a few drops of spirits of turpentine to the center of the print. Then wipe the liquid over the surface with a tuft of absorbent cotton and polish it with a pad of canton flannel or soft cotton cloth. This removes nonchemical finger marks and visible and invisible sludge adherence. Some beeswax (about the size of a pea) dissolved in two ounces of turpentine and applied in the same manner will improve the brilliance of the dull blacks of matte- or rough-surfaced papers.

For many years carbon tetrachloride was used for removing fingerprints and smudges from negatives and prints. But carbon tetrachloride has been found to be highly toxic when the fumes are inhaled. Therefore, lighter fluid or naptha is now recommended for this purpose.

Figure 5. *Germain Photo Specialties retouching stand.*

Lighter fluid may also be used to remove thick, sticky, and improperly applied retouching medium from negatives. Sprinkle a few drops of lighter fluid on the surface to be cleaned, polish off with a soft cloth, and repeat the cleaning changing to a new portion of the cloth until no streaks show on the negative.

The ruling pen is used to draw straight lines. The *Gillott's fine-drawing pen* is used for lettering on negatives and prints. Waterproof *drawing ink* is used with the ruling and drawing pens. The *French curve* is used mainly for opaquing negatives. Variously shaped curves and contours can be accurately outlined when this curve is used as a guide.

Black masking tape is often used where there is a predominance of straight lines in an opaquing job. Cut in narrow strips so the masking tape can be accurately guided around curved portions of a negative. After outlining the image, the opaque is bruished on up to the outline.

The Grumbacher black gamma pencil can be used for outlining preliminary to opaquing. It can be used on either side of a film negative for straight or curved contours with full assurance of drawing opaque lines without asserting too much pressure on the negative. Again, the opaque is brushed on up to the outline.

Abrasive reducer is used as a mechanical reducer on all types of negatives. Dense portions can be reduced locally and print detail will

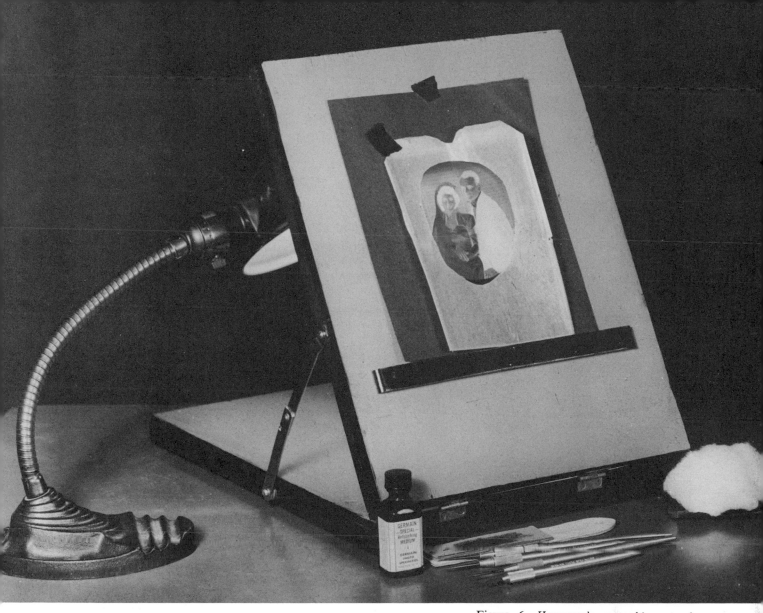

Figure 6. *Homemade retouching stand set up for retouching with the gooseneck-lamp illumination in place.*

be revealed that would otherwise have a soot and whitewash character. The reducing pencil is used for the same purpose as the abrasive paste. It is an abrasive in pencil form. It can be used in smaller and more localized areas than the paste.

MATERIALS FOR RETOUCHING AND SPOTTING PRINTS

The Payne's-gray, burnt-sienna, lampblack, blackish, and brownish *water colors* are used for matching color and texture of all types and surfaces of paper prints. A white palette or small flat dish is prepared with these colors. The black and sepia *crayon sauce* and the *pumice-stone powder* is used for sketching backgrounds on negatives and prints.

PORTRAIT-NEGATIVE RETOUCHING

For your first retouching experiment select a close-up portrait negative, the head measuring between one and one-half to two inches from the tip of the chin to the top of the forehead. A critically sharp negative is best, preferably one that shows many freckles, lines, and skin blemishes. Make a fully timed and developed glossy enlargement or contact print to be used for comparison as the retouching progresses. The retouching medium is now applied.

Formula for Retouching Medium (Dope)

Spirits of turpentine   4 ounces
Powdered resin   1 ounce

Dissolve the resin in the turpentine. Let the mixture stand for several days with occasional shaking until dissolved before doping a negative.

With prolonged use the medium may become too thick. This can be corrected by adding a few drops of turpentine. If a negative becomes messy with repeated doping or the use of medium that is too thick, it can be cleaned with a wad of absorbent cotton and a few drops of spirits of turpentine, benzene, naptha, or lighter fluid. If the first attempt leaves visible streaks on the negative, repeat the cleaning as often as necessary using a fresh tuft of absorbent cotton each time.

The very first attempts at doping

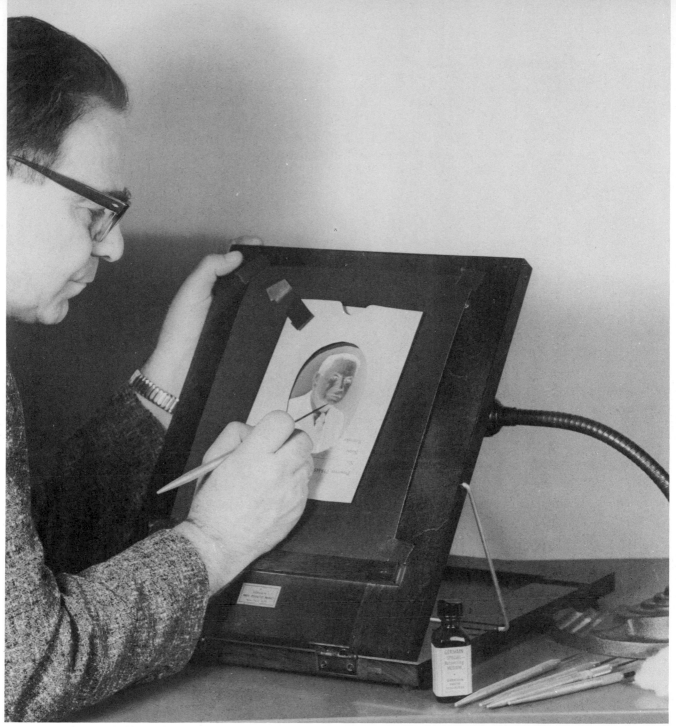

Figure 7. *Seated at the retouching stand. For best results the retoucher should never sit too close to the negative. All other incidental illumination in the working area should be turned off or subdued.*

the negative may result in a streaked mess which will retard the best retouching efforts. However, this will not ruin the negative permanently. Clean off the medium as described above and redope the negative. Be sure the medium is applied in a smooth manner without visible streaks. Do not leave a defined ring on the circumference of the doped area.

It is not necessary to cover the entire negative with retouching medium. The medium is applied only where the retouching will be localized. However, some retouchers dope the entire negative area on the premise that lead may have to be applied to other areas later.

The doped negative is now placed on the retouching stand and the light turned on. A sheet of opaque paper or thin cardboard, in which a hole has been cut matching the area to be retouched, is placed under the negative so that only the area to be retouched is illuminated by transmitted light. During the prolonged time spent retouching, the negative must be protected from fingerprints. Therefore, insert the negative into an envelope in which an opening has been cut revealing the area to be retouched.

The process of portrait-negative retouching consists of three major steps. The first consists of cleaning away the skin blemishes on the entire face. The second consists of

Figure 8. *Various stages in retouching a portrait negative. A) Completely unretouched and extremely uncomplimentary. B) The results after the skin blemishes have been cleaned away. C) Slight modification of the character marks. D) The final step with modeling accomplished. The good retoucher will stop here. The greatest aid to retouching, of course, is proper lighting in the first place.* (Retouching photos: Helen H. Dieterich)

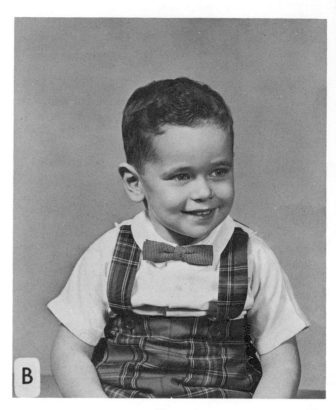

Above: Figure 9. *Spotting a print. The left-hand print (A) has numerous black-and-white spot defects, most of which have been successfully removed in the right-hand (B) spotted print. Spotting colors and the etching knife were used.*

Left: Figure 10. *Spotting color palette. A piece of opal glass or a small palette can be charged with the various water colors to be used for print retouching. Notice the homemade easel. Two drawing boards, 12×17 inches, hinged together, plus two stay brackets which adjust to a 30-degree angle when in use. This easel arrangement alleviates physical fatigue when long periods are spent retouching prints. When not in use the easel can be folded flat and stored.*

Right: Figure 11. *A complete complement of scraper etching-knife corrections, plus facial pencil retouching. (Artwork: Helen H. Dieterich)*

the modification of the character marks. The third step, called modeling, consists of properly tying together the first two steps and blending or modeling in harmonious union the contours, half-tones, highlights, and shadows of the face.

SKIN CLEANING

Blemishes, freckles, and skin spots are common in all faces. They are never desirable in any portrait. In all cases an effort must be made to get the skin texture smooth and clean. This cleaning or first step

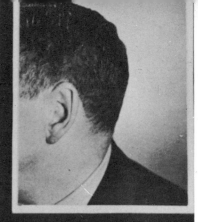

BEFORE
ETCHING AND
RETOUCHING

HAIR
ETCHED
IN

CIGARETTE
ETCHED
OUT

KERCHIEF
ETCHED
OUT

SLEEVE
AND LAPEL
CORRECTED

FINAL KNIFE
CORRECTIONS
PLUS FACIAL
RETOUCHING

has little to do with resemblance to the subject. The beginner should not fear getting the skin too smooth or overdoing the retouching at this stage.

Start retouching on the forehead, working across from left to right. Then work down the right side, across the chin and up the left side of the face and finish where you started. Fix your attention upon one little individual transparent spot at a time. Place the sharp pencil point in the center of the spot and move the point through it with a light feathery stroke. Make the spot invisible by filling it up with lead strokes until the density is equal to the density of the area around the spot. The shape of the stroke may be rolling or circular.

There is no special stroke for the beginner to acquire. In time you will aquire a stroke that will be characteristic of your retouching. The desirable stipple or pleasing grain which characterizes the work of the skilled retoucher is acquired by practice.

A common fault of the beginner is that he sits too close to the retouching stand. The proper distance is not the same for all individuals. Eyesight, volume of light used behind the stand, size and density of the negative—all influence the distance to be maintained. At all times the distance must be

Figure 12. *The first step in sharpening the scraper-type etching knife. Place the flat of the blade in perfect contact with the smooth side of the Norton India combination stone, and grind it back and forth as indicated by the double-pointed arrows until the surface is perfectly flat. A wooden model of the blade was used on the overlay image to facilitate description.* (Photography and art work: Helen H. Dieterich. Copyright © 1963, Germain School of Photography)

just far enough so that the actual pencil strokes cannot be seen (Figure 7).

Anything that is not a character mark must be treated as a skin blemish. Fill the spot with many delicate pencil strokes. Make them blend with the surrounding density. Apply your strokes in such a manner that they do not become obvious. When properly done the lead strokes become an integral part of

the image. After enough persistent practice a uniform, clean skin texture is produced.

When the skin cleaning is smoothly done and finished, study the effect. See how well you have avoided encroaching on the character marks. It is vitally important during the first step not to pencil stroke upon the character marks. Now the character marks stand out in greater contrast against the smooth skin texture that has been produced by the preliminary cleaning. Next make a print for comparison with one made before retouching (Figure 8).

CHARACTER MARKS

You are now ready to start the second step in retouching, the modification and treatment of the character marks. It must be understood

Figure 13. *Second step in sharpening the scraper-type etching knife. Place the bevel face on the stone and grind it back and forth as indicated by the double arrow. The surface of the bevel must be absolutely true. Repeat this operation and the previous one as in Figure 12 on the smooth Pike Arkansas stone, being sure to lubricate the stones with light oil during all sharpening operations. The duplication of the sharpening on the Arkansas stone is for the purpose of creating a razor-sharp edge.* (Copyright © 1963, Germain School of Photography)

that the properties or nature of the character marks are indicative of resemblance. Proper retouching treatment will result in correct retention of resemblance. Whether we are aware of it or not, we recognize resemblance by means of the character marks. As a general rule and depending on the lighting used, the negative registers the character marks 100 percent too deep and those character marks which are diagonal register on the negative about one-third too long. Retouching will reduce the depth of these marks to half, and shorten the diagonal marks one-third.

Character marks sometime require more protracted and discriminating treatment than these two simple rules indicate. No matter where it is located in the face, every character mark has a lighted and shaded area. The retouching is started by shading down from the highlights towards the shadows, taking care the pencil strokes follow the direction of the character mark, never at right angles to it or diagonally across it. Working from the highlights towards the shadows will help retain natural conformation and prevent obliteration of the character mark.

To facilitate pencil stroking, it is proper to rotate the negative in its envelope while retouching. The retoucher soon learns that a little discretionary over-retouching of the character marks pleases most customers; therefore, never carry it to the obliteration point. If some detail of each character mark is retained in the final print it is safe to assume that the retouching has not been carried too far.

Start with the wrinkles on the forehead. Tone them down or reduce their depth to an agreeable smoothness and modify any vertical lines between the eyes. Now start retouching under the eyes. Notice that under each eye there usually are two or three depressions. The first depression, located immediately under the eye, is retouched the least because it represents the natural fold of the lower eyelid. Taking out too much in this area gives the appearance of puffiness or swelling.

The next depression, right under the first, usually has more of a diagonal direction in the face. It is considerably modified and in many instances it is almost completely obliterated.

The third depression quite often does not appear at all; when it does appear it is frequently completely removed. In the character-type subject or very old subject, this third depression suggests the subject's age and should not be reduced to any great extent. In a younger person it would be quite proper to obliterate this third depression, as you can do so without loss of resemblance.

Where the character marks repeat themselves, as under the eyes from the corners of the nose to the corners of the mouth, and from the corners of the mouth downward towards the chin, they must be retouched in their respective pairs. This procedure assists greatly in keeping retouching of the character marks balanced so that one side of the face is not overdone or underdone when compared to the opposite side.

The next character mark is the one that starts at the lower corner of the nose and runs diagonally downward and outward to the corner of the mouth. If you gently obliterate the lower quarter or third of this character mark and reduce the rest of it about half, you will notice what an improvement this makes as compared to the untreated line on the opposite side. Modify and correct his opposite line in the same manner. Here you have a very clear example of what we mean by balancing character marks. The same treatment applies to the two character marks that run from the corners of the mouth downward and outward.

The depression in the chin under the lower lip always requires some

Figure 14. *Third step in sharpening. Figures 12 and 13 describe the creation of a sharp cutting edge. We must now convert the sharp edge to a scraper by feathering it. Place the blade on the lubricated Arkansas stone, the bevel surface facing away from you, and draw it towards you with a slight rocking motion as indicated on the left. A wooden model of the blade was used in the overlay print. The keenness of the blade must be tried on discarded negatives while learning how to properly prepare the blade for knife corrections without digging or scratching the negative image.* (Copyright © 1963, Germain School of Photography)

treatment. Here you must take into consideration the sex, age, and character of the subject. In a masculine type, it is altered as little as possible. A deep depression will give masculine strength to the chin. For most older people the same treatment is required. With women, full-faced men, and young subjects, the treatment is just the opposite, you take out a good deal of this depression. Remember that the more you obliterate this depression the more you create the effect of a receding or weak chin. If you overdo this area, disregarding the anatomical structure, you will produce an unnatural bulge or outward swelling under the lip. Good judgment is of prime importance and the type of face must be studied carefully to determine the amount of correction necessary.

A prominent lower lip is often encountered. In this instance the lower lip registers too wide in the vertical dimension. In addition there is usually a deeper horizontal crescent-shaped shadow immediately under it. The first procedure is to blend this shadow into the lower border of the lip to such a degree that you obliterate the original outline of the lip. Then you carefully recreate, a little higher up, a new lip line and judiciously build it up with delicate horizontal strokes, thus creating a narrower lower lip. It is now appropriate to make a test print for comparison with those made previously (Figure 8).

MODELING

Assuming that the student has practiced on many negatives and has become proficient up to this point, his work on casual inspection will take on a finished quality at this stage. However, the expert retoucher at this point would notice the necessity for modeling, or the final step. Sit back at a greater distance from the negative than required in the first two steps and notice that although the skin texture is nicely done and the character marks are properly modified, there is a disconnected effect between the highlights, shadows, halftones, and contours of the face. Although the retouching seems to have a finished appearance, the experienced eye will notice the patchy effect.

At the proper distance (where you can see this disconnected effect) begin to make a harmonious blend. Great care must be practiced when weaving the densities together so as not to lose the identity of the individual densities. Just weave them together in a *belong to each other* manner. If you overdo this step you will undo all the good work you have accomplished up to now. By becoming overambitious you will create an inflated or puffed-up effect in the face that will not be at all natural. Be satisfied with a little of this work at a time in the beginning. Follow up your efforts with many carefully studied test prints until you are more experienced and more certain of yourself (Figure 8).

PINHOLES

Despite all care in processing, negatives will frequently have some pinholes that require treatment. This is done with pencil or with brush and spotting water colors, or both. The brush-and-ink technique is best.

Quite often a pinhole can be obliterated with a retouching pencil. An HB or a B pencil is applied in the same manner as in cleaning the skin texture. If the pencil lead does not take, don't force it to the breaking point; instead use the 00, No. 1 or No. 2 spotting brush. The size of the brush depends on how large the hole is. The brushes are used with the Eastman spotting colors.

SPOTTING NEGATIVES

In spotting, the color is thick and heavy, never watery. The brush is semidry with color, not filled with color solution.

First, the brush is drawn across a thoroughly wet piece of cotton to work up the color. Then the brush, charged with wet color, is tested on a discarded negative. The brush is rotated to a point with just the right amount of spotting color. The result

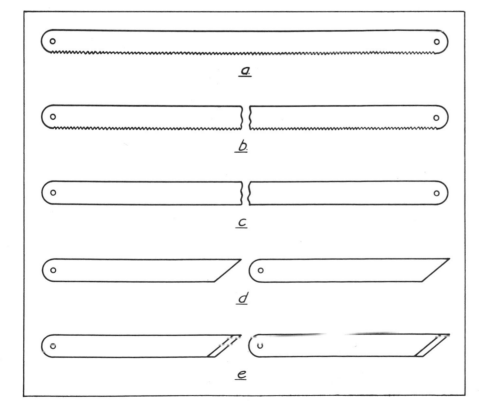

Figure 15. *Steps in making an etching knife from a hacksaw blade. a) High-speed hacksaw blade b) Same blade broken in two halves. c) Saw teeth ground off. d) Broken ends ground to proper angle of about 50 degrees. e) Bevel of 20 degrees put on both pieces, making two very good etching knives. (Drawing: Helen H. Dieterich)*

Figure 16. *Handmade background.* Left, *print from negative without sketching.* Center, *background design sketched on separate piece of groundglass.* Right, *image and background combined.*

is a brush that is pointed and almost dry. Touch the brush to a piece of white paper and you will see that it leaves a small spot of the most delicate gray tone. This is the proper condition for use. If the brush leaves a spot of water or moist color it is too wet. Stroke the brush a few times on a piece of white blotter or a discarded print or negative to remove the excess moisture and repeat the conditioning as described above.

Try the brush on a clear edge of the negative. If a tiny spot of color is left by the brush, carefully touch the brush point to the spot in the negative. Never try to fill a pinhole with one stroke of the brush. Touch it lightly once, let the color dry a moment, apply another stroke, and so on until the proper density has been built up. In treating a larger transparent spot the proper method is to fill it in with small dots in a scattered manner. This filling of a large area with small dots, known as *stippling,* is decidedly superior to a flat wash of color.

After spotting out transparent pinholes, there is one final step. There may be a few opaque or dark spots on the negative which will appear as white spots in the print.

With the toe or point of an etching knife shave these spots down very carefully. Do not try to reduce them with one stab of the knife. Etch them down with many light

shaving strokes until they take on the density of the surrounding area. If you shave too deeply, fill it in as you did in the previous spotting.

SPOTTING PRINTS

The same procedure is followed for spotting prints as for spotting negatives (Figure 9). For negatives one type of color, black, can be used at all times. For retouching or spotting prints the colors must be matched to the texture or surface and tone of the paper. A proper palette must be made to meet the requirements of glossy, semiglossy, matte, rough, white ivory, buff, black-and-white, and sepia prints. A white saucer or piece of opal glass makes a good palette (Figure 10).

With a brush or fingertip dipped in water, apply daubs of color in order. The Winsor - Newton lampblack or Payne's gray and burnt sienna are used for matte and rough surfaces. The Talens blackish and

Figure 17. *Handmade background. The same technical procedure followed as described in Figure 16.* (Church-window background drawn by Helen H. Dietcrich)

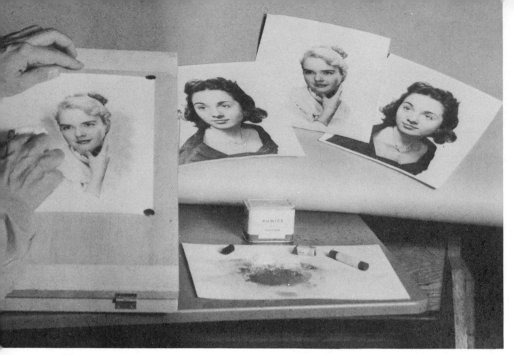

Figure 18. *Hand sketching white backgrounds. The dry crayon sauce being applied to the background of the print.*

brownish are used for semi-matte and glossy surfaces. Cold-toned colors are used for spotting on white-base papers; warm-toned colors, on ivory or buff papers. Burnt sienna and the brown sections of the spotting pads are used for working on sepia prints. They can be blended with any of the other colors to match any tone in sepia. Payne's gray can be mixed with any color to produce lighter shades.

Gum arabic is added to any color to make it more glossy. It is usually used with the Talens colors. Wet a lump of gum arabic and rub some

on the palette. When needed, mix it with the color required. Mucilage is a vegetable glue made from gum arabic and is sold in small size, convenient glass bottles with a rubber dispenser top. It is more convenient to squeeze a few drops of the liquid on the palette instead of trying to work up the dry gum with water.

In addition to all the colors and spotting materials mentioned, Spotone is used by many professional photographers. Its popularity stems from the fact that a print will readily absorb this dye from rough

Figure 19. *The sketch effect being created with a pencil eraser.*

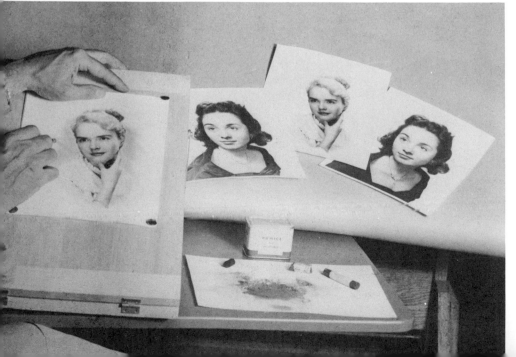

to glossy surfaces without any visible residue. Spotone is supplied with full instructions for use.

The 5H, 6H, 7H, and 8H retouching leads are used on negatives or prints where light gray strokes are required. Their use on prints is restricted to glossy surfaces only. For very fine hairlines on glossy paper, first dope the surface of the print in the same manner as you would prepare a negative for retouching. If properly done the paper will not show dope stains. Then proceed to retouch out the lines with one of the hard leads. You must remember that this is practical only on lighter areas.

ETCHING

The etching knife plays a major part as an adjunct to negative retouching. Figure 11 illustrates a complete complement of knife corrections. For print treatment its use is limited. Only the smaller black spots can be scraped away with some measure of success without showing even when the print is examined at an angle.

There are two types of etching knives commonly used. One is the scraper type and the other is the cutting type. Both can be used interchangeably for negatives and prints. Figures 12-14, illustrate the method of sharpening the scraper-type etching knife. It has a diagonal bevel edge similar to a wood chisel with the cutting edge turned over like a furniture scraper. One can be purchased from the photosupply store, or can be made from a hacksaw blade (Figure 15). The surfaces are ground true on a Norton India combination stone, 1B-134 and a Norton Pike Arkansas stone, HB-13 (Figure 12-14). Both stones are necessary to sharpen an etching knife. After surfacing the blade on the India stone, you then repeat the sharpening on the smoother Arkansas stone. A thin oil must be used to lubricate the stones.

The cutting knife may be a safety-razor blade, pen-point scraper (stencil cutter), or X-acto knife. The author prefers the No. 11 blade used with the X-acto knife handle. All these cutting implements are best for use on prints, and can be used to some extent on negatives. Kodak abrasive paste and reducing pencil can be used on negatives, but not on prints.

HAND-SKETCHED BACKGROUNDS

For sketched backgrounds on portrait negatives you will require negatives with black or dark-gray grounds. For similar backgrounds on prints, you must use prints with white backgrounds, preferably vignetted prints.

A hand-sketched ground on a portrait negative (Figure 16 and 17) is made by binding a sheet of groundglass, matte celluloid, or traceolene to the back of the negative with bits of Scotch tape, with the shiny surfaces in contact with each other. Place the backed negative on the retouching stand (emulsion side down, matte side up) in preparation for sketching in the background. The materials required are: black crayon sauce or powdered graphite, 4, 5, or 6B lead pencil, art gum, kneaded eraser or soft eraser, and a paper or chamois artist's stomp.

The powdered crayon sauce or graphite is applied with a stomp, or with a soft cloth which has been tightly twisted around the index finger. The sauce or graphite is applied on the back of the negative, directly upon the matte surface, in liberal but irregular daubs. To produce a heavy enough coating, it may be necessary to apply the black powder with somewhat heavy stomping strokes.

When a coating has been applied, certain portions of the colors are removed in a sketchy manner with an eraser. Keep in mind that you are working on the negative, that the black crayon sauce produces whites and the erasures cause blacks or shadows in the final print. It is advisable to make progressive test

Top: Figure 20. *Crayon sauce applied to the background in preparation for the eraser strokes.*

Bottom: Figure 21. *The final sketched print completed. Hand-sketched backgrounds are also called abrasion-toned prints.*

prints. The soft pencil is used to accentuate highlights. Its use is optional and can be deferred until the simpler sketching with the eraser is mastered. The same process is used for working up backgrounds on commercial subjects.

For sketching on a white-background print (Figures 18-21), mix about two-thirds crayon sauce or graphite with one-third powdered pumice. Keep this in a convenient container or small tray. Twist a piece of soft cotton cloth tightly around the index finger. Rub the covered finger into the powder, shake off the surplus powder, and try it on a discarded print to determine the depth of color it is going to leave.

When you have adjusted the correct shade on the covered finger, apply the color to the white background of the print in a free, sketchy manner. Localize the color in the vicinity of the head and shoulders. The sketch is emphasized with a soft eraser.

The author prefers a common eraser on the end of an ordinary lead pencil. The solid tone of the rubbed-in powder is broken up with the eraser to produce the sketch effect. After the eraser stroking is completed, wipe the sketched area lightly with a tuft of absorbent cotton to soften the sharp pencil strokes.

Use sepia crayon sauce with powdered pumice for sepia prints. Traces or small portions of black crayon sauce or graphite may be added to match dark sepia-toned prints. Appropriate shades of dry pastel colors can be used for matching other tones. On certain occasions delicately blue- or red-toned prints can be enhanced by sketched grounds.

Dead-matte or medium-rough surface papers are best. Glossy, semiglossy, or semi-matte papers are not suitable for sketching. To prevent the sketching from smudging, the print can be sprayed with a nonglossy, transparent plastic which can be purchased in a pressurized can. There are a number of reliable brands on the market.

STRIPPING BACKGROUNDS

Stripping away backgrounds is extensively practiced in commercial photography. It is used when objectionable detail must be eliminated and a solid-black ground is required. Objects with sharp outlines such as motors cars, furniture, statues, cut glass, and machinery are suitable for this process. There are two methods practiced by professional retouchers, physical and chemical.

The physical method is to go around the object with a sharp knife, cutting through the emulsion to the celluloid or glass base. When working on a film negative, scrape away the dry-gelatin background until it will show black in the print (Figure 22).

With a glass negative the peeling method is best. After the outline is cut, wet the background by daubing it with a tuft of wet cotton, being careful not to wet any portion of the image. The background will absorb the moisture and swell. In a short time the gelatin can be raised using the end of a sharp knife at one corner of the negative. When the gelatin is loosened, the entire background can be removed by rolling the swelled gelatin with the fingers. Be careful not to rub the edge of the image especially if it has been inadvertently moistened.

The second method requires the use of Farmer's reducer. This method is suitable for both film or glass negatives. Cover the entire image with Maskoid, leaving the background exposed. Use a 0 or No. 1 spotting brush to outline the image and fill in thoroughly with a larger brush. Be careful not to leave any uncovered spots.

After the Maskoid is thoroughly dry, immerse the negative in Farmer's reducer until the entire visible detail in the background disappears. The image will not be affected in the slightest degree, because the Maskoid acts as a repellent. After the background is bleached away, wash and dry in the usual manner. When dry, the Maskoid is easily rolled off with the fingers. The Kodak Farmer's

reducer (in powder form with full instructions for mixing and use) can be procured in photosupply stores. The Farmer's reducer removes only the silver image.

An alternate method for stripping a background, is to cover the image with Maskoid as described for use with the Farmer's reducer. It is then soaked in a solution of three-parts water and one-part Clorox or Rose-X bleach. This will remove the gelatin from both sides of the film including the silver image of the background. When the background is completely cleared, wash the negative for about five or ten minutes and hang up to dry. When dry, the Maskoid can be removed by rolling off with the fingers.

BLOCKING OUT

Opaquing or blocking out commercial negatives produces pure-white backgrounds in prints (Figures 23 and 24). Eastman Kodak or Grumbacher opaque is used for this purpose. It is supplied in glass jars and must be thoroughly stirred before use.

Thin the opaque with a little water and try it on a discard negative. When dry, the opaque must be smooth and show solid-white in the print. If it dries lumpy and shows cracks and pinholes by transmitted light the opaque was not stirred enough initially or was applied too thickly.

Use an 00, 0, No. 1 or a No. 2 brush and work carefully around the edge of the image with the opaque. Use the smallest brush that is consistent with the size of the negative image. In the case of delicate contours or intricate patterns, the initial outline may be made with a B or BB pencil (soft leads) or drawing ink and a Gillott's letter-

Figure 22. *Removing a background. To produce a solid-black ground in the print, the etching knife alone can be used to accomplish the job. The illustrations show: A) Before treatment. B) Skillful and accurate outlining of the image. C) The emulsion is progressively shaved away from the image. D) The complete removal of the background, producing a pure-black ground in the print.*

A

B

C

D

Figure 23. *Treatment by chemical reduction and opaquing to produce a black or a white background. A. Before chemical treatment with Farmer's reducer to eliminate the objectionable background. This treatment produces a clean black as in C. For a white background as in B, the opaquing method is used.*

ing pen, and the opaque worked up to this line, not over it. Using a larger brush for convenience, the entire negative background is then painted in with opaque.

The Grumbacher Gamma Retouching Pencil works well on negatives and prints. It is a nonlead pencil particularly good for outlining negatives when opaquing. It makes opaque lines with very little pressure and works equally well on both sides of a film negative.

Sometimes the gelatin may repel the opaque and will not permit it to take evenly. In such cases rub the surface of the negative gently with a tuft of absorbent cotton dipped in rottenstone or very fine pumice powder. Be careful for too much rubbing will cause scratches. If you do not wish to risk scratching the negative or if it is small in size, you can treat it in the following manner: soak the dry film in wetting agent for ten minutes to half an hour, after a brief rinse in running water hang up to dry. Masking-paper or plastic strips are cut to size and fastened in proper position around the image. Any curves in the negative are outlined with a ruling or lettering pen guided with a French curve. The ruling pen guided with a straight-edge ruler is used for opaquing straight lines. Opaque or drawing ink works well when used with a ruling pen. The use of black masking tape is a time saver.

LETTERING ON NEGATIVES AND PRINTS

Experience in drafting or lettering is obviously of value in lettering by hand on negatives and prints and sometimes necessary when identifying, signing, or copyrighting a picture. However, efficiency can be mastered by tracing from an alphabet or lettering chart.

Lettering on glass negatives must be done on the emulsion side and from right to left (mirror-image fashion), otherwise the lettering will be in reverse on the print. Lettering in regular order (from left to right) can be done directly on the back of film negatives. Light tracing can first be made with a pencil to insure straight lining and proper spacing and then gone over in black drawing ink. This will produce white letters in the print.

If black letters are required, the lettering is done with a hotpoint-pyrograph needle. This device resembles a small electric soldering iron and is used for burning-in decorations on leather goods and wood. This hotpoint sears through the gelatin emulsion and makes a transparent line which prints black. When used on a film negative, care must be exercised not to burn through the celluloid base. It would be wise to first practice on a discarded negative.

A large darning needle fixed in a retouching-pencil holder may be used for lettering. The needle can be heated in the flame of an alcohol lamp as a hotpoint or it can be used cold to scrape or cut away the gelatin.

Black waterproof ink, lettering pens, brushes, and opaque are used for lettering on negatives. Lettering on prints and photographic mounts is considerably easier. The materials commonly used are pens or brush, soft lead pencils, crayon pencils, and carbon or charcoal pencils. A lettering pen used with waterproof ink is a favorite method.

Chemical bleaching is sometimes employed for lettering on negatives and prints. The following formulas will be found to work as perfect bleaches:

Water	2 ounces
Iodine crystals	5½ grains
Potassium iodide	20 grains
Gum arabic	65 grains

(Alternate formula which is simpler to make:)

Drugstore tincture of iodine	1 ounce
LePage's mucilage	10 to 15 drops

Apply this solution with brush or pen, being careful not to let it spread on unwanted areas. After lettering, rinse the negative in running water for a few minutes and immerse in a plain fixing bath without acid hardener until the whites are cleared. Wash for half an hour and hang up to dry. This bleach will produce transparent clear letters on negatives and pure white on prints.

If the solution spreads too readily

in spite of all care exercised, add more gum arabic or mucilage to the bleaching solution. For best results, use a 20- or 25-percent solution of plain fixing bath that has not been used for any other fixing purpose, discarding it when lettering is accomplished.

All the techniques described about lettering have been practiced for many decades by the profession, and are still used extensively. However, as time goes on new technical improvements are being developed to aid the photographer. A new type of prepared-lettering sheets have been in use for some time. They are sold under the name of "Letraset-instant lettering." The letters and numerals are easy to transfer to negatives and prints and are available in a number of styles and sizes. Art-supply stores have them for sale. All the numerals and letters in Figures 1-3, 8, 9, 15, 22-24 were made with the "Letraset-instant lettering" sheet. It is a dry-transfer method which leaves no trace of adhesive or smudge.

Figure 24. *Clorox treatment to eliminate objectionable backgrounds from negatives. This method is suitable for commercial negatives. A) Before Clorox treatment. B) Clorox treatment produces a clear-black ground. C) For a white background the opaquing method is used. See text for additional instructions on negative treatment.*

REVERSAL PROCESS

JOHN S. CARROLL
Editor "The Photo-Lab-Index"
[Normal processing, development, fixing, and washing produces a negative from a camera exposure. By adding several steps it is possible to reverse an image during processing so that the film exposed in the camera becomes a positive. The method is used for both black-and-white and color photography. In this article the process as used for black-and-white is explained step-by-step.]
• *Also see: Development, Motion-Picture Film.*

WHILE ATTEMPTS AT POPULARIZING movies for home use began almost as soon as the motion picture was invented, the greatest drawback to its acceptance was the cost. A roll of film was exposed in the camera, developed to a negative, and then a second roll of film was exposed in a printer to form the positive for projection. This is an excellent method for commercial films where many copies of an original film are needed. However, the amateur usually requires only a single copy of his movie and the need for two rolls of film to produce one copy—

plus the cost of processing both rolls—made movies for home use extremely expensive.

The breakthrough came with the introduction of the reversal process. The film used in the camera became the final projection copy by a system of development which converted the image from negative to positive during processing.

DEFINITION

There is nothing very mysterious about reversal processing. When a film is developed to a negative, a good deal of unexposed- and undeveloped silver bromide is left which must be dissolved out in hypo. The reversal process is simply a system by which the film is first developed to a negative and then printed directly on the remainder of the unused halide.

The negative is next removed by a bleaching bath and the positive latent image is developed to form the final positive picture. Since all this is done on a single film in one process, it eliminates the cost of the film needed for the positive print and the cost of printing and developing the positive.

When color films were first introduced for home processing, a similar method was applied. The negative image was first developed in a

normal-reversal developer, the positive was exposed and developed in a special developer forming both silver and dye, and finally the silver images produced in both stages was bleached out, leaving a positive color image.

PRACTICAL REVERSAL

In theory, all there is to reversal processing is to develop the film in a negative developer, expose the film to light, bleach the negative image, and develop the film a second time to produce the positive image.

In practice it is not quite this simple. It depends for one thing on how heavily the original film is coated; if too much silver is left after the negative has been developed, the resulting positive will be far too dense.

Also, emulsions always contain a small percentage of practically insensitive grains. Thus even after full development of a thin-emulsion film some undeveloped grains remain in the highest lights and clear positives cannot be obtained.

CONTROLLING RE-EXPOSURE

There are two approaches to the problem of controlling re-exposure. The first was used by Kodak when they processed black-and-white reversal films for amateurs.

The film was developed normally in a special machine. As the moving film left the developer, it passed under a special photocell exposure meter, which controlled the strength of the re-exposing light. Where the negative was dense, the film received more exposure; where it was thin or underexposed, the film received less re-exposure.

After leaving the re-exposure station, the film was bleached and developed. However, the second developer did not develop all the re-exposed silver—it was controlled to produce an image of proper density for good projection. Finally the film passed to a regular hypo bath where all silver grains that had not been affected by the previous stages were removed.

The procedure had several advantages. It was capable of correcting for under- or overexposure as much as two stops either way. It produced images of excellent contrast and gradation, since the film was actually going through a true-printing stage in the process.

It had disadvantages, too. The automatic exposure control tended to eliminate all special effects. For instance, if the photographer tried to underexpose deliberately to give the impression of a night scene, the film would be corrected by the photocell device and would come out looking nearly normal. Fades were also affected; if the camera shutter was slowly closed down to produce a long fade-out the compensator would automatically keep bringing up the image and the first part of the fade would be completely lost. When the image finally did fade out, it became a milky gray instead of black. Thus a long smooth fade was often changed into a short, abrupt one.

REVERSAL FILMS

Obviously, it is much simpler if the film can simply be developed, heavily exposed, and all the remaining silver developed to produce a positive of correct gradation.

A number of such films are available. Kodak supplies Plus-X and Tri-X in reversal types. DuPont also supplies a number of reversal black-and-white emulsions, and there are several imported types made by Gevaert and others. These films have a thinner emulsion coating than normal negative-type films. If correctly exposed, reversal films can be processed without need for controlled second development or controlled re-exposure.

Ordinary cine-positive film can be reversed, but the results are contrasty and usually suitable only for titles. A 35 mm Kodak Direct Positive Panchromatic film, a reversal emulsion similar to Plus-X, which is used to make black-and-white positive slides in miniature cameras, is also available.

REVERSAL PROCESSING OF BLACK-AND-WHITE FILMS

Even with the thin coating there are some insensitive grains in the emulsion which will cause a foggy positive. To avoid this, the developer used is very strong and contains a silver solvent such as potassium thiocyanate.

The silver solvent has two effects. First, it assures clean highlights in the final film. Second, since the silver solvent eliminates the insensitive grains from the emulsion the effective emulsion speed is somewhat increased. The same film is usually considerably faster when processed by reversal, as compared with the exposure required if the film is used as a negative.

For processing Kodak reversal films, the first developer usually used is a modified Kodak D-19, containing an addition of sodium or potassium thiocyanate. The modified formula is known as *Kodak D-67,* and follows:

REVERSAL FIRST DEVELOPER

Warm water

24 ounces (750 cc)

Developing tanks, such as this Nikor model for 35 mm film, that utilize a spiral reel for the film can be easily used for reversal processing. This type of reel design facilitates exposing the film evenly before the second development.

Kodak Elon
30 grains (2 grams)
Sodium sulfite, desiccated
3 ounces (90 grams)
Kodak Hydroquinone
¼ ounce (8 grams)
Sodium carbonate, mono.
1 oz. 290 grains (50 grams)
Potassium bromide
73 grains (5 grams)
Sodium thiocyanate
30 grains (2 grams)
Add cold water to make
32 ounces (1 liter)

If packaged Kodak D-19 is available, this developer can be prepared simply by adding two grams of potassium or sodium thiocyanate to each liter of developer (30 grains to each quart).

Exact developing time cannot be specified because it depends on the film and the equipment used. It will be about 12 minutes in most immersion-type tanks, 10 minutes for the open-drum type of equipment, and 15 minutes for rewind tanks. These calculations are for Kodak Plus-X and Tri-X films and do not apply to the DuPont emulsions which are designed for much shorter developing times.

After development the film is washed for a few minutes in cold water so that an excessive amount of developer will not be carried into the bleach bath. The film is then bleached in the following bath (Kodak R-9):

BLEACH BATH

Water
32 ounces (1 liter)
Potassium dichromate
140 grains (9.5 grams)
*Sulfuric acid (concentrated)
³/₈ ounce (12 cc)

*Caution: add the acid, very slowly to the water. Never pour water into sulfuric acid as it may boil explosively.

After the film has been immersed in the bleach and agitated two or three times the room lights may be turned on. Bleaching continues until all the black silver image has been removed and highlight areas are clear against the creamy background of unexposed silver bromide. After bleaching is completed, the film is again washed for a few minutes to

eliminate the yellow coloring resulting from the bleach. However, some stain will remain and the next step is clearing:

CLEARING BATH

Kodak sodium sulfite, desiccated
3 ounces (90 grams)
Cold water to make
32 ounces (1 liter)

This bath removes any remaining yellow stain from the film and restores the sensitivity of the remaining halides so they can be re-exposed for the final positive.

The film is then exposed to light. The light must be quite strong; for instance, a Photoflood. (Remember, the film must be protected from heat.) Exposure should be long enough to assure that all remaining silver will be exposed and developed, producing the final image. Diffused daylight can be used, but direct sunlight must not as it will cause a purple over-all stain on the film.

DEVELOPMENT OF THE POSITIVE IMAGE

Next stage is development of the positive image with a straight Kodak D-19 developer, or the D-67 formula with the sodium thiocyanate omitted. *Important:* the final developer must not contain any thiocyanate. Development is continued until the film is apparently black all over; examining it against a light will show a good, bright positive image, if exposures were correct. There is nothing critical about development here; it is simply important to be sure development is complete.

Theoretically, the finished film should not require fixing, since there should be no unexposed or undeveloped silver halides remaining after the above process. Actually there are always a few insensitive grains which will have escaped the action of the first developer and succeeding stages, and a more brilliant image will result if these are removed. Also, the gelatin of the film is tender after the two developing baths and the bleach. It is good practice, therefore, to end the process with five to ten minutes in a good hardening-fixing bath such as Kodak F-5, which clears the image and hardens the gelatin.

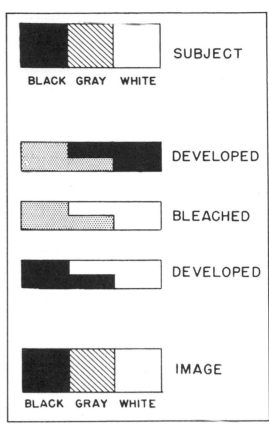

Diagram showing the steps in reversal development from the original subject to the final image that corresponds to the original.

After fixing, the film must be thoroughly washed to remove all traces of hypo. Finally, it is dried in the usual way. An antispot rinse may be given after the final wash and before drying to eliminate the need for squeegeeing and to avoid possible damage to the film.

NOTES AND COMMENTS

Each film manufacturer has his own formulas for processing of reversal films. In general, better results will be obtained if the formula supplied by the manufacturer is used, but the above formulas will do quite well on any film provided:

1. The film is a reversal type.
2. The time in the first developer is adjusted to the specific film being used. A small reel holding a few feet of film can be made and used for tests.

The density of the final positive can be controlled only in the exposure of the original film in the camera. Thus films to be developed by reversal must be accurately exposed. Even if you use a meter, there is a chance of incorrect exposure due to equipment errors and tests should be made at various emulsion-speed settings to determine the working film speed for your purposes.

Certain universal films are intended for either negative or reversal processing. In general, they will apparently have a higher speed when processed by reversal. Note, too, that many of these films have a gray antihalation coating in the form of a dye located in the cellulose base which cannot be removed. This produces a light-gray tone over the whole film, which should not be mistaken for fog. Fog reduces the contrast of the image because it deposits mostly on the lighter parts. However, the gray of the base is an even addition over-all and has no effect on the contrast of the image. It merely reduces screen illumination somewhat.

Some Kodak reversal films intended for machine processing, have the "Rem-Jet" (removable jet) antihalation coating. This coating is usually softened by the first developer and washed away completely in the rinse. It is important not to use a hardening rinse after the first developer with these films, as it will interfere with removal of the jet backing. When developing on a drum, the film should be loosened slightly after the developer and while rinsing, and a cloth or sponge slipped underneath. The cloth may then be run along the back of the film to wipe off any bits of jet backing which remain. This should be done at this stage for later these bits of backing may harden and be difficult to remove.

One of the great advantages of reversal processing is that the most sensitive grains in the film are also the largest. The large grains make up the negative image and are the ones removed by the bleach. Thus the finer grains form the positive and the result is a beautifully fine-grained, smooth image.

This effect also applies to color films which are processed by reversal. The dye image has exactly the same grain structure as the silver image which formed it, but the reversal process assures that the dyes will be formed by the smallest grains.

The procedure for processing color-reversal films is almost the same as for black-and-white. The composition of the baths is different and formulas are not generally available. The chemicals required for processing color films are supplied in kits, and the kit required for each film is the one recommended by the manufacturer. Unlike black-and-white films, the color films of various makers are very different in structure, and the color film of one maker cannot be processed in baths designed for another.

However, there is no difficulty in processing color reversal film once the black-and-white process has been mastered and the amateur can very easily process his own reversal color.

□

MARC RIBOUD
Biography

Marc Riboud of *Magnum* is a globe-trotting photojournalist whose assignments for major magazines in Europe and America have taken him to the most remote corners of the world.

Riboud was born in Lyons, France, in 1923 where he was later to work as an industrial engineer before becoming a professional photographer. His interest in photography started when he inherited an old Leica from his father. Almost immediately he began doing picture stories in his spare time. In order to finish one such assignment he took a week's leave of absence from his job at the factory. "I am still on that leave of absence," he says.

An important moment in Riboud's early photographic career came in 1950 when his brother introduced him to the French photojournalist, Henri Cartier-Bresson. Eventually, Riboud showed Cartier-Bresson some of his pictures with the result that Riboud was invited to join *Magnum,* the cooperative picture agency, of which Cartier-Bresson was a founder. At about this same time Riboud moved to Paris where he shot stories on speculation (later distributed by *Magnum*). It was during this period that Riboud had the opportunity to observe Cartier-Bresson at work, an experience that was to have an important influence on his own work.

Although he was (and is) still based in Paris, it was not long before Riboud had built a considerable reputation as one of the most widely travelled photographers. In London in 1954 he photographed Winston Churchill at the Conservative party conference; also in London in the same year the dock strike and the hydrogen-bomb protest. In 1955 he made trips to Dalmatia and Turkey on assignments, and a year later he was working with Mike Todd on *Around the World in 80 Days.* Later that same year (1956) he drove overland by Land Rover from Paris to Calcutta stopping along the way on the five-month trip for assignments in Turkey, Iran, and Afghanistan.

Riboud was to remain for one full year in India. "This was the first time I was completely cut off from the world I knew—and taking lots of pictures. Because of the intensity of the change, I was forced to observe. I find it difficult to work in a place like Paris because I am too familiar with it. When I am completely engaged in work and in a new and stimulating place, my mind is free to see and to discover."

In 1957 Riboud went from India to China and covered assignments on Peking and on Chinese industry and agriculture for such magazines as *Holiday, Life, The Saturday Evening Post, Fortune,* and *Paris Match.* In 1958 he did stories on such diverse subjects as the Sumatran rebels, the funeral of Pope Pius XII, and Rockefeller's election as governor of New York. In mid-winter of 1958-59 he made another one of his long automobile journeys, this time from Fairbanks, Alaska to Acapulco, Mexico.

More recently Riboud has been an accredited correspondent-photographer in Soviet Russia (1960).

Christmas in Provence, Marc Riboud / Magnum

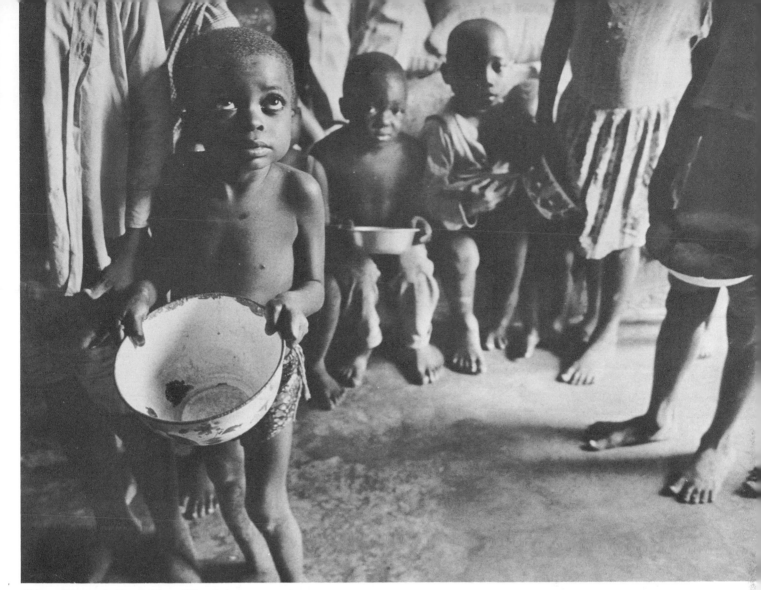

Above: *Famine in Kasai, Marc Riboud /
Magnum*

Left: *Algeria, 1962, Marc Riboud /
Magnum*

He has followed his U.S.S.R. assignments with two trips to Africa for the Nigerian Independence celebration (1960) and the Congo famine (1961).

To understand and appreciate Riboud's aims, one need only review the subjects he has chosen to photograph. Once examined, a definite pattern takes shape indicating that here is a man who is concerned with people, their unique portion of the earth, and their continually intense interaction upon each other. Significantly, Riboud rarely photographs the individual man, preferring instead the urgency and excitement to be found in the group.

Like Cartier-Bresson, Marc Riboud works only with 35 mm cameras. He tries to hold his equipment to a minimum, working with two Leicas (one for color and one for black-and-white) usually with 35mm and 50mm lenses, and one Pentax with a 180mm telephoto. He also carries a third Leica as a spare in case one of his other cameras should break down.

Early in his photographic career, Riboud developed and printed all his own work, but because of the pressure of assignments, he now has all his darkroom work done by a lab. He prefers to work in black-and-white but has found in recent years that more and more of his work must be in color.

Of his own philosophy, Riboud has said, "For me, the photographer is a witness. His job is to record real events rather than to stage or create something in front of the camera. Unfortunately, this kind of photography is sometimes hard to sell because magazines often have preconceived ideas of the particular pictures they want. Another problem of the magazine photographer is that he must often work too quickly, when it would be better if he could spend a longer time in a place and have the chance to know it better.... In all my work I am not very interested in my old pictures. The photographs that interest me the most are the new ones I am going to take."

Riboud has done one book *Femmes du Japon* (Japanese Women) and is currently working on a book about an African family in transition from the traditional life of the bush native to that of a modern 20th-century city.

—Charles R. Reynolds, Jr.

H. P. ROBINSON
Biography

From the birth of pictorialism in the 1850's to its climax in the early 1900's, Henry Peach Robinson was so great a figure that his contemporaries regarded him as the uncrowned king of photography.

Born in Ludlow, Shropshire, in 1830, he began life as a bookseller with a lively interest in the arts and sciences. He contributed early in his life to botany, natural history, and archeology. In painting, etching, and sculpture he was so precocious that his paintings were hung in the Royal Academy before he was twenty-one.

In 1850 he added daguerreotype to his other interests. Two years later he was in London, still selling books but now preparing seriously for a photographic career by learning first calotypy and then wet collodion, the medium in which he was to do his most famous work.

Pictorialism was in the very air of London, and it was doubtless Dr. Hugh Diamond, leader of an important photographic group, who convinced Robinson that a brilliant career lay before him in combining photography with art. It was a time when the awe and respect which greeted photography in 1839 was wearing off. Painters and other people with artistic pretensions were becoming increasingly irritated with photography—not only was it still obstinately wrong about color, recording red as black and leaving skies blank, but it was by its very nature exasperatingly literal, including things that nobody noticed and offering no means by which motifs could be selected, combined, and emphasized. Instead of accepting this challenge to their ways of seeing, these well-intentioned people wished to make the process malleable enough to raise it to the height of an art—by which they meant academic painting.

The next year, 1853, at the first meeting of what was to be the Royal Photographic Society of Great Britain, Sir William Newton, miniature painter to the court, declared that sharpness was not everything and that photography could and should be improved by the hands of qualified artists. In 1865 Gustave Le Gray, a painter, printed sky negatives with his seascapes. In 1857 O. G. Rejlander, a painter, exhibited in Manchester his "Two Ways of Life" which was composed of 30 negatives.

In this same year, Robinson

When The Day's Work Is Done. 1890, from Sun-Artists. *This sentimental type of genre picture flattered the taste of the time and was so widely imitated by photographers with none of Robinson's charm and experience that photographic salons reached an unparalleled low.* (Photo: Museum of Modern Art)

turned professional opening a studio in Leamington and producing his first known work, "Juliet with the Poison Bottle," one of a series of his vignettes now in the collection of the Royal Photographic Society. In 1858 at the Crystal Palace, he exhibited a combination print called "Fading Away." This represented a young girl dying and caused such an uproar of discussion as to whether such subjects were too emotional for photography that Robinson became famous overnight.

Following this success he made the annual practice of issuing to subscribers one large picture, usually a combination print averaging 18×24 inches. Like the fashionable paintings they imitated, these pictures were anecdotal and sentimental, although of a certain charm and taste. Each was regarded as the photographic climax of the year.

Asked to lecture on his methods before the Royal Photographic Society in 1860, he told how most of the foregrounds in his pictures were made in the yard of his house at Leamington, where he had raised a bank of earth, planted it appropriately, and even made a brook of his darkroom drain.

He also explained that he found real peasants and fisher-folk too awkward, self-conscious, and stupid for genre work, and admitted that he was compelled to enlist young ladies in rustic costume as his models, since they alone had the grace and intelligence necessary for posing. The story is told that one day as he was photographing some young ladies on the grounds of their father's estate, the gardener came up in high dudgeon, and not recognizing his young mistresses in their disguise, told them to be off before the master should find them.

His famous composite, "Autumn" appeared in 1863 and was destined to become "the most bemedalled photograph in the world." Photographic salons were still scarce, yet Robinson won some 100 medals, many of them from the Royal Photographic Society. Even the furor caused by Mrs. Cameron (See *Julia Margaret Cameron*) and her magnificent portraits left him compara-

Autumn, 1863. From Pictorial Effect in Photography. *In Robinson's own opinion the joints in this, his most famous combination print, are clumsily handled. He deplored the line in the grass that separates the dark figure on the ground from the group at the left. Four pictures were used; the foreground figures break into three and are of course silhouetted upon the background, also taken at a separate time. Robinson planned and sketched all his combination prints in advance and, as his skill increased, it becomes difficult to discover how they were put together. Yet not even his skill in lighting and printing can restore the emotional impact of a true photograph. Compare this with the work of Emerson.* (Photo: Museum of Modern Art)

tively unshaken. He recognized her ability, but recommended that she learn enough technique not to make "smudges."

Nevertheless, Robinson was one of those who petitioned Dallmeyer for a diffusion-focus lens in 1866. Photographs taken by Robinson with this lens exist, but he continued to prefer the sharpness and slickness that resembled the academic painting of the day. In this Robinson was reinforced by Adam Salomon, a sculptor whose "creatively retouched" portraits were exhibited in Paris in 1867. The following year this idol came to visit Robinson at his new studio in Tunbridge Wells.

By 1869 the clamor for Robinson's recipe for success was so great that he produced *Pictoral Effect in Photography: being Hints on Composition and Chiaroscuro for Potographers, to which is added a Chapter on Combination Printing*. In this book, he borrowed from an 1830 treatise on academic painting a few of its more outworn formulas and illustrated them with spots and diagrams, little scribbled etchings of popular paintings, and even actual albumen prints from his own work. These he garnished with choice quotations from Sir Joshua Reynolds, Ruskin, and others. He also gave advice on the proper bedside manner for getting the best from a sitter and similar matters.

Robinson's studio methods distinctly foreshadow Hollywood and *Vogue*. He described how to get an outdoor effect indoors; how to combine, under careful lighting, movable platforms heaped with earth and grasses, props such as gates and stumps, and carefully painted backdrops. His preference for "attractive ladies playing at haymaking and fishwives," as a contemporary dubbed them, is still shared by casting directors and fashion editors. His opinions on focusing, lighting, and retouching remain

Two Little Girls, 1869. From Pictorial Effect in Photography. *This charming picture clearly shows how accomplished a photographer Robinson was and how little he needed to resort to tricks. Subtle variations are worked in the familiar pyramid form. The dark spaces above and below the figures emphasize their littleness, and the lighting of the delicate faces is brilliantly handled.* (Photo: Museum of Modern Art)

those of glamour photographers everywhere.

Nevertheless, he was not without flashes of insight into the true character of his medium. Had he been less comfortable and successful and, above all, less preoccupied with academic art, the history of photography as a medium might be very different.

During the seventies *Pictorial Effect* went through many editions. Robinson was elected to the Council of the Royal Photographic Society and was awarded the gold medal of the Paris Exhibition of 1878. In the early '80's, his influence was reflected in the incredible depths of cheap slickness and sentimentality in the salons. In 1881 he brought out, in collaboration with Capt. W. de W. Abney, *The Art and Practice of Silver Printing;* in 1884, *Picture-Making by Photography;* in 1885, *The Studio, and What to Do in It.*

OPPOSITION BY EMERSON

In 1886, the first signs of a great revolt appeared. An intense and dogmatic young man, Dr. P. H. Emerson, gave a lecture at the London Camera Club in which he trumpeted the claim of "straight" photography as a fine art independent of other mediums, and thundered against Robinson and his works, calling them "a senseless jargon of quotations." Emerson's own photographs, being direct and sensitive observations of nature, were as great a challenge as his theories. Robinson at first contented himself with making good-humored fun of Emerson and his followers. But Emerson was a master of invective and was, moreover, in deadly earnest.

Robinson meanwhile was elected to the Vice-Presidency of the Royal Photographic Society in 1887, he had a one-man show at the Camera Club in 1889, and he brought out four more books, all essentially rehashes of *Pictorial Effect: Portraits and Pictures Produced by Photography and Art,* 1887; *Letters on Landscape Photography,* 1888; *Art Photography in Short Chapters; The Complete Photographer,* 1890. The victory nominally lay with Robinson, for Emerson suddenly retracted his theories in 1891. Actually, Robinson himself was caught up in the revolution Emerson had started and was to acknowledge with kindly dignity the good that Emerson had done.

Emerson's projected exhibition reforms caused a growing dissatisfaction with the Royal Photographic Society. A quarrel about hanging, precipitated by an officious secretary, led to the withdrawal of Robinson and several others who then founded, in 1892, the great international society known as the Linked Ring. The Linked Ring elected to its ranks only those whom it considered artists. Its esthetics began by being a blend of Emerson and Robinson, but gradually a greater artistic license crept in until most of its members regarded a photograph as merely the foundation for handwork. By 1899 the Linked Ring had begun its slow decline. Robinson returned to the Royal and was elected an Honorary Fellow in 1900. In 1901 he died at his home, Winwood, in Tunbridge Wells.

RODEO PHOTOGRAPHY

CAL GODSHALL
Photographer and Rancher
[In this article, an experienced photographer outlines some important facts to keep in mind when photographing the rodeo. And he adds some interesting points in regard to rodeo etiquette—an important factor in this field.]
• *Also see: Action Photography; Horse Photography; Sports Photography.*

RODEO-ACTION PHOTOGRAPHY IS DIFferent from any other form of photography because of the constantly changing range of action, the element of danger to the photographer, and the fact that the contestants are competing for valuable cash prizes. For all these reasons the photographer must not interfere with the action or use equipment that will frighten the animals.

A knowledge of animal behavior is also essential. Standing directly in front of a bucking horse is not safe for the photographer unless he can anticipate the action of the horse. Daylight photography of bucking horses will not spoil the action of the animal as would flashlight photos taken during a night performance but the photographer should remember that he can out-turn a bucking horse. His reactions must be fast enough to enable him to turn inside the *loop* of a bucking horse if he wants to avoid injury.

Bucking steers and bulls of the Hereford strain, or other strains or range animals, are not likely to charge or attack a person. If they do charge, they can be effectively avoided by lying prone on the ground. Fighting brahmas, however, are a different matter. Usually they are taught to fight and charge any person afoot. Lying down won't protect you from this animal. If a brahma can't pick you up with his horns, he is apt to kneel on you. Therefore, when you are photographing brahmas and they come toward you—run fast for the fence. Brahmas are best photographed from the side, and at a safe distance say 25 feet.

In bulldogging, or in any roping event, the photographer should never get in front of the animal to be roped or the roper's horse. This may alter the running animal's course, causing the contestant to lose precious seconds which could mean the loss of prize money.

The best way to catch the action of a roping event or of a bucking horse or bull, is from the side—

Bulldogging a steer. The best way to photograph this exciting event is from a three-quarter front angle, showing all three participants: the hazer, the steer, and the bulldogger. (Photo: DeVere Helfrich)

possibly just a little in front of the side, getting a three-quarter angle. Bulldogging pictures are best from a three-quarter angle towards the front. This will show the bulldogger, the steer, and the hazer.

RODEO ENTRANTS

The cowgirl plays an important part in rodeos and is excellent photographic material. There are few girls now roping or riding bucking animals, but the girls do participate in the trick riding—a form of riding originated by the Cossacks of Russia but perfected by the American cowboy and cowgirl.

Stock or cowhorse exhibitors use cowgirls for showing off the workability of a well-trained cow horse. Many of these girls, called "Queens of the Rodeo," are selected in competition for horsemanship and appearance. With their colorful western costumes, they offer the greatest opportunity for beauty around a rodeo and, in action, are the pictures sought by newspapers and magazines.

TYPES OF SHOTS AVAILABLE

Audiences see the action in front of the chutes and in the arena, but they never see what goes on behind the scenes. Dozens of opportunities exist there for providing a series of pictures of the livestock getting ready, the saddling in the chutes, the handling of the livestock behind and in the chutes, and many other activities. For these pictures, it is necessary to get permission from the livestock owner or the arena director. A promise of finished prints is usually sufficient to obtain this permission.

A summary of pictures obtainable at a rodeo might be as follows: saddle-bronc riding; bareback-bronc riding; brahma-bull riding; steer riding; bulldogging or steer wrestling; calf-roping; single-steer roping; team roping and typing of steers; wild-

Calf roping is usually one of the biggest events in the rodeo. This provides many opportunities for obtaining the best action and also an interesting photoseries of the event. (Photo: Les Walsh)

Plenty of wild gyrations here as cowboy Jack Buschbom takes to the air on "Sleeper" who lunges into peak action with all four legs in the air. (**Photo: DeVere Helfrich**)

cow milking; wild horse saddling and racing; trick and fancy riders and ropers.

SPEED AND FOCUS

Speed, of course, must be determined by lighting conditions, but the range from 1/350 to 1/500 of a second is best to stop this fast action. Focusing is difficult because the photographer wants to catch the best action of the animal and the contestant, and therefore must wait until that action occurs before shooting.

The best time to catch a bucking animal is on the peak of the upward jump. This is usually during the most violent action when all four legs are off the ground. If taken from the front, the photo will show the face of the rider. If the rider bucks off at this peak, only luck will determine whether he falls off on the side of the photographer or on the side away from the camera.

Another important feature in photographing rodeo action is to try to shoot from the knees so that your subject will be wholly or partly framed against a sky background instead of a grandstand full of people. In some rodeos this is not possible, but in most arenas it can be accomplished. In getting to your knees for a good action shot,

keep sufficiently alert so you can quickly jump to either side if the animal turns towards you.

Most shots of rodeo action should be made at an estimated distance of about twenty-five feet (with normal lenses). Try to get the action at its peak, or as near that point as possible. If it is impossible to get close to the action, use a longer focal-length lens with a 35 mm or 2¼ × 2¼ camera. When using a fast film, and the day is clear, the diaphragm can be stopped down to

The best pictures come at the peak of action and here the cowboy takes off for some personal sky diving from the last violent buck. (Photo: Les Walsh)

f/11 or smaller with shutter speeds around 1/500 of a second or faster.

YOUR ATTITUDE

Photographers can be very unpopular in rodeo arenas or they can get along with no trouble at all, depending on how thoughtful they are of others. Interference with contestants, will put a photographer in wrong with the cowboys. To be constantly standing up in the arena poised for something to happen, always in the way of the spectators, will make the man with the camera unpopular with the audience. There-fore, keep down low at all times except just at the time of shooting.

CAMERA

Photographing rodeo action with a camera that requires the photographer to look into a hooded finder is very dangerous because the bucking or performing animal looks far away in comparison to its actual distance. The best type of camera is the Speed Graphic—because one can keep both eyes open and use the large wire finder at the same time. The image can be practically centered and you can still accurately see just how far away the animal is.

Another important factor in this type of photography is the film size. A 4 × 5 film with a 5½ or 6-inch lens will give the best results. Since the action of a bucking horse can not always be centered on the film, a large field of film surface is a tremendous aid when small portions of the negative must be enlarged.

On the other hand, the 35 mm rangefinder is very effective for rodeo work. Focusing is easier depth of field greater, shooting quicker, and there are 36 exposures to each loading. The individual photographer must decide which camera to use by weighing the advantages and disadvantages of each.